KU-526-357

The Last Secrets of the Silk Road

The Last Secrets of the Silk Road

Alexandra Tolstoy

P
PROFILE BOOKS

First published in 2003 by
Profile Books Ltd
58A Hatton Garden
London EC1N 8LX
www.profilebooks.co.uk

Copyright © Alexandra Tolstoy 2003

10 9 8 7 6 5 4 3 2 1

Typeset in Galliard by
MacGuru
info@macguru.org.uk
Printed and bound in Great Britain by
Clays, Bungay, Suffolk

The moral right of the author has been asserted.

All rights reserved. Without limiting the rights under copyright reserved above, no part of this publication may be reproduced, stored or introduced into a retrieval system, or transmitted, in any form or by any means (electronic, mechanical, photocopying, recording or otherwise), without the prior written permission of both the copyright owner and the publisher of this book.

A CIP catalogue record for this book is available from the British Library.

ISBN 1 86197 393 4

For Mummy and Papa
With fondest love

Contents

Acknowledgements

THERE ARE MANY PEOPLE to thank and our adventure owed much to the support and enthusiasm of others. The most important are our parents, all of whom showed great loyalty despite no doubt feeling sceptical and worried at times. They never questioned what we were doing, which lent us the confidence to pursue our dream and achieve things we would never otherwise have done. It was not only our parents but also grandparents, aunts, uncles, godparents and friends who showed great generosity and support.

We are much indebted to our sponsors who took the risk of assisting an unknown and inexperienced team of young girls. In particular, the Registrar of Chinese Herbalists showed incredible generosity. At the time of our expedition they were fighting a battle in the EU against a proposed ban on the importation of Chinese herbs without import licenses, which would have been prohibitive to the sale and use of these medicines in the UK. Our journey along the Silk Road sought to illustrate the importance of such remedies, which have been traded between East and West along this route for millennia.

Rathbones, Amec, Sedgewicks, CLC and Sir David Barnes all gave generous financial support. DHL provided us with parcels at several points along our journey, which proved invaluable in replacing vital equipment and satisfying our cravings for chocolate and Hello! Magazine. Mountain Horse equipped us with jodhpurs, boots, chaps and coats that were put to the ultimate test of five thousand miles through the most extreme terrain and thankfully proved invincible. Terranova lent us tents that survived ferocious hail, snow and sand storms. Datadial built us a website, which charted our progress along the Silk Road. Panasonic and ICS lent us a laptop and satellite telephone that enabled us to contact home in case of emergency, and many other companies contributed equipment that helped to make our arduous trip a little easier.

We also benefited from much valuable advice: notably from Shane Winser at the Royal Geographical Society and the well-known explorers James Greenwood, John Warburton-Lee and John Labouchere. Monument Oil in Ashgabad helped to smooth our way through the bureaucracy of Turkmenistan, while the Meredith-Jones cotton company did the same for us in Uzbekistan.

Paul Marsh and Leyla Moghadam, my literary agents, and Peter Carson, my editor, must be thanked for the great chance they took in enabling this book to be published. Without them, I would never have had the confidence to write it and I owe them much for their faith in me.

For myself, I would like to thank my travelling companions above all: Mouse, Wic and Lucy. None of us could have completed this journey without each other and I will always remain indebted to them for one of the happiest and most exciting years of my life. They were perfect companions and I look back with great nostalgia to the fascinating and, most of all, fun months we had together. The first questions everybody asked on our return were, 'are you still friends?' and 'did you fight?' Of course we did at times, but we laughed a lot more than we argued, and most importantly returned better friends than we set out. An experience like this creates an incomparable bond and I know I will always have a particularly strong affection for them.

Without them I could never have written this book and it is only through use of their diaries that I have been able to create an account of our journey. At many points I use or paraphrase their words so that this book is really of joint authorship. They each contributed very different and individual aspects to the account, making it far more colourful than I ever could have done alone. The amusing anecdotes generally stem from Wic and Mouse while Lucy provided me with lyrical descriptions and historical knowledge. I am extremely grateful for the generosity they have shown not only in this respect but at all times.

The last person I must thank is Shamil, our guide in Central Asia, who has become one of my closest friends and constant travelling companion. Each year since the Silk Road Expedition we have ridden together somewhere in Central Asia or Russia and I hope we will continue to do so for many years to come. None of these journeys would ever have happened without his vast knowledge and experience of horses and nature, as well as his good humour and charm. I will always be indebted to him for everything he has taught me and it was one of the luckiest chances in my life that led me to meet him.

Illustrations

The photographs, apart from numbers 1, 2 and 13, are by Sophia Cunningham, Lucy Kelaart and Victoria Westmacott.

Introduction

AFTER GRADUATING from the University of Edinburgh in the summer of 1996, I gained a place on the graduate-training scheme at Credit Suisse First Boston, the American investment bank. I was fortunate enough to be sent to New York for the initial three months' training, before returning to London to join the Eastern European equities desk as a broker. From a worldly point of view, I had found an enviable job; well-paid and interesting, but to me it became more and more painful as each long day passed. Waking at five each morning and sitting at a bank of desks with telephones ringing and traders shouting for twelve hours a day was not as exhilarating as many had led me to believe. I looked back at my university days with regret, wishing that I had made more of my freedom. Finally, after just under a year of joining the bank, I handed in my resignation, with no more definite plan than to travel or work abroad. My parents were surprised but sympathetic, and I spent the next couple of months on holiday or doing odd jobs.

One of these was working at the Chelsea Flower Show for a friend who was running the Country Life Garden. She had employed several of her friends to hand out leaflets and I found myself working alongside a girl called Sophia ('Mouse') Cunningham, whom I had known slightly at Edinburgh. We spent much of those few days chatting and at one point she told me of a dream she nurtured, that of riding the ancient Silk Road on horses and camels. Having studied religion at university and written her dissertation on the movement of Buddhism along the Silk Road, she had been inspired to retrace this great trading route. I was excited by the idea, but did not think of it much more until a month later when I went on holiday with some friends to Paxos, the Greek island north of Corfu. Early one evening Lucy Kelaart, an old friend of mine from prep school, and I decided to go for a walk along one of the shepherds' paths that meander through the stony hills, out towards the sea. It was one of those lovely balmy summer nights when life seems infinitely perfect and happy. We were laughing and talking when she told me that she was bored with her job as a literary agent and thinking of moving to live in South America. I immediately told her of Mouse's idea and she was completely captivated: together we decided to call Mouse as soon as we returned to England.

Lucy had studied at Edinburgh with us but she had also spent seven years at school with Mouse, until the age of eighteen, so they were old friends. Mouse was thrilled that we were so keen on her idea and suggested that we ask another friend, Victoria (Wic) Westmacott, to be the fourth member of the Silk Road Expedition, as we quickly christened our project. Wic also had studied at Edinburgh but while I had only met her briefly, Mouse and Lucy were both firm friends of hers. She took no persuading and in the winter of 1997 we had our first official 'expedition meeting'. That evening we decided on our route: five thousand miles through the desert, steppes, mountains and forests of Central Asia and China, travelling only on horses and camels. As we pored over the map in Mouse's cosy Chelsea flat it was almost impossible to conceive galloping through these wild and unknown regions.

These meetings continued until the spring of 1999, but rarely were all of us able to attend. Mouse spent a couple of months in China researching the Chinese section of our journey, organising camels and guides, while I spent a winter in Russia organising horses and guides for the Central Asian half. Wic, Mouse and I also spent stints of this time working abroad and one spring I walked five hundred miles through northern Spain, along the famous Camino de Santiago pilgrimage route. But somehow we managed to co-ordinate, and despite having no experience in such work were able to organise the logistics and vast sponsorship required for such an expedition. We knew it would take us at least eight months to complete and animals are always an expensive way of travelling, so this last aspect was the most demanding. Against great competition, Mouse won a Winston Churchill travel fellowship while the rest of the sponsorship came from companies or individuals. Lucy, Wic and Mouse worked particularly hard for the six months leading up to our departure in order to achieve this end.

We also decided to raise money for Merlin, a British medical charity which provides emergency relief to disaster zones around the world. Friends, relatives and companies generously gave donations and we succeeded in collecting over £15,000.

Each of us has very different characters and adopted varying approaches to the expedition. Small, athletic and blonde, Mouse loves the outdoors and is always eager for adventure. Having hunted all her life with the Flint and Denbigh Hunt in North Wales, she was a far more experienced rider than we three were. She also possesses much determination and ambition, and it was clear from the beginning that her interest lay in the successful completion of the journey and overcoming its physical challenges. I think Mouse's imagination was stirred by the idea of a sporting adventure, and the fact that we would be the first people to retrace this historic route on horse and camel. Not liking to admit weakness, she was very keen for the journey to appear as strenuous and demanding as possible back at home and on occasion we had to restrain her enthusiasm in the name of truth! She is also even-tempered and kind and was a skilled diplomat in moments of conflict when we were less able to cope with the stress. I was greatly impressed by the self-control Mouse is able to exert and her demure exterior belies a steely character as well as physical strength. She rarely showed irritation and almost always appeared happy, although there must have been occasions when she was keeping her true feelings concealed.

Tall with large brown eyes, Wic was definitely the animal lover of our group. She adored both the horses and camels and derived immense enjoyment from this element of the journey. Extremely solicitous for their welfare, she showed them constant attention and at times we were worried she would walk the Silk Road in order to spare her horse or camel the extra burden! Her compassion led to some unhappiness, because she felt that at times the guides were not as indulgent towards the animals as they might have been. Wic has a dreamy, happy-go-lucky personality and it was only through distress for her horse or camel that she gave vent to uncharacteristic explosions of anger. She has a vivid imagination and was clearly much affected by the magnificent scenery and colourful people we encountered. Wic instantly became fascinated by the filming, and spent many happy hours capturing our exploits on camera.

Lucy was described as an 'Amazonian' by our guide, Shamil. She has a long, slim figure and exotically dark looks. I felt that my interest in the expedition coincided more with that of Lucy than the others. She was, I think, drawn by the excitement of retracing this historic trading route, as well as a curiosity for the unusually remote regions of the world we would be passing through. Lucy is always passionate about everything she does and read avidly about the history of the Silk Road before we left, intrigued in particular by Tamerlane and Genghis Khan. Incredibly kind-hearted and sympathetic, she is selfless to an extreme. She is also very self-analytical and at times could become low and quiet. But these occasions were rare and it was mostly her incisive sense of humour and distinctive laugh that punctuated our days.

Inspired by Peter Hopkirk's evocative books, I was greatly drawn by the romance of travelling through the territory of the Great Game, one of the most colourful periods in history. It was during the 19th century that two of the world's greatest empires, Victorian Britain and Tsarist Russia, fought a secret war in the plains and mountains of Central Asia, each vying for control of this wild hinterland. My personal history also drew me towards this area, in particular Central Asia with the role it has played in the Russian and Soviet empires. As the head of the Tolstoy family and an indirect descendent of the legendary author of 'War and Peace', my father was always eager that we should understand the history of our family and country. From a young age he emphasised our Russian heritage and in common with my brother and sisters I was christened and brought up in the Orthodox Church. We maintained close links with the other White Russian émigrés and their descendants, meeting at church and in houses and flats in Kensington and Chiswick, where the traditional Russia of the Romanovs was preserved. I remember Russian visitors from all over the world appearing in our house throughout my childhood, and our home is full of Russian icons, books and memorabilia. This additional thread to our family life had always made me feel different from my English friends, and I am sure was partly responsible for my later urge to travel.

In 1992 my father decided that, as the eldest child and having only recently left school, I should spend six months studying Russian in Moscow before going to university. My grandfather had escaped from the clutches of the Bolsheviks in 1920, sailing to Portsmouth with his English nanny and my father was born in England, during Stalin's terrible regime, so that I was among the second generation to be brought up outside Russia. It was only after the collapse of the Soviet Union that we were free to return to the *rodina*, or 'motherland'. As a historian deeply critical of Communism and in particular Stalin, it would have been dangerous for my father and family to travel to the Soviet Union. Although nervous at first, I soon fell in love with Russia and have spent considerable periods of the last decade living in Moscow.

It is obviously difficult for me to describe my own character but I will do my best in order to complete the picture of our group. 'Strong' is an adjective I have heard used frequently in reference to myself and I know that I have an often-insurmountable will and determination. I am also impatient and possess a hot temper, but on the other hand am quick to forget an argument. My parents, three siblings and I could not be closer but at the same time we are very outspoken with each other, and visitors are often amused by the dramas they encounter in our home. However, we have a lot of fun and discuss everything under the sun, so that if I brought difficulties to the Silk Road I trust that I also contributed some entertainment. The other three were often bemused at the intense interest I could show in the smallest events of their lives or most distant relatives but I think it helped to pass the time during those long desert days.

On our return to England, we all went on to do things that in some way arose out of the expedition. We gave lectures together at the Royal Geographical Society and Mouse and Wic spent a year giving lectures at schools all over Britain. Mouse then moved to India where she is working for a children's street charity, Youth Reach, while Wic has become a successful camera operator and researcher for a Channel 4 production, drawing on her experience from the Silk Road. Lucy completed a Masters in Central Asian History and Russian at SOAS the year after we returned, and then moved to Almaty in Kazakhstan where she works for a regional health reform project. I received a contract to write this book and decided to write it in Moscow rather than London, making it easy to spend my summer holidays riding in Central Asia. Having viewed the Silk Road as the adventure of my life, a year ago I began to long for the open skies and steppe once more and became intrigued by the idea of riding through Mongolia and Eastern Siberia. Together with another university friend, Katherine Turner, Shamil and I have just spent the last six months riding 2,500 miles on horseback through these similarly wild parts of the world. My taste for adventure is nevertheless still not sated, and in 2004 Shamil and I are planning to retrace Genghis Khan's 1219 campaign from Mongolia to Uzbekistan, once again on horseback, only this time in the form of a race. I now cannot imagine life without Central Asia or horses, and feel immensely fortunate to have discovered these passions through a chance conversation at the Chelsea Flower Show.

1

In the beginning

WE ARRIVED IN MERV by dark, having driven several times around the modern city of Mary that has grown up beside the ancient oasis town. Finally, having asked directions to the archaeological site of ancient Merv in the town's only hotel, we found ourselves bumping down a dusty desert track. In the headlights we spied a figure waving animatedly. Our driver stopped the mini-bus and, opening the door, we were greeted by a young man who introduced himself in broken English as Evgeniy. Clambering on to the bus, he explained that he was our guide and that our camp was just a little further on. Five minutes later, we saw a large building silhouetted against the flatness of the desert and beneath it six tiny figures – our horses.

In the camp Evgeniy introduced us to Sacha the cook, Igor the driver and Dzhuma the horse guide. They shook our hands rather awkwardly, then showed us the two tents they had erected for us and produced some bowls of warm soup. We sat in silence, eating our soup and looking out to the desert, barely discernible beneath the weakly lit night sky. Going to sleep that night I did not know whether to feel excited or nervous. Everything felt so alien; I seemed to be living in a dream in which nothing was quite real.

The next morning we climbed eagerly out of our tents to find that the weather was warm and sunny. What had on the previous night seemed a vast and endless landscape now appeared smaller and less mysterious. The building that we had seen the night before (the mediaeval Sultan Sinjar's mausoleum) no longer seemed so imposing and we realised it was actually some distance from our camp. Unfortunately, the horses also looked less statuesque by daylight. They were very thin, and one had a pendulous, bleeding growth hanging from its neck.

'Evgeniy, what's wrong with this horse?' we asked.

'Oh, they were brought here in a lorry and that one hit itself on the side of the lorry.'

'But why are they so thin?'

'That's normal.'

They were clearly underfed, but there was nothing we could do beyond encouraging Dzhuma to feed them as much as possible. Soon after breakfast Evgeniy, or Zheniya as he told us he preferred to be called, suggested we visit the remains of ancient Merv.

Merv, known as 'The Pearl of the East', had been a Silk Road city and (after Baghdad) the greatest city in the Islamic world. It reached its zenith under Seljuk rule in the eleventh and twelfth centuries, the period during which the mausoleum looming over our camp had been built for one of its rulers, Sultan Sinjar. A site just north of the city, known as Margush, had first been inhabited in the ninth century BC. Three hundred years later, some of Margush's inhabitants had moved lower down the river Murghab to Merv, while others had crossed into Persia and Afghanistan. This dispersal has given grounds for a controversial new argument, propounded by our archaeologist guide, Victor, which asserts that Zoroastrianism originated here in Merv. A temple has recently been unearthed at Margush which he claims demonstrates that the roots of Zoroastrianism can be traced back more than three hundred years before the life of the founder of the religion, who lived in sixth-century Persia.

Alexander the Great spent a couple of years in Merv in the third century BC before appointing Antiochus, his favourite general, the son of Seleucus, to rule the city. Antiochus rebuilt Merv, naming it Antiocha Margiana, after which it enjoyed a relatively peaceful existence until the seventh century AD, when the Arabs conquered it. But in the twelfth century came an even more terrifying conquest, by Tuli, the favourite son of Ghengis Khan. Having broken down its well-protected walls by destroying a dam in the Murghab, which flows through Merv, the Mongol horde sacked the city.

The sites of ancient Merv contain a Buddhist temple, a mosque, a Nestorian church and a Zoroastrian temple: a unique combination of faiths in Central Asia. Set on a dusty flat plain, looking out over the edge of the Kara-Kum desert, it is an imposing place – Sinjar's mausoleum inspires deference among even the infidels.

We walked back to our camp after a long day exploring ancient Merv, tired out by the heat, dust and wealth of information Victor had fed us.

Our horses seemed even more dejected than before. We went to bed in nervous anticipation, for the following day was to be our first day of riding. However, having woken up early, we did not set off for three hours. The smallest horse, which had been intended as a packhorse, was completely incapable of walking; its legs crumpled beneath it as we tried to lead it forwards. So, after some discussion, Evgeniy agreed that he and Sacha would find it a new home, while we set off on the other horses with Dzhuma.

It was a strange anti-climax finally to be riding, especially as our morning was spent passing through the outskirts of the modern town. The road was lined by shabby, one-storey buildings peopled by men, women and children dressed in bright Turkmen robes. They all stared at us, sometimes giving us an inquisitive smile, revealing a flash of golden teeth. We plodded slowly along, feeling self-conscious in our Western clothes with our garish new saddlebags. Consequently, we were glad to leave the town, even though it was only to be replaced by a flat scrubby landscape dotted with acacia trees.

Expecting not to see a spot of natural beauty for many weeks, we were overjoyed when Dzhuma led us into a grassy clearing enclosed by small trees casting dappled shadows. Our first day over, I felt disappointed that it had passed in such undramatic fashion. The next day we woke to see that our horses had found a surprising store of energy. We left the scrub for the small sand dunes that line the edge of the Kara-Kum desert and the horses hurtled up and down them, avoiding the tortoises that were basking in the warm sun. Later on we joined a railway line that runs between Ashgabad and Chardzhou, and on to Bukhara in Uzbekistan. We rode alongside its tracks, never once seeing a train, only the never-ending telegraph poles and rippling dunes.

The following day we rode into the former Red Army post of Ravnina, now a small Turkmen village. Here we decided to have our first rest day, which coincided with the Muslim festival of Kuban-Bairam. This feast day, which celebrates Mohammed's offering of his son to Allah, is marked by all Muslims slaying an animal before daybreak as well as keeping an open house until sunset. Evgeniy told us tradition dictates that each person must visit forty homes during the day in order to absolve their sins. Dzhuma, a Turkmen, had friends in Ravnina who invited us into their home, where we sat cross-legged on the gaudily carpeted floor of the main room with all the extended family – about twenty people altogether – and looked in amazement at the feast laid before us. Ominous-looking bowls of mutton floating in greasy water were placed in front of us by one of the older women, who wore a multi-coloured long dress and headscarf. We made our politest attempts to swallow all the meat and broth. Luckily it was accompanied by the most delicious apricot jam I have ever tasted and exquisite sweet cakes. We drank tea with camel's milk – slightly richer and more pungent than cow's milk. During lunch we were shown the full outfit of a Turkmen bride, which included a metal headdress and hand jewellery. Wic was then invited to try it all on. It suited her very well, she was told, and would she like to marry one of the sons?

Apparently we were the first English people to have visited the village and after lunch we were trailed around the village by a crowd of dusty children. I was surprised by how few people spoke Russian and what little imprint the Soviets had left here. We were led to a lethal-looking swing, which would, it was explained, in conjunction with the forty visits, cleanse every imaginable sin. Mouse and I stood on it as they pushed us higher and higher until I felt we were piercing the clouds and began to scream.

After this one of the old men, a friend of Dzhuma's, offered to take us out into the desert to visit the remains of an ancient gold mine and a well. We walked for a couple of miles through the dunes until we reached a spot that did not look very different from its surroundings. But the old man pointed to a place where he said the well had been before it dried up. The gold mine was even less visible, but he pointed out every tiny flower and plant, naming them all. He told us, in simple Russian, that his grandparents had lived as shepherds out here until they were 105 and 118; they had never visited a town or village, except to be buried, and when they saw an aeroplane passing overhead they thought it was an iron eagle. I asked if people still lived a nomadic lifestyle. He told us the Soviets had made it impossible by rounding everybody up into the dreaded *kolkhozes*, or collective farms. However, the present generation obviously still feels immense pride in, and love for, the desert, cherishing all its history and legends. They could recognise every patch of scrub and find their way perfectly across a horizon seemingly free of landmarks.

It was now the end of March and the desert was beginning to wake. After leaving Ravnina, we had our first glimpse of a thin, brown sidewinder snake, flexing its body after the winter's hibernation. The dunes were covered in holes and burrows and loose-rooted grass. Now, for the first time in the desert, we saw trees like small willows. Eagles circled overhead, and desert rats and tortoises often crossed our path. Less welcome were the ticks which suddenly appeared everywhere – hopping into our ears, crawling up into our jodhpurs, leaping up from the sheepskins on our saddles and venturing beneath our shirts. Our horses' bellies were soon covered in them, bloated to the size of almonds.

Wic noted in her diary at this point: 'I can't remember the last time I heard "nothing". Having lived in London for so long, my idea of peace is usually accompanied by an orchestra of piercing car alarms, screeching cat-fights and bickering neighbours. Here the highlight of my day was when Fang (my jaw-snapping nag) and I climbed to the top of a sand dune to survey the vast expanse of scrub and to savour the wonderful, almost tranquillising sensation the silence induces.' It was indeed strange to be in this empty landscape, particularly after all the frenetic organisation of the last few months back in England. My response however, was not as positive as Wic's. Had we really worked so hard to be stumbling through these scrubby sand dunes? I remembered the beautiful rolling hills around my parents' home in the English countryside and thought maybe I had been stupid to want to explore so far afield. But this disillusionment lasted a very short time. Within a day or two I never wanted to live any other way.

The next morning Zheniya woke us with bad news: Mouse's horse had been bitten in the night by a scorpion and only had hours to live. We jumped out of our tents in panic to see Dzhuma shaking with laughter – Turkmens also observe April Fools Day. We spent the day riding to the Repetek reserve, a small enclave of the Kara-Kum desert dedicated by the Soviets to monitoring its climate, plant and animal life. Our guide was not physically prepossessing, with a bulbous nose and thick glasses, but he proved very interesting. He took us on a tour of the small museum, where he entertained us with tales of the local snake life. Cobras are apparently the most dangerous, but three times more poisonous are the Karakul (Black Widow – *kara* means black in Turkic) spiders, who eat their husbands on their wedding night. He told us that the males have grown wise to this and sometimes smuggle a fly along on the fateful night. Having performed his conjugal duty, the husband then flees, leaving the unsuspecting fly behind as a substitute. The guide pointed out local herbs, flowers and grasses. A flower Lucy had thought bore a resemblance to burnt popcorn proved to be sedge. It is an essential ingredient in the Karakul sheep's diet, keeping their fur perfectly curly. When some of these sheep were taken to Kazakhstan, their fur grew straight. We also learned about the holy saksaul trees – white ones grow everywhere but black ones only where there is water.

The flora of the Kara-Kum desert is unique in the world because of its resistance to heat. In other deserts plant life stops at 50° Centigrade, whereas here life actually increases at that level and plants photosynthesise at a higher rate.

After leaving the Repetek reserve we rode for two days through the dunes to Chardzhou, some twenty-two miles from the Uzbek border. Our first feeling on entering the small, grimy town was one of excitement. It had been two weeks since we had passed through any settlement containing more than two households and a handful of chickens. We suddenly felt a great sense of importance as people stared at us, shouting in Russian '*Otkuda*?', 'Where are you from?' However, we were greeted not only by curious questions and looks, but also unfortunately by stones and sticks. The situation reached a point where a group of young boys who had surrounded Lucy and her horse started whipping it around the head with a long bamboo shoot. Wic and Mouse pulled back, shouting at the boys to stop and surrender their weapon. In response, the biggest boy brought the cane down with an almighty thwack onto the flanks of Wic's horse. Wic wrote later that her 'skin turned green and her seams began to split' as she transformed into the 'Incredible Wic'. She spun round in her saddle to face the boys and, uttering a shrill war cry, kicked her horse on to stampede through them. They turned on their heels. By now we found ourselves in a torrential rainstorm, which distracted us, and we trotted through the main street of Chardzhou, eager to leave the town and find our camp.

That night we slept on the banks of the Amu Darya, the great Oxus of ancient times. This river, which marks the western border of the historical region of Transoxiana, or Alexander the Great's Sogdiania, is one of Asia's most important water sources. We crossed it over a rickety metal bridge that reverberated with every step of the horses' hooves. The banks of the river were lined with dilapidated buildings and the water was a murky brown – all of which helped to dispel its romantic image. We pitched camp on the opposite shore, while Igor set up his fishing rod, sitting patiently until the sun began to set and we could see his cap and rod silhouetted against the pink sky.

The next morning, having waged war against the gluttonous ticks which had settled on our horses, we began riding out towards the Uzbek border, along small roads where the green of the wheat was rendered even more brilliant by the dust surrounding it. Each wheat field was attached to a smallholding that looked almost biblical, with stables constructed of branches and roofs thatched with straw. Camels, oxen, sheep, dogs and people stared at our novel procession from fields and neatly hoed vegetable patches. An old woman draped in layers of quilted patchwork heaved a sheet full of faggots on to her back, saluting an old man in similar dress and tall fur hat, who sat cross-legged on the muddy ground.

At lunchtime we arrived at a mosque built in 1996 on the site of a holy man's house. We were ushered into its courtyard lined by shady trees, under which had been placed some low wooden tables. The caretaker spread out tablecloths and cushions on them, littering them afterwards with little cakes. He gestured to us to sit down and, having first removed our boots, we clambered on to the tables, where we sat cross-legged.

After lunch the caretaker took us inside and offered up a prayer for a safe journey. We left the mosque in a blaze of heat and the poor horses began to fade quickly. Lucy's horse was suffering the most. She could only walk two paces before stopping, so Lucy decided to dismount and lead her on foot. Before long, the heat was dispersed by a crack of thunder and soon, as we trudged along the straight road towards the border, we were bombarded by gargantuan hailstones. A couple of miles from the border we met our back-up truck, from which Igor greeted us with the news that the truck's Turkmen permit had expired. We decided to cross the border that night. As we walked slowly on, the horses dragging at every step, the sun appeared from behind a screen of clouds and created two rainbows against the leaden sky.

We finally reached the border, after what seemed an eternity, where again we found Igor, Sacha, Zheniya and the truck waiting. Zheniya told us that we had to leave our horses to join us the following morning because their paperwork was not ready. Dzhuma led them away and as we were whisked off by several border officials we saw the horses grazing among some reeds.

Six and a half hours later we emerged after an exhausting investigation of both us and our baggage. We had shown our passports twelve times. The customs guards, dressed in Soviet army uniforms, then insisted on rifling through every one of our bags. Next Lucy was escorted off alone, deep inside the building into a small room, furnished with an iron bed and two tall desks, in which a Turkmen began to interrogate her. He took down details of exactly where we had stayed in Ashgabad and then drew out a diary in which, on the pages for 26–30th May, he scribbled down the essential events of our lives up to this point.

'Where were you at university?'

'Edinburgh.

'What were your specialities?'

Lucy talked him through our different degrees.

'Where have you lived since?'

'Sorry?'

'WHERE HAVE YOU LIVED?'

'London.'

'What did you do there?'

'I was a literary agent.'

Incomprehension.

'Bookseller,' she qualified herself, eliciting a page of hurried notes.

He went on to ask exactly what we had filmed in Turkmenistan. Fortunately at this point Zheniya entered the room. He explained how beneficial our filming had been to the Turkmen nation and what advantages it could bring to their country. With these words of flattery, Zheniya and Lucy were finally allowed to go back to the main hall. Here a pot-bellied official broke the bad news to us that the horses would on no account be permitted to join us over the border the following day, on the grounds that they were 'Turkmen national treasures'. We were tempted to challenge him to ride them from Merv to the border and see whether he did not change his mind, but there seemed little point in aggravating him. It was night time by now and we were sick of this interrogation, so we decided to resign ourselves to fate and the only restaurant in no man's land. Here we found some delicious *pelmeni,* or Russian dumplings, smeared in sour cream, and washed down with cans of warm beer. Feeling a little better, we moved on to the Uzbek border in our truck. A smiling official who asked our names, on hearing Wic's, exclaimed, 'Victoria!' in admiring tones. Five minutes later we bumped into him again whereupon he began a long eulogy to Wic. 'How tall she is!' 'What eyes that light up and pierce the night!' 'So little hair – how very Uzbek and beautiful!'. He then began to question her. 'Is your mother beautiful? What does she do?' All this time a large poster of the fourteenth-century tyrant Tamerlane frowned down on us, as if he were the current ruler of Uzbekistan. Perhaps thanks to the official's fervent admiration for Wic, we were allowed to pass through the border with only three passport checks. We camped a mile from the border, both exhausted and worried about our horses.

2

First staging post

WE FELT A HUGE SENSE of relief to be safely in Uzbekistan. As we had five whole weeks ahead of us before we would encounter our next border crossing, bureaucratic officials already seemed agreeably remote to us now. Zheniya had gone back to the border early in the morning to try and retrieve our horses, but on no account would the Turkmens release them: they were still 'national treasures'. Although we felt guilty for having abandoned them, we knew that parting had become inevitable because they were so exhausted and incapable of travelling much further with us. We would very soon have had to exchange them for new horses and it may have been more difficult to find them a new home while on the road. Wic was particularly insistent in her enquiries about the horses' future. Where would they go? Who would feed them? What would they be used for? Zheniya told her that Dzhuma would take them back to his farm in northern Turkmenistan where they would have a good life and be well looked after. Wic was somewhat appeased.

Our next challenge was clearly to find new horses. It was important that we complete our journey before winter set in; we knew it was going to take us a minimum of eight months and we had only set off in late March, so we could not afford to waste days. The toughest part of our route in western China lay ahead of us, in the Taklamakan desert, so we wanted to allow for delays there. Therefore, while we stayed behind in the camp, we sent Zheniya off immediately in the back-up truck to Bukhara, where he said he could probably find horses in the hippodrome. It was always better to have a local negotiating on his own because the moment a foreign face showed up the prices escalated.

We had still not left the Kara-Kum but there was a river running just behind a small hill to one side of our camping spot, so we decided to take advantage of this rarity and wash our clothes, which were filthy and covered in dust from the desert. Wic was crouching in the rushes, scrubbing her shirt, when thunder began to crash and great grey clouds came rolling in from the horizon. Fat, round drops of rain started to fall and fierce winds materialised out of absolute calm. Lucy, Mouse and I were in the camp, where we watched powerless as the winds tore down our tents and ripped up their pegs. All our belongings – sleeping bags, rucksacks and clothes – became submerged in pools of water. It seemed the most terrible event at the time; the thought of nothing ever drying and everything being dirty was utterly depressing. In our insular little camp where we lived looking no further ahead than each evening, small disasters like this assumed vast proportions.

However, the storm disappeared as quickly as it had arisen. As the skies cleared we draped all our sodden clothes on the tamarisk bushes to dry in the evening sun. Zheniya had still not returned when we went to bed.

When I woke the next morning I heard a familiar movement outside, but it was not until a small whinny broke the silence that I realised its implications. I stuck my head out of my tent to see five horses tethered around us. Healthy and shiny, they looked almost frighteningly large and powerful after our scraggy Turkmen ponies. By contrast with those poor, dejected animals, who had needed a kick at every step, these ones tugged at their ropes and pawed the ground. They looked like they could gallop the rest of the Silk Road without stopping.

Zheniya was standing by one of the horses with a dark-skinned young man. 'This is Abbas, the horses' owner and your new guide,' he told us. Abbas gave us a disdainful nod before immediately turning back to inspecting a cut on the horse's head. He was tall and good-looking, with dishevelled black hair. His clothes were equally striking: a shabby but colourful striped silk coat, or *chopan*, baggy trousers and high boots. He looked so natural in this wild, scrubby landscape that I suddenly felt very self-conscious in my jodhpurs and chaps. His scorn for us could only have been exacerbated by our inability to vault on to our horses, as he did, in one agile jump. In fact, not only were we humiliated by having to ask Zheniya to help us mount, but Lucy and I also displayed an unmistakable lack of courage. Abbas had told us to choose our own horses – he was on a magnificent German stallion and the remaining four were all mares, accompanied by one foal. I chose what I thought looked like a docile mare, but when I stuck my foot in the stirrup, she suddenly darted forward, forcing me to hop along the ground and almost fall over. I yelped and Mouse grabbed the mare's head so that I could extract my foot. Mouse then offered to exchange my horse for hers, which I managed to mount without further indignity. Meanwhile, Lucy had chosen a black mare whose appearance also belied its character. As soon as she was sitting in the saddle it started prancing around and pawing the ground. Wic suddenly noticed that she was crying and suggested that they too switched horses, which Lucy agreed to after some persuasion. Lucy always hated making a fuss and I think despised herself for not being braver – later in the day, as we were riding along next to each other, she told me she wished she could be as fearless as Mouse and Wic. I tried to reassure her – Mouse and Wic had ridden far more than either of us and bravery naturally comes with experience. But she was not completely consoled. I noticed several times during the expedition that Lucy became very cross with herself for not behaving as she would have liked.

Our awe of Abbas was soon to be dispelled, however. For the first part of the day he rode ahead of us, only turning around to see if we were keeping up with him. If we were lagging behind, he jerked his head forward and waited for us to overtake, shouting at the mares as they passed. He always seemed to choose a place to do this where he could be on a higher piece of ground than us. He would make his stallion, Pasha, cavort backwards and forwards, showing him to his full advantage. Almost too self-consciously, he would then lean back in his saddle to stroke Pasha's arched tail, dropping his reins so that the horse would rear slightly.

But this impressive spectacle soon began to lose its allure. Lucy's horse became very lame and Abbas got completely lost, so we were forced to walk. We had left the fringes of the Kara-Kum and were now passing through apricot orchards and small farms, intersected by dusty paths. They all looked the same as each other and we must have taken several wrong turnings before we realised we were miles from the point where we had agreed to meet the truck. Abbas had been directing us without looking at his map and we had passively trusted his authoritative manner. But now we insisted on his taking out the map while I asked each person we encountered for directions. Abbas was very affronted by this. Suddenly he turned to me saying, 'You shouldn't talk to people in Uzbekistan, or smile at them.'

'Why?'

'Because they're dangerous, even children.'

I translated for the others, who snorted with laughter because the

Uzbeks we had seen so far had all been agricultural workers who did nothing more aggressive than smile at us and ask where we were going.

'You don't understand,' said Abbas defensively. 'This is an eastern country.'

I pacified him by not speaking to any more Uzbeks and he seemed to regain some of his pride. However, he obviously did not include himself in this perilous category because in place of the aloof silence he had maintained all morning he suddenly became very garrulous. After telling me that he had identified all our characters immediately he told me with great confidence that 'all four of you will get to Bukhara but only three will leave'. The fourth member – he had not yet decided which – would remain as his wife.

Finally, as the sun was setting, we entered the tiny village where we had agreed to meet the truck and camp for the night. Zheniya had found an idyllic farm with a small white-washed house and thatched, open stables full of sheep, goats, chickens and cows. It was owned by an old Uzbek man who had agreed to stable our horses there for the night. We left Abbas to guard them while we camped a few miles away.

The next morning we returned to the farm. The sun was streaming down and the house looked even whiter and cleaner than the night before. A woman in a headscarf, the old man's daughter, was squatting in the doorway, squinting as she stared at us. Her husband was playing with their little girl in the courtyard, swinging her up above his head to make her laugh. They stopped to stare at us, too, as the child hid shyly behind her father's legs. We found Abbas with all the horses, except the foal that belonged to Mouse's mare, which the day before had trotted behind her all the way. Suddenly our host appeared from behind one of the stables, leading the foal. Apparently, he told us, he had woken up in the night to find it in his bedroom, depositing an unwelcome present. Having removed it, he found it a few hours later in a neighbour's field, chewing its way through their prize crop. Despite this, the old man begged us to join him and his family for breakfast. We were shown into the house, where we removed our boots and sat cross-legged on quilts. The room was very basic but clean and each object, from a greying photograph of the son-in-law during his military service, to the pillows piled against one wall, was obviously cherished. The daughter brought in fried eggs, with bright yellow yolks, fresh bread and cucumbers. The food was simple but delicious, and there was such a cosy atmosphere in this happy and uncomplicated home.

As we set off it became quickly apparent that there was something seriously wrong with Lucy's mare. From the moment of her arrival we had been worried by the fact that she was heavily pregnant but Abbas had continually assured us that she was not due to deliver for at least three months. Her lameness the day before seemed to have become worse and now her back legs were struggling to support her vast weight. She could hardly move. After Lucy had ridden her a few hundred yards, I shouted at Abbas to stop. He was very dismissive – 'She's just lazy and you need to kick her on.' We tried again, with Lucy lagging further and further behind. Mouse then offered to ride her but she was no more successful. The poor mare was obviously in great pain. Finally Mouse could not bear it: she jumped off and with tears in her eyes, said, 'I can't do this, it's terrible.' Abbas looked very surly. He evidently thought we were being overly sentimental. But Mouse insisted that we go no further with the mare. Grudgingly, he admitted that she had an old wound in one of her hind legs; then he suggested that we tether the horses where we were while he went off for help. He cantered away on Pasha, returning an hour later to tell us that he had found a farm where the mare could be left until he returned to collect her after our arrival in Bukhara. He then led the mare away on foot, which seemed to take an eternity. Fortunately, leaving his own mare as collateral, Abbas was able to borrow a horse from the farm so that we could continue. This creature was more like a small donkey than a horse. Mouse bobbed along at the back of the line on it, but it was full of energy and managed to keep up with us.

For the next couple of days we continued through the agricultural land and uncultivated scrub which surround the route to the oasis of Bukhara. The landscape here is flat and dusty, with few distinguishing features. It was no longer hot and spring began to feel far away again. As we approached the outskirts of Bukhara our path took us through white plastered villages and orchards of apple blossom. For the last few hours of riding the minarets and domes of Bukhara were visible on the skyline. We trotted and cantered solidly without a break, desperate to arrive in the city after several weeks in the desert. We were to take the horses to the hippodrome on the outskirts, then spend two days exploring the city and enjoying the unusual luxury of hotel beds before setting off for Samarkand.

During these last days the others had become very irritated by Abbas's arrogance and confidence in his good looks. He had also exchanged his *chopan* for a lurid green nylon jacket and cowboy boots, which went far towards dispelling his romantic image. But I was still impressed, so as we reached the hippodrome I listened with great excitement when I heard Zheniya invite him to join us for dinner. However, Abbas gave a very dismissive 'no' and pushed us into the truck. I was mortified, but as we drove into the centre of Bukhara my disappointment disappeared under a wave of nausea and crippling stomach cramps. That morning I had woken up at 5.00 am with the worst headache of my life, but after taking some pills and drinking a lot of water I had felt better and forgotten about it. Now I could hardly think, I felt so sick and weak. As soon as we reached our hotel I collapsed and spent the rest of the evening and night running between my bed and the bathroom. I was sharing a room with Mouse, whom I must have kept awake all night. But she showed no irritation and every time I got up I just heard a little voice in the dark ask, 'Are you all right?'

Bukhara appeared a huge landmark to us – it was the first staging post on our journey. Only now that we had covered a sizeable distance did we feel that we had really begun. For over two millennia travellers and merchants passing along the Silk Road must have felt similar relief on arriving in Bukhara. Whether they were covering a short stage of the trading route or had travelled all the way from the other end of the Roman Empire, this ancient oasis offered respite after the heat and aridity of the Kara-Kum desert. Built out of clay, its mosques, madrassahs and caravanserais are havens of coolness. Huddled together among narrow dusty streets they cast delicious shadows in which it is possible to finally escape the fierce desert heat. But in the midst of this shadiness are dramatic open squares where the sun beats down in summer, as if to remind you that the desert is not far away.

The Poi Kalyan, where Silk Road merchants traded goods for centuries, is the most remarkable of these squares. Rising up from one side of its plaza is a gargantuan minaret, said to have been the tallest building of its time in Central Asia. Genghis Khan was so impressed by it that he allowed it to be spared during his destruction of Bukhara. This 155-foot structure towers over the town, acting as a beacon to travellers, visible from afar. Built by Arslan Khan in 1127, during the Kharakanid empire, its foundations were dug 53 feet deep, and bound with eggs (apparently extremely resilient glue).

The minaret's inner stairs are shut to visitors, but in the late afternoon Wic ventured back alone with the video camera. She managed to find the caretaker and, after a lot of gesturing and smiling, was allowed in. Having climbed the 105 stairs she emerged onto a covered balcony which affords a panoramic view: a carpet of small vaulted roofs, interspersed with turquoise domes and lofty minarets, in stark contrast to the searing blue sky above and the flat desert around. Wic was overjoyed and probably relieved not to have the rest of us with her to hinder her. After our first day of riding, as we left Merv, she had written in her diary: 'I would never have been able to envisage a couple of days ago what sort of effect a camera would have on me, but since I arrived here I haven't been able to think normally. Everything I view has to be beautifully composed, focused, framed and exposed ... I'm constantly thinking about the editing, the sound, the light, and the story.'

That evening Wic continued to film until the sun had set, and then descended the tiny spiral staircase to the foot of the minaret. But when she reached the door she found it was locked. She was trapped inside. However hard she banged and shouted, nobody responded. She despaired of ever being let out when she suddenly heard a creak as the door handle was pulled from the other side. Minutes later she was free again, saved from her visions of the legend we had been told earlier in the day. According to legend, Arslan Khan killed an imam after a quarrel. That night in a dream the imam told him, 'You have killed me; now oblige me by laying my head on a spot where nobody can tread' – and the tower had been built over his grave. However, her relief diminished when she saw that her liberator was dressed in the robes of an imam.

Flanking the Poi Kalyan on either side are the Kalyan mosque and the Mir-I-Arab Madrassah, whose portals are decorated in blue, yellow and white faience. Rising up from the madrassah are two turquoise domes, which we had seen the day before, nestling in the shadow of the minaret. In the sixteenth century, when the Uzbek Shaybanids made Bukhara the capital of the Bukhara khanate, the Kalyan mosque had been the leading mosque of the city, prayed in each Friday by 10,000 Bukhariots. Nowadays it is only used on Islamic holidays, its large courtyard empty but for a solitary tree. Its friezes were restored in 1996/7 by Unesco but, as Lucy wrote, 'looking at the old postcards this saddens me a little as some of the faience seems untrue and too garish. However, the brickwork and turquoise domes are faultless, their size, shape and colour exceeding expectation and the scope of human creation.'

We spent the rest of our first day wandering through the dusty streets and bazaars, where salesmen caught our eyes, hoping to attract our attention to their 'unique' and 'most special' *suzani*. These wall-hangings, for which Bukhara is famed, are intricately embroidered with silk threads and boast the most beautiful swirling patterns. Sadly, nowadays it is more fashionable among Bukharans to have modern, nylon carpets hanging on the wall of their homes, so these delicate, handmade cloths are sold readily to tourists.

My favourite part of Bukhara was Labi-Hauz, an outdoor restaurant, or *chai-khana*, looking out over a square pool of water. We ate lunch there, sitting cross-legged on one of the low wooden beds, or *topchans*, that fill every restaurant. These beds are enclosed on three sides by low wooden railings and covered in cushions, with a small table balanced in the middle, on which the food is placed. Mulberry tree branches budding with green spring leaves hung over our heads as we lay lazily back on the cushions, watching some ducks splashing in the pond. Sitting at the next *topchan* was a group of old men dressed in the ubiquitous *chopans,* or robes, of Uzbekistan. They were eating mutton kebabs and large, round *lepyoshkas* (bread), which they washed down with bowls of green tea. They exuded an air of complete repose. Although the setting was idyllic and the food looked exquisite: succulent kebabs, fresh bread, green salad and dumplings dripping in melted butter, I could not appreciate it. I was still in great discomfort, with searing pains and constant nausea. The others tried desperately to hide their enjoyment in order to spare my feelings, but surprisingly it actually gave me vicarious pleasure to see how delicious those simple dishes obviously were.

That night I developed a fever. I could not stop shivering, despite the five blankets Mouse had managed to purloin from other rooms in the hotel. In the morning I woke her up by screaming from the bathroom: I was terrified to find that I was now passing blood and feeling even weaker and more dehydrated than the day before. I was becoming depressed by the fact I was not getting any better. Having finally managed to make an international phone connection to my mother, I started to cry at the sound of her voice. It was almost a month since I had spoken to her and I felt so far away and removed from home. But she reassured me that I was doing the right thing by not eating, and 'starving out' the bacteria in my stomach.

Somehow I managed to drag myself out of the hotel with the others to visit the legendary Ark of Bukhara. The citadel, which dates back to the first century, was destroyed twice before today's monumental fortress was erected in the sixteenth century by the Sheybanids. Serving as a city within a city, it was completely self-sufficient, with a well, mosque and bazaar. From the imposing main gate a path leads up into the interior, flanked on either side by a series of cells measuring no more than five feet high. Each one would have incarcerated four or five unfortunates in complete darkness. The Emir's horses were stabled above in such a way that their droppings fell into the cells below. Beyond these cells the passage emerges into the heart of the Ark, where the Dzhuma (Friday) mosque can be found, as well as a vast open-air throne hall, the oldest surviving part of the citadel. A small wall hides the entrance from the throne so that the Emir never had to see his subjects standing in front of him – they emerged from behind this wall on their knees. Mouse recreated this uncomfortable scene, crawling the full forty feet towards the throne.

But the most memorable feature of the Ark is the 'Sia Chat' or Bug Pit, where, in the early nineteenth century, amid the intrigues of the Great Game, Lieutenant Colonel Charles Stoddart and Captain Arthur Connoly of the British Army were detained for the last few months of their lives by the despotic Emir Nasrullah. Stoddart had been sent with a letter from the Governor-General of India to try and form an alliance with the Emir against the Russians. For different reasons, one of the more ridiculous being that the letter had not come from Queen Victoria herself, Stoddart was thrown into the stinking black pit, rife with every kind of insect life. Two years later, Connoly arrived from England in an attempt to rescue his compatriot, only to be thrown into the pit, too. For months they were kept here with fleas, ticks, rats and scorpions as their only companions. Eventually two filthy, emaciated figures, their bodies almost unrecognisable for sores, emerged blinking in the sunlight to face the executioner's axe. The machinations of the Great Game, a phrase coined by Connoly himself, continued with renewed vigour.

On our way out of the Ark we encountered a cockfight taking place under the trees which grow in the shadow of the walls. A huge, vociferous crowd had gathered to watch two scrawny cockerels battling with each other. It was a pathetic sight, but I could not feel too condemnatory because the spectators showed such exuberance. We left as quickly as possible, preferring at least not to participate in this mediaeval scene.

As the day came to an end we remembered that this leisurely routine of sightseeing was only a brief pause in our journey. I particularly dreaded continuing. I felt so ill now that I did not know how I would cope being on a horse for ten hours a day. I had already lost at least half a stone in the last couple of days and consequently felt faint all the time. The others were very worried about me, but there was nothing we could do.

Our two days in Bukhara had been grey and rainy, but on the morning of our departure the skies cleared, so we returned to the hippodrome with excitement, looking forward to seeing our new horses, which Zheniya had promised would be waiting for us there. I was also rather eager to see the elusive Abbas again, even only fleetingly, before we set off for the hills that divide Bukhara from Samarkand.

The hippodrome was in fact more farmyard than horse stud. It consisted of a dusty yard with a few chickens pecking at the ground and some ramshackle buildings housing the twenty or so horses which allowed it to be categorised as a hippodrome. There was also a small pen where two Bactrian camels were enclosed, looking vacantly over the fence at us. But that morning we only had eyes for the five horses we found tethered around the yard. There was not one wart, flesh wound, bloated tick or lame leg in sight. Furthermore, there was a reassuring lack of expectant mothers and accompanying offspring. But we were sceptical: our suspicions were confirmed when Wic mounted a pretty black stallion. Its problem was not related to any physical deficiency but rather to its temperament. Before she had even landed in the middle of the saddle it had begun skipping wildly around the yard, flaring its nostrils and flattening its ears at anyone who dared to come near. However, Wic was enjoying the unaccustomed energy and savoured every fly-buck it made as it bolted out of the farm and down the lane. Mouse, Lucy and I were allocated three other horses by our new guide, Shamil, who had brought the stallions from Dzhizak in the Ferghana valley, and Zheniya introduced as our 'horse expert'. The blue-eyed Shamil immediately seemed more competent than either Dzhuma or Abbas and we readily followed his instructions. Mouse ended up on the largest horse, because she had the most experience, while I was given a stocky chestnut and Lucy the supposedly most docile horse. We were warned several times by Shamil not to approach each other because the stallions would kick and bite each other at the first opportunity, so we all sat nervously at opposite ends of the yard, waiting to leave.

Here we said goodbye to Zheniya and met Vadim, whom we had

arranged would replace him as our camp manager for the next section of the journey (Igor was to continue as our back-up driver and Sacha as our cook). Zheniya had not only found Shamil for us, to act as our horse guide, but also a blacksmith, whom we were introduced to as '*Dyadya*' (meaning 'Uncle' in Russian) Tolik. They set off in the truck as we tried to prevent our horses from bolting.

Shamil, who had taken the youngest horse, led the way out on to the ring road of Bukhara. We were edging our way gingerly along, keeping as far away from each other as possible and using all our strength to restrain the horses, when a rather impressive black Zhiguli car drew up alongside us. A familiar pair of cowboy boots stepped out. We watched in astonishment as Abbas marched into the middle of the road, pulled a whistle from his pocket and brought the traffic to a standstill. His intentions at first seemed honourable – he was simply helping us to cross the roundabout – but as I rode past him, last in the line, he leaned over and planted a kiss on my ear. Wic saw me turn completely scarlet. Abbas then disappeared, only to reappear minutes later parked on the side of the road again. Lucy was convinced he had watched too many James Dean films, for there he was leaning on the bonnet with his legs and arms crossed, giving me a final rehearsed wink as I rode past him for the last time. I forgot about being ill and spent the rest of the day daydreaming.

Our journey continued into the countryside once more. At times it felt as though we were in the south of France, for our track was lined by fields full of apple trees and grape vines. That night we camped at the most idyllic spot to date, on the shores of a turquoise lake. Its motionless surface stretched out to hazy mountains on the horizon, behind which the sun set, leaving streaks of orange and pink in the night sky. But sadly for me this beautiful scene was marred yet again by my illness. I was losing more blood and weight. Lucy and Wic, who had completed a wilderness medical training course before they left England, were thrilled to have an opportunity to practise their knowledge. They produced a thick tome called 'Where There Is No Doctor' and, after much analysis, concluded that I had amoebic dysentery. The book suggested a course of antibiotics, which we were fortunately carrying with us. I swallowed the first pill, hoping its effects would be quick.

I felt both resentful at being ill and mystified as to why I was the only one to have succumbed to the dysentery. Amoebic dysentery is caught from bacteria in water; we had all been drinking the same water, which we had filtered religiously, so why had I been singled out? Mouse, however, had a theory.

'Alex, it's probably because you've never been camping before and we all have.'

'But I've lived in Russia for two years, where the water is notoriously filthy.'

Moreover, I did not see how a few camping trips in Scotland, or even Africa, could have made them immune to dysentery. Lucy and Wic nodded sympathetically. Mouse is generally very relaxed and the last person to boast. However, some aspects of our journey appeared to bring out a competitive streak in her and she often seemed keen to prove that she was the most adventurous and experienced traveller of us all. Because the expedition was her idea I think perhaps she had been encouraged to view it as 'her thing'. I remember on one occasion when she was annoyed with me because I had made a decision without consulting the others, she shouted at me: 'Alex, this is MY trip!' Although we were very much a team, Mouse was nominally the leader and had indeed been our inspiration, as well as finding the majority of the sponsorship. It was perhaps natural that she should feel defensive of her position and I no doubt antagonised her by being too domineering at times.

The next few days were spent skirting the shores of this and a second lake. We forded rivers, navigated swamps, jumped ditches, frightened flocks of pelicans and ducks and did our best to outpace a particularly nasty breed of giant mosquitoes. We lunched in small groves of trees by the lakes' shores, where Shamil took the opportunity to dive into the water. One afternoon we rode through what appeared to be a deserted holiday resort which, we learned, had been a Soviet 'rest home' where officials had come on a break with their colleagues. The nights were spent on the water's edge, and one evening we were treated to dogfish, which Igor had caught among the bulrushes. Shepherds often passed by our camp, herding their long horned goats back home, beneath the ebbing sun.

One morning, however, was interrupted by a frightening incident that set a precedent for the rest of our time in Uzbekistan. We were riding in single file behind Shamil along a path flanked to our left by the second lake and to our right by open scrub. In the distance we suddenly spied a small light object accelerating towards us at incredible speed. As it became bigger we discerned a grey, riderless stallion, charging at full pelt. Its front legs were hobbled, but this seemed to pose no restraint on it, as it lunged forward, lifting its head to release a shrill neigh. There was also a *chopan* flapping from its sides, which made it look wilder. The moment Shamil realised what was happening he yelled at us to turn around and, dismounting, tied his horse to a tree. We stood huddled together while Shamil pelted the loose stallion with stones. By now it had reached us and was circling our group, trying to charge but being kept back by Shamil's assaults. Our horses were pawing the ground, desperate to fight back, but Shamil shouted at us to keep them with their heads facing into the centre of the group, so that they were unable to see the stallion. However, our horses also hated each other and mine, which was particularly aggressive, kept trying to bite and kick the others. Feeling weak from my dysentery, I became frightened and jumped to the ground, holding my horse by his reins. Shamil was furious, screaming at me to remount because I now had no control over my horse, which was kicking out and pulling to get away. Then Shamil's attention was suddenly distracted by the appearance of a shepherd bearing a huge stick, who fended off the grey stallion until I was able to remount, by which time he had managed to grab its head collar and jump on to its back. Once the stallion was mounted he became controllable, and although he was still flaring his nostrils and occasionally pawing the ground, we could stand within speaking distance of him and his rider. Shamil talked to the shepherd in Uzbek – we could not understand what he said, but from the tone of his voice we guessed that he was reprimanding him. The shepherd did not look very contrite as we rode off.

In Uzbekistan, Shamil told me, stallions are not gelded, so they are either extremely aggressive towards other stallions or overly amorous towards mares. Our horses were apparently particularly bad because they had been trained in the Uzbek national game of *ulak*, similar to polo, played on horseback but with the body of a dead goat instead of a ball. The aim of the game is for any rider to hoist the goat from the ground, lodge it under his leg and gallop as fast as possible towards the goal posts, without any of the other riders wresting it from him. Consequently, one man can be competing against an infinite number of opponents and the horses are trained to be as aggressive as possible so as to repel any other horse that comes near. Obviously, speed and acceleration are essential too, so we spent these first few days teaching our Uzbek horses to trot – they were so used to going straight from a walk to a gallop. Mouse had a particularly difficult time, although it made for amusing viewing. Her horse insisted on cantering at all times, with its head straining at a right angle to its body as she tried to restrain it. This meant it could not see where it was going, as its head was almost turned back on its neck, and therefore it was constantly stumbling. The horses had another awkward habit: whenever we bent down to avoid branches they were convinced we were leaning down to grab a goat and would shoot off, almost leaving us suspended from the branches.

Shamil terrified us by recounting the story of a man he knew who had been killed by a stallion attacking him when he was riding. For the rest of our time in Central Asia we broke into a sweat every time we saw a solitary horse tethered. We were convinced it would break free and attack us.

After the excitement of our battle with the stallion we turned away from the lakes, across a seemingly infinite flat plain, towards the mountains. By the end of the day I was beginning to flag, my stomach writhing with cramps and nausea. I tried everything to relieve the pain: riding sidesaddle, walking and leading my horse, undoing my jodhpurs, but to no avail. When we arrived in our camp, I collapsed on the ground. The others made me a bed of sleeping bags outside, under the shadows of an avenue of trees, and I tried to sleep.

That night I was getting up every half hour, so the next morning we all decided that I should not ride that day but travel in the back-up truck. I had been ill for almost a week now and only seemed to be getting worse. Mouse decided to send emergency e-mails to the British embassy in Tashkent and a doctor in London. Answers came back reassuring us that I was taking the correct antibiotics and that it was only a matter of time before I would get better. It was miserable travelling in the truck that day; not only was it extremely uncomfortable, but I hated the feeling of cheating. I decided that the following day, whatever I felt like, I would start riding again.

But the others had different ideas. They became very cross with me, saying that I was stupid not to rest, as advised by the doctors. I was annoyed because I knew I could manage, and travelling in the truck, with the combination of Igor's chain smoking and the very bumpy terrain, was almost worse for me. Mouse and Wic kept trying to persuade me to eat, which I found almost impossible because of the acute nausea the antibiotics were giving me, so we set out on rather frosty terms. However, I was very glad to have held out against them because that day proved to be our most beautiful so far. The grey morning skies had cleared, allowing the sun to illuminate a dazzling sea of green hills covered in bright red tulips and poppies, yellow buttercups and primroses, blue campanulas, forget-me-nots and irises. The beauty of the scene was so overwhelming that Wic wondered out loud whether the shepherds we passed took the hills for granted or, like us, they never tired of them. On the top of the higher peaks stood cairns made by the locals for navigation. We passed a shepherd on horseback at one of these whom Shamil asked for directions. He stared at us for a while, completely mystified as to who we were, then pointed with his leather whip across the valley.

At the foot of the hills were adobe villages, their mud-baked houses scattered across the valley bottoms. Some houses boasted tin roofs, others mud, cemented to the walls by clumps of grass. The former signified the wealth of the owners. The small dusty streets were awash with blossom and vivid green leaves. Poplars, willows, apricot, apple and mulberry trees dripping with glutinous fruits filled the tiny but verdant gardens. As we passed, the locals came to watch from windows, behind gates, across fences held together by scrap metal, staring unashamedly at our unusual procession. Stopping to buy milk, we received numerous invitations to drink tea from these supremely hospitable people.

Now, having experienced a few days of searing heat, we were suddenly engulfed by sheets of unrelenting rain. Shamil attributed this to Mouse lighting a cigarette from a candle – apparently a bad omen. Riding further through the steppe, we passed through more idyllic scenes of pastoral life: flocks of astrakhan and angora sheep and goats tended by shepherds incongruously dressed in kagouls. Curiosity often drove them to follow us for a mile or so, casually abandoning their charges.

When we had first met Shamil in Bukhara he had seemed extremely serious and responsible. For the first few days he had ridden solemnly in front of us, only talking to point out an interesting plant or animal. I had been far too preoccupied with feeling ill and the memory of Abbas to pay him much attention, but Lucy and Wic swooned over him. He was very good-looking but in a completely different way from Abbas. He had light hair and bright blue eyes, his nose crooked from being broken so many times by the horses. He also dressed in a completely different way from the rest of the back-up team in their shell suits. It was obvious that he could not care less what he wore but had inadvertently chosen the most flattering clothes possible: old-fashioned baggy fawn jodhpurs, faded in the sun, and a pair of chaps improvised by sawing off the feet of a pair of long boots; when it was hot he wore a white scarf on his head, tied at the back of his neck in a knot, and he never wore a shirt, so his chest and back had gone completely brown in the sun. He had a boyish but broad figure, with a smooth chest and wide shoulders. I remember noticing his hands in particular: they were very strong looking, with rounded fingernails. He always stood with his chest slightly pushed out and spine arched back, his feet set firmly on the ground, about a foot apart. He had a distinctive habit of rubbing his chest with one hand as he spoke and he would always break into laughter in the middle of a conversation, slapping his leg as he did so. Everything about him exuded a nonchalant and masculine self-confidence.

After a few days Shamil grew more familiar with us. We realised that his gravity at the beginning hid a much more light-hearted and ebullient character than we had assumed. He began to tease us, playing practical jokes and using his few words of English to make us laugh. As I had to act as interpreter, he would often interrupt our conversations to ask me to translate something for the others. If we did not pay him enough attention he launched into conversations of his own, usually fairly tangential. One day he loudly announced he had a name for each of us and had analysed our characters. His inferences proved quite perceptive: Mouse was told she was 'Tiger' because of the efficient way in which she had killed a chicken for our supper a few days before. Shamil said he thought she had a strong character and that he could see in her eyes the potential to be competitive. Lucy, who was given the name 'Panther' because of her black hair, he said was extremely kind-natured. Wic became 'Jaguar' because of her speed on a horse; he also told her he thought she could be determined. I then waited my turn but Shamil went silent, so I asked expectantly, 'What about me?' 'You're cat food,' he replied, and burst out laughing. Then I asked him for my character analysis, hoping that this would be more complimentary, but he replied ambiguously, 'You look Russian'. I am sure he would have liked to have said something more acerbic but was embarrassed because I alone could understand what he was saying.

By the time we reached the outskirts of Samarkand, I was beginning to feel better and had started to eat normally. It was a huge relief not to wake up ten times a night and no longer have crippling stomach pains. I relished the days more than ever. Abbas had vanished from my mind and, despite his comments, Shamil's charms were fast taking precedence.

After eight days of riding from Bukhara, within ten miles the peace and simplicity of rural life gave way dramatically to the tumult of the city. When we could ride no further into the city we dismounted and stood guard by our horses. Shamil instantly became very wary. 'These people are wild,' he said. 'Cities are where civilisation ends and crime begins.' We kept our eyes firmly on our saddlebags while we led the horses to another hospitable hippodrome.

3

Samarkand and beyond

'WELCOME THE BRAVEST GIRLS to Samarkand!' cried Max, our city guide, enthusiastically. Like most Russians, he could not understand the attraction of riding along the Silk Road. Living in the open and travelling on horseback represent normal life to local Uzbek farmers, but to the urban Russian population in Uzbekistan these appear uncivilised habits. Max asked us incredulously why we wanted to spend eight months of our lives in such 'undeveloped' countries when we could be lying on the beaches of the French Riviera.

To me Samarkand conjures up more romance than Paris or Rome ever could. Its very name suggests adventure, intrigue and the mystery of the Orient. Over the centuries it has been a focus of some of the most powerful empires in history. Alexander the Great conquered Samarkand in 329 BC; 1,500 years later Genghis Khan and his hordes sacked the holy city. In the fourteenth century the mighty Tamerlane made it his capital, and in the nineteenth-century Great Game, when Britain and Russia were contesting the vast mountainous regions to the north-west of the Indian Empire, it became part of the rapidly expanding Russian Empire. It was the Silk Road that gave Samarkand its exotic reputation, for the city lay at the heart of the trading system, and virtually all the Chinese caravans with their outlandish wares passed through it. Under Tamerlane Samarkand acquired the towering mosques and dazzling turquoise domes that have gained it world renown. Before the nineteenth century its isolation caused it to be rarely noticed in Western travel writing. (Marco Polo famously referred to Samarkand in his Travels, but it is uncertain whether he actually visited it.) It is this inaccessibility that lends mystery to the legend of Samarkand.

Until the collapse of communism in 1991, Samarkand was visited only by Soviet citizens and the occasional privileged tourist. Back in England, we had found it difficult to obtain much material on its history, and that which was available appeared to focus exclusively on Tamerlane. I had expected a city similar to Bukhara, with its atmosphere of serene antiquity, but Samarkand is a vibrant, majestic place, where history impinges directly upon the present. We met old Uzbek men with long beards, in their striped, padded *chopans* and *tipi-tekes* (skull-caps), walking beside Russian girls wearing tiny skirts and gaudy make-up. The incongruity was obviously not apparent to them, and the disparate worlds seemed to cohabit happily.

We spent two days visiting mosques and madrassahs accompanied by the still bewildered Max. He told us Nature was glad to see us in Samarkand, where the sun shone continually, shimmering upon the turquoise domes and minarets. UNESCO has recently been restoring many of Samarkand's monuments, replacing the intricately patterned tiles where they have disintegrated. But modern craftsmen have been unable to unearth the secret of the turquoise, blue, green and yellow dyes used by Tamerlane's craftsmen, and the restored panels have already lost the vitality of colour retained by the originals.

Samarkand is famed for the Registan square with its mosques and madrassah, said to be the most spectacular architectural ensemble in Central Asia, but I preferred the Bibi Khanum mosque. According to legend, Tamerlane's Chinese wife Bibi Khanum, seeking to surprise him on his return from his Indian campaign of 1398–99, commissioned this colossal monument. In Tamerlane's absence, the Persian architect fell in love with Bibi Khanum. She attempted to dissuade him from his infatuation and presented him with twelve decorated eggs, saying that although they looked different, essentially they were the same, as is the case with women. The architect replied by presenting Bibi Khanum with a glass of red wine and a glass of white wine. 'They may seem similar', he explained, 'but I prefer one to the other.' On his return, Tamerlane became suspicious, declaring that only a man in love could have created such a magnificent monument. When he saw the scar left on Bibi Khanum's cheek from her admirer's kiss, Tamerlane sent a detachment to seize the architect dead or alive, but he fled up one of the soaring minarets, leaped off, and, so the story goes, flew back to Persia. The mosque, which was undoubtedly designed to supersede anything of its kind ever built, today towers gloriously over the city. Its belittling splendour inspired in me something of the awe and fear Tamerlane evoked in his day across half the world. Fully in scale is a giant Koran holder, which stands in the courtyard opposite. In it used to rest the Osman Koran, whose script was so big the imams could read it from the balconies along the colonnade. Max told us that crawling beneath the lectern causes a woman to bear many children, although Lucy later read a Victorian account which suggests it is a good cure for sciatica.

The two days we spent in Samarkand provided a good rest for us. We enjoyed what were to be our last beds until Kashgar, three long months later. We also ate in restaurants, sitting on the ubiquitous *topchans* of Uzbekistan, relishing the relatively sophisticated food of *laghman* (spaghetti soup) and *shashlik* (mutton kebabs). At the other tables old Uzbek men played chess while their wives, swathed in the traditional Sogdian bright red, yellow and green zig-zag patterned silk, sat gossiping. We also visited the bazaar, pressed up against the east wall of the Bibi Khanum, which was teeming with peasants who had come in from the countryside to sell their wares. The heat and noise were almost overwhelming, and we could not take a step without being assailed by somebody pressing their goods on us. It is still called the *kolkhozniy bazar* (collective farm bazaar), but collectivisation has never really affected what is sold here, by whom, or at what price. Each alley is devoted to a specific product: fresh fruit, dried fruit, dairy produce, spices, meat, live chickens, bread, clothes.

Samarkand is famed for its painted *lepyoshkas* (round, flat loaves of bread), which are said to keep for two years. Traditionally, the last thing an Uzbek son does before leaving home on a long journey is to take a bite from a loaf freshly baked by his mother. She hangs it in a safe place and then, when he returns, sprinkles it with water, puts it in the oven and invites relatives and friends round to help him finish it. Max told us that when he went to serve in the Soviet army for two years his mother followed this tradition.

We bought bags of apricots and apples, glass phials of saffron, as well as a striped silk *chopan* each. Every villager in Uzbekistan, male and female, wears one of these padded, knee-length coats, as they have done for hundreds of years. Modern clothes have now become available, thanks to the influx of cheap goods from China and Turkey, but the *chopans* are luckily still universal, and in our experience far more practical against cold and rain.

Sadly, the weather changed as we left Samarkand, with a biting wind chafing and agitating the horses. My horse and Mouse's were particularly fiery. Shamil was convinced that they had been used to cover two mares in our absence. He was meant to have been responsible for watching the horses, but several bottles of vodka had obstructed this duty, and apparently the farmer we had left them with had made good use of the opportunity with our horses, half thoroughbred and half Karabair, a hardy Uzbek breed.

It was a freezing day, and also Lucy's twenty-sixth birthday, so instead of camping we decided to stay in an Uzbek home for the night. We found a family willing to lend us one of their rooms and provide tethering ground. Theirs was a typical Uzbek house: one-storey and set around a courtyard, where the goats and sheep are kept at night. We were lent a room stacked on one side with the floral quilts which an Uzbek bride always brings to her marital home. The family joined us for supper, as we sat cross-legged on the quilts eating soup and the ever-present *plov*. *Plov* is a rice-based dish, served with mutton and vegetables, which can be found all over the Caucasus and Central Asia. There are said to be over two hundred ways of cooking *plov*, with variations on how many carrots and spices are used and how the rice and mutton are cooked. It can be delicious, when made with good meat, or rendered inedible, from use of rancid mutton fat. Luckily this was one of the better ones. It was accompanied by home-brewed vodka and toasts were made to everything under the sun. The mother of the host was tiny, almost toothless, and wholly silent. However, she smiled continually as she drank numerous shots of vodka.

Lucy seemed to be enjoying herself until about midnight, when she suddenly went silent and withdrew from the circle. As we lay down to sleep Mouse tried to sympathise with her but she rolled over and closed her eyes. The next morning she continued to look grim and refused to speak to us. We attempted to discover what had upset her but she remained completely unresponsive and rode alone at the back of our procession. We were worried that we had done something to offend her and the whole incident dampened the atmosphere, so that we spent most of the day in a depressed silence. Luckily, she had recovered by the evening and we never saw one of these black moods again.

For the next couple of days we rode through wheatfields thick with poppies. The only incident to interrupt our routine was when a van of soldiers carrying AK47s challenged us in a small town near the Uzbek–Tajik border. Having interrogated Shamil, they grudgingly let us pass when they realised we were not the spies they had taken us for. Had that been the case, there must surely have been more artful ways of disguising ourselves.

The wheat fields soon gave way to an ominous-looking mountain range. We clambered up a winding path to a plateau at the top, looking out to a range of snow-capped peaks on the horizon, which became pink in the setting sun. I could just imagine some of the struggles of the Great Game being fought out there, as nothing in this savage wilderness can have changed since the nineteenth century. But the wind was bitterly cold, so we descended as quickly as possible into the valley below, where we found a small adobe village, very pretty, with all its orchards still in blossom. When we stopped at a farm to buy some milk, the owner ran inside and brought out five bowls and a bucket of fresh *kefir* (yoghurt). We tried to pay him but he refused to take anything, telling us it was an honour because we were the first Westerners to pass through his village.

By this time, we had developed a fairly rigid routine of riding about twenty-five miles a day for three days, then resting for one. In this way, the horses became fitter and stronger, and we had time to repair any broken equipment. We did not expect our rest day up in the mountains to be very enjoyable – it was so bitterly cold, and there was nowhere to shelter. However, we woke to find the sun streaming into our tents. What had looked grim and oppressive the day before had become in the sunlight an idyllic alpine valley. That morning, we walked back to the village along the valley bottom, seeking an iron welder to repair the broken frame of a saddle. Shamil directed us into a courtyard, where, beneath the shade of a walnut tree, a small crowd had collected to watch the village welder ignite his torch. Sparks leaped from the electrical box, which was connected directly to the pylons above, as he rammed wires seemingly at random into the live plugs. There was a lot of bickering about which wire was which – earth, live or neutral – with Shamil shouting louder than anybody; convinced, as always, that he knew best! But miraculously there was no accident, and our saddle was soon mended. By this time the crowd had tripled; even the local mullah, in his white robes and skullcap, was there gravely eyeing us.

We spent the remainder of the day in our camp, lying in the sun eating the yoghurt and honey we had bought in the village. Igor and Shamil had polished off several bottles of home-brewed vodka by lunchtime and now begged Wic and me to join them on a mushroom hunt in the hills. They were far too agile for us, though, leaving us behind as we struggled up the vertical slopes. When we finally reached the highest peak, we found our guides holding bunches of the wild tulips that grow in the crevices of the rocks.

Suddenly we heard an eerie wailing and spied a solitary figure seated cross-legged, staring out across the hilltops. The man did not stop his haunting song as we approached him. I addressed him in Russian, but he could only answer falteringly, so Shamil continued in Uzbek. Apparently he was a shepherd who lived up in the hills with his two brothers for the six months of the year between spring and autumn. Although they came from the neighbouring village, barely five miles away, they did not return home during this time, but only met their parents once a month at the foot of the hills to collect food. By day, they each wandered over different parts of the hills, tending their sheep and goats. At night, they herded the animals into a stone pen they had built high up in a valley, and slept in an open-ended tent guarded by several half-wild dogs. The moment we left him, the shepherd lapsed once more into his plaintive song.

I recalled the experience of one of my wilder relatives, Feodor Petrovich Tolstoy, who in 1804–5 walked the length of Asiatic Russia, from Kamchatka to our home province of Kazan. In later life he described his encounter with an old man (probably a political or criminal exile) somewhere in those vast wastes, who chanted strange verses piteously to the sound of his balalaika. Feodor Petrovich declared that 'rarely in the theatre or concert-hall have I been so deeply moved as by that absurd song'. Now I imagined how he must have felt.

We visited the shepherds' tent after dusk. They could have been living in biblical times as they sat round their campfire, wrapped in sheepskins, watching the stars. They hardly spoke, even to each other, for solitude had obviously become a way of life for them. We seemed to make little impact upon them and they displayed no curiosity about our way of life. They clearly possessed no concept of any world beyond their hills, unquestioningly accepting their solitary existence. Such a simple, pastoral way of life had always seemed enviable to me, but I was suddenly overwhelmed by a sense of how lonely and bleak it must be in reality. Carrying jars of goats' milk, we returned to the camp, where the noise of Lucy and Mouse chatting and playing cards provided a dramatic contrast to the scene we had just left.

Those days in the hills were some of the most enjoyable of our journey. They seemed carefree and timeless, and all I can remember is laughing and laughing. By this time we had been riding with Shamil for almost a month, so had come to know him well. He had such a strong and appealing character, and was so talkative and animated that, although he could not speak a word of English, he somehow managed to communicate with the others. There were many occasions when the days might have become dull and repetitive, but he was so enthusiastic about everything we saw, from the smallest spider to the carcass of a dead horse, that we were never bored. I can see him now, swinging from his saddle like a Cossack to pick mushrooms – he always carried a saddlebag, just in case we passed some on the way. Because I was the only one who spoke Russian, he would become very restless if I did not speak to him for half an hour and interrupt my conversation with the others, on the pretext of showing me something interesting. Once he shouted with excitement as he pointed out what he took to be a huge eagle crouched upon a post in the distance, where it remained motionless. We all burst out laughing when we cantered up to it, to discover an old tyre hanging from the post.

Shamil had an excellent sense of humour and, although he had had a difficult life, made a joke of everything. But he also worked incredibly hard, often spending whole nights awake guarding the horses. He adored the horses, and was completely in his element with them. Every rest day he would spend sewing up broken bridles and saddles as well as solving any problem we ever had with our equipment. He was also incredibly inventive, on one occasion even adapting an old car seat-belt he found lying on the road into a girth for Lucy's saddle.

Shamil is a Tartar, whose ancestors were among the Golden Horde that invaded Russia in the thirteenth century. Although blue-eyed and fair-skinned, he still strongly identifies himself as a Tartar, and at home he speaks the Turkic dialect. His family left Kazan in the 1960s, during a dreadful famine, and moved to Tashkent in the hope of finding work and an easier life. As a child he decided to become a show jumper, and in his twenties he competed for Uzbekistan, becoming the national champion. However, as a result of the break-up of the Soviet Union, it became increasingly difficult for him to gain a place in the team. Uzbekistan had now become an independent country, striving to reassert its national identity, which required being represented by indigenous Uzbeks, rather than Russians or Tartars as before. So Shamil turned to training horses and making saddles. His time with us was his first work as a guide, and he told us it allowed him to fulfil the dream he had always harboured of riding through Central Asia.

Shamil seemed to know everything about horses, as well as the flowers, wildlife and history of Uzbekistan. Fascinated by the figures of Alexander the Great and Enver Pasha, the Ottoman general who dreamed of uniting the Turkic people, he spent hours recounting stories he had read about them, as we rode across the very land on which they had fought. The landscape has barely changed since the Russian Revolution, so it was not difficult to picture the bloody battles that took place on horseback between the Basmachi, under Enver Pasha, and the Bolsheviks. He was enraptured by his heroes' bravery and the reckless lives they led. I sometimes felt he should have been born in a different era, when he too could have played a dashing role in those Buchanesque adventures. To me, Shamil embodied all that I had always envisaged a Cossack to be: a free spirit, living every moment to the full, accountable to nobody – very like Lukashka in Tolstoy's *The Cossacks*, in fact. Shamil drank and rode with equal enthusiasm and, like his famous Caucasian namesake, the nineteenth century hero of the fighting against imperial Russia, considered his honour more valuable than life itself. Shamil was such a romantic figure, with his bright blue eyes, proud and passionate nature, and complete fearlessness, that he seemed wholly out of place in his everyday life in the dreary Soviet-style city of Tashkent.

From the mountains we descended to the 'Hungry Steppe', which until the 1930s had been uncultivated but is now a grid of artificial canals and wheat and cotton fields. Stalin envisaged in his first Five–Year Plan that cereal production in Uzbekistan should be reduced so as to concentrate on an enormous increase in the output of cotton. In order to realise this hopelessly misconceived policy, there began the rapaciously wasteful use of water that has depleted the Amu Darya and Syr Darya rivers, which in turn has lowered the water level of the Aral sea, whose very existence is now threatened by the ever encroaching salt marsh and desert. We saw direct evidence of this, with water gushing from unsealed joints in the canals and other sections bled dry. The land is so unsuitable for cultivation that vast tracts of it lie half-ploughed, and the wheat fields are filled with weeds and poppies.

For a week we plodded along the canals, the monotony only relieved by Shamil's jokes. It had become very hot and, save for rare avenues of poplars and mulberry trees, there was no shade. The horses tired very quickly, and were plagued all day by flies. At lunchtime we lay in the grass, fighting off the gnats, while Shamil jumped into one of the canals, undeterred by the stagnant water. By day we never escaped the loud croaking of the bullfrogs who lived in the canals, and frequently loped across our path, only just avoiding the horses' hooves. By night we camped in the fields. As we fell asleep and the camp became silent, the bullfrogs' chorus grew ever louder.

It was on one of these long days that Shamil christened all our horses. In order to keep him quiet for five minutes I had given him an

English/Russian dictionary, which seemed to absorb him completely. Taking advantage of his uncustomary silence we began to chat among ourselves. Minutes later we were interrupted by his familiar loud tones.

'You, Lucy, hossie, fleet-footed reindeer!' He hooted with laughter. We could not help but join in and encourage him to name the rest of our horses. The results were as follows: Lucy's horse became not just a fleet-footed reindeer but a 'mottle-backed, fleet-footed reindeer'. Later he was re-christened 'Gay Donkey' because of his long ears and partiality for the other stallions. Mine became 'Ginger Lion' because of his chestnut colouring, Wic's 'Black Pampers' as a zany alternative to 'Black Panther' and Mouse's 'Big Ben' because of his size. Shamil's own horse was the smallest and youngest of the group, so he became simply 'Malish', meaning 'little one'.

At the end of this week we passed through the town of Gulistan, where we spent a day resting in the hippodrome. Almost every town in Uzbekistan has one, such is the importance of horses in this country. This one consisted of a row of twenty or thirty white-washed stone stables surrounded by a few scruffy paddocks. Some of the stables were empty but the rest were occupied by mares and occasionally their foals. These horses are used for breeding and to compete at a local level. Some of them have thoroughbred blood – there was even one Akhal-Teke, the famous Turkmen breed that Alexander the Great is alleged to have ridden – but most were from local stock. The owners of the hippodrome were friends of Dyadya Tolik's, so we were treated as guests of honour. After a week of hot and dusty weather we were overjoyed to be able to use their *banya* (sauna), which under Russian influence has become a feature of every Uzbek village. In the evening, our hosts set up tables under the trees and all the local dignitaries were invited to join us. They cooked a huge *plov*, but instead of the usual mutton they used larks, which they had caught in their fields.

The next day we crossed the second great Central Asian river, the Syr Darya, or Jaxartes, which forms the eastern boundary of Sogdiana. It was much more beautiful than its southern sister, the Amu Darya, with poplars and silver birches lining its banks. Storks rose up as we clattered across the bridge. Here in 329 BC Alexander the Great laid his plans for Alexandria Eschate (Alexandria the Furthest) when ill tidings arrived from Samarkand. Spitamen, an ally of Bessus, the Persian regicide who had murdered the last Achaemenid ruler, Darius III, whose fate Alexander had chosen to avenge, had incited the Sogdians to attack Samarkand. Alexander sent 2,000 men to crush the rebellion, but they were butchered by Spitamen's soldiers. The rebellion was quelled only when Alexander himself marched back to the city and Spitamen fled, to be killed later by his own men. His head was presented to Alexander on a plate. Consequently, the famous conqueror never crossed the Syr Darya. Having camped on its banks, we continued our journey through flat fields of wheat and cotton in blazing heat. The road seemed to go on for ever, with next to nothing to distract us. Along the way we passed an inquisitive farmer who shouted out, 'Who are you? I don't understand!' Shamil turned round in his saddle and called back: 'People!' Apparently content with this succinct response, the man returned to his work.

The next day we decided to ride for half the day and allow the horses to rest for the remainder. It had become oppressively hot and Mouse's horse, Big Ben, was slightly lame. We set off early for Ahangaran, where Dyadya Tolik had more friends with whom we could stay. Our path led us through wheat fields full of peasants working with wooden ploughs dragged by donkeys. Shamil asked one how far it was to Ahangaran. 'Three kilometres,' came the answer. We felt relieved that it was so close, and trotted on. Ten minutes later Shamil asked a man mounted on a mule the same question. 'I'm not sure,' he began, adding however in a decisive tone: 'actually, it's fifty kilometres.' '*Churka*!' This was Shamil's favourite term of abuse, meaning 'blockhead' in Russian. The fact was that nobody seemed to know the way, and we retraced our steps over and over again. There was a small incline, where a group of tall poplars stood over the banks of a river, which we rode through several times. On one side of the river was a hollow in which a group of old men sat engaged in conversation. Each time we passed they laughed delightedly at our predicament.

By midday the sun was blazing down from its zenith in a dazzlingly blue sky. The heat was stifling: the heavy sultry air never stirred, our burning faces longed for a breeze – but no breeze came. The yellow glare of the wheat fields shimmered in the sun as our horses walked slowly on, stirring up clouds of dust. Finally we found our way to a railway bridge that crossed the river Angren, which divided us from Ahangaran. There were no paths on either side of the track, so we had no choice but to dismount and lead the horses along the lines. Only seconds after we had gained the other side, a huge freight train came thundering past. When we reproached Shamil for taking such a risk, he said he knew precisely when the trains crossed the bridge. We knew that he had never been there before in his life, but he advanced his claim with such assurance that we could not help laughing. The hippodrome was just ahead of us, and an hour later we were in the *banya*, sluicing ourselves with deliciously cold water.

We had thought of exchanging Big Ben, because of his lameness, for another horse at the hippodrome, but Shamil was adamant that we would never find a good enough replacement. As we rode out of the stables, a man beckoned me over. 'That horse is the best horse you'll ever find – he's so strong,' he told me, pointing at my horse. 'He used to belong to me. Do you want to sell him back?' Shamil had been listening and, before I could answer, shouted, 'NO!', jerking at my reins to move off.

From Ahangaran we headed once more into the mountains. It continued to be overwhelmingly hot, although snow was visible on the peaks. Streams gushed down the valleys to merge with the tumultuous, muddy Angren river. The only people we met were shepherds, who sold us milk and *kefir*. Shamil was overjoyed to find more mushrooms. He spent the days leading us up and down valleys in search of them. After a week we reached the foot of the 8,000-foot Kamchik pass, which divides the north of the Ferghana valley from Uzbekistan. The day before we crossed it was Russian Victory Day, so we spent it drinking vodka with Igor and Shamil. Both had lost at least one grandparent in the Second World War, which seemed to justify their becoming more and more maudlin as the day went on, until by the evening they were barely able to stagger to their tents.

Instead of following the road that zig-zags its way around the base of the Kamchik pass, Shamil decided that we should follow tracks created by wild boar and goats to pass directly over the mountains. We were forced to dismount and ascend on foot, dragging our horses behind us. We began to climb slowly along one of the tracks, but before long it disappeared, so we were forced to scramble over rocks and scree on all fours, until we found a ledge where we could stop and rest. The gradient was so sheer that we could only clamber in short bursts, and each time we gained a summit we would find another peak soaring higher still. The sun was scorching, and sweat dripped from us and our horses. After about three hours we reached the very top, when all the strenuous effort suddenly seemed worthwhile. We were surrounded by a range of snow-topped mountains that met the clouds, while the hills we had climbed in the last few days appeared like molehills on the horizon. Complete silence reigned as a magnificent eagle appropriately circled the valley below us. It glided towards us, with its huge wings outspread and unblinking eyes scouring the rocks far beneath.

From here we followed a ridge that linked a succession of towering peaks. We were able to ride along it, but it led us on to heights where we could no longer avoid the snow, compelling us to dismount once more. The snow was much deeper than we had expected, reaching up to our thighs, and the horses began to lose their footing. They panicked and, instead of continuing across the glissade, floundered downhill into ever-deeper drifts. It required tremendous efforts to pull them out. Shamil had to run backwards and forwards, helping us to struggle across. We were able to begin descending, but the slope was extremely steep and covered in loose scree. Lucy, Mouse and Wic decided to edge further along the ridge in order to find a more gradual slope down. However, Shamil and I had already gone too far to change our route.

I became increasingly alarmed to feel the ground slipping below me. When I glanced back I was yet more terrified to see a landslide crashing towards us. The rocks above us, which had obviously become loosened by our passage, had generated a gathering avalanche of scree and small boulders. Our path was fairly narrow, on either side of which the ground looked stable and firm. But Ginger Lion stopped and jerked his head back, his ears flat against his head and the whites of his eyes showing. He pawed at the ground, trying to secure his footing, then refused to move across the slope out of the path of the tumbling rocks. He was so strong that there was nothing I could do but attempt to soothe him. I yelled at Shamil, who was just ahead of me and having the same trouble with Malish. He turned around and, leaving Malish standing on his own, clambered back to grab Ginger Lion's rope. With me goading Ginger Lion on with a stick, we managed to get both him and Malish off the scree and on to a patch of firm ground. We stood for a while, calming the horses. I had to sit down because I was shaking so much from shock, but Shamil seemed completely untroubled by this frightening incident. From here we slowly made our way to the valley bottom, where we found the others waiting triumphantly for us. Shamil was too proud to concede that they had used a better route, although he confided to me later that they were cowards! By now it was 3.00 pm. We had taken seven hours to cross the mountain pass. It was sobering to think of all the merchants who must have performed similar journeys with whole caravans of animals.

That night we camped by a small stream, in a glade of poplars. In the morning an old shepherd appeared, waving his stick and yelling at us to leave. He claimed our camp was on his best pasture and that we should have sought permission from him before setting it up. Shamil told us it was common ground but that the shepherd had used it so often, he regarded it as his. However, Shamil remained obsequiously polite even as he protested, for in Central Asia you must never contradict someone older than yourself. We rode off, following a road that was filled all day with Daewoo vans. After the Second World War, Stalin relocated peoples throughout the Soviet Union, and a large number of Koreans were deported to Uzbekistan. Now they have become a fully integrated part of the population, even taking on Russian-style patronymics. There are Korean restaurants in most towns and links are still kept up with Korea – a huge Daewoo factory has been built in the Ferghana valley.

The road was lined with stalls, manned by tiny children, which were piled high with pyramids of white balls that looked like gobstoppers. Shamil was very excited by these and bought an entire bag of them. He did not tell us until after we had put them in our mouths that they are an Uzbek speciality, called *kurak*, made from sour cheese. He was rather offended that we all spat them out.

Now we left the road to turn back on ourselves, towards the Kamchik pass, through the orchards of the Upper Namangan valley. It was mid-May and walnut and apricot trees swam in a sea of dog roses, the scent of which made us think nostalgically of high summer in distant England. We had only just erected our tents on a hill above a village when it began to pour with rain. It continued until after dark, when lightning blazed across the sky, illuminating our line of sodden and dejected horses.

The next morning Shamil woke me at 5.00 am to tell me he had found Ginger Lion covered in swellings. One eye was so swollen that he could not open it, and a bag of fluid was hanging between his front legs. By now I had been riding him for almost a month and had grown very attached to him. He was bad tempered and had already kicked the other horses several times, as well as biting Lucy quite badly on the leg. However, I admired his spirit and in some ways felt an affinity with him. We are both hot-headed, with strong characters. I am not overly sentimental about animals, and Ginger Lion's independent nature meant that he did not like to be fussed over, which suited both of us. Although he could be aggressive to me, I felt we respected each other's ways. He was also physically the strongest of all the horses, with the most stamina, so it was particularly upsetting to see him in this weakened state.

Within an hour Ginger Lion's other eye had swollen up, too; he had become completely blind. He stood motionless, with his head bowed to the ground, refusing to eat or drink. Shamil had never seen anything like this before, but was convinced that several ticks he had found on Ginger Lion's stomach had caused this reaction. Dyadya Tolik walked down to the village to find a vet, returning with one an hour later. The vet borrowed our stethoscope and pronounced that the Lion's heart was functioning normally but that he could not be ridden for a while. He was unsure why the swellings had arisen, but agreed with Shamil's idea of giving him several injections of penicillin.

Having covered Ginger Lion in blankets, we climbed back into our tents and tried to while away the time playing cards and reading. All day there had been a very thick fog, which made everything damp and cold, but luckily we had a bottle of whisky, carried carefully all the way from England, to warm us up. Every hour I checked on Ginger Lion's swellings, but there was no sign of their decreasing.

Dyadya Tolik lay in a doze, exhausted from the worry, while Shamil refused to state an opinion without his approval. Shamil, whose own alcoholic father had abandoned him and his mother when Shamil was five, listened to nobody except Dyadya Tolik, who exerted a powerful influence over him. They had worked together since Shamil had first trained as a showjumper at the hippodrome in Tashkent, where Dyadya Tolik had been a blacksmith, and they behaved like father and son. I only once saw them disagree, when Dyadya Tolik was drunk. They often laughed for hours together, though Dyadya Tolik could be very gruff with Shamil. However, Dyadya Tolik would also occasionally reveal, almost accidentally, how fond he was of him. Once, after a very hard day's riding, we met Dyadya Tolik in the camp, and he asked Shamil, 'How are you?' Shamil replied, 'Oh, the horses are exhausted but the girls seem all right.' 'No, but how are you?' I could see that Dyadya Tolik was worried about Shamil, and that they would be loyal to each other through everything. It was a very endearing relationship.

By the evening a whole procession of men from the village had come to inspect Ginger Lion. Each shook his head, saying he had never seen such a case before. Finally, one man told us that there was a fly living in the hills whose bite could cause such a strong allergic reaction. This seemed to reassure Dyadya Tolik, although the swellings were still no smaller. He told us that we could continue the next day.

I was overjoyed to find that Ginger Lion looked much better the next morning, but it was decided that I should ride without a saddle. We set off on foot, leading our horses into the hills behind our camp. The track wound up into the foothills of the Tien Shan mountains, then back down into the more fertile plains of the northern Ferghana valley. They seemed incredibly flat and featureless after the rocky mountains, so it was very comforting when eventually we saw a small village on the horizon, bathed in the evening sunlight. As we approached, we were joined by children wielding sticks larger than themselves herding their cows, goats and sheep home for the night. The village street was filled with life: small children and old men squatting in the dust under the shade of the mulberry trees, girls carrying buckets of water, women journeying home on donkey carts driven by their young sons, and boys charging up and down bareback on their ponies. At the end of the street was parked an old, battered lime-green car. It had no driver, but the back seat was crammed with five babies and a calf, which had its head stuck out of one window.

A little beyond the village we set up camp in an apple orchard. After we crossed the Kamchik pass, Dyadya Tolik had suffered from altitude sickness for a couple of days. As a result he had decided to return to Tashkent, because we were to spend the following six weeks in Kyrgyzstan, crossing the Tien Shan, where we would have to ascend even higher. This was to be his last night, so he cooked us a farewell *plov* which we ate under the trees, accompanied by numerous vodka toasts. We asked Dyadya Tolik about his home and his family, and whether he was excited about returning to Tashkent. We were extremely touched when he suddenly looked very sad, telling us how much he had enjoyed being with us, and how much he would miss us. 'I love you all,' he declared. 'You are always welcome in my house, any time.' Tears rose in his eyes as Shamil poured him another shot of vodka.

The conversation then changed to marriage. It seems that, since the collapse of the Soviet Union, Muslim laws have begun to wield more influence in Uzbekistan, and it is now quite acceptable to have more than one wife. In fact, if a husband can afford it, he is permitted to have up to four wives. Dyadya Tolik chuckled when we asked him if he takes advantage of this law, and proudly told us that he has two wives. Later I asked Shamil more about this, but he refused to elaborate, saying it was not his business. I could not tell whether he disapproved or was simply being loyal to his friend.

The next day we rode to the outskirts of the town of Chust. We stopped at midday to rest and, leaving Wic and Mouse to look after the horses,

Lucy, Shamil, Dyadya Tolik and I set off for the bazaar. Chust has become a term employed to classify settlers, as opposed to nomads. Thus, Tajiks and Uzbeks are Chust peoples, whilst Kazakhs, Kyrgyz and Turkmens are nomads, known also as *Kara-Kum* people, a name derived from the Turkmen desert. Settlers live in towns and are traders, while nomads live in the countryside and are subsistence farmers. Traditionally, traders speak Tajik, an Indo-European language related to Persian. We were none the less amazed to find that all the traders in the bazaar at Chust still spoke Tajik, despite its being in the middle of Uzbekistan. Lucy and I were told to hide ourselves while the men negotiated prices for some knives, for which Chust is famed. During the time when the Silk Road flourished, the main exports of the Ferghana valley had been horses, armour, oil and knives.

Now came the moment to say goodbye to Dyadya Tolik. I felt very sad, as I had grown so used to him and his farewell seemed to mark the end of something. He had become a real friend to us, looking after our horses conscientiously. I also felt worried about how Shamil would cope without his calming influence, knowing that he would miss him bitterly. That night Shamil drank a lot of vodka and became very melancholy.

The following day was our last in Uzbekistan as we approached the border with Kyrgyzstan. We had lunch beside a stream and tried to cool ourselves off in its murky waters. Downstream we were joined by some little naked boys, playing and splashing in the sun. After lunch I was standing talking to Shamil, who was helping me to tighten Ginger Lion's girth, when I felt a sharp bite sink into the front of my shoulder. I looked down to see a piece of flesh hanging beneath my ripped shirt, and screamed with pain and shock. Shamil immediately grabbed Ginger Lion's head and kicked him hard in the groin. The assault, and the sight of so much blood, had given me such a fright that I could not stop crying. However, the others took control, drawing the wound together with butterfly stitches. Shamil, who was mortified that one of his horses could have bitten me, carefully converted his handkerchief into a sling. For the rest of the day he rode beside me, giving Ginger Lion threatening looks if he even slightly moved out of line.

We spent the night in no man's land. With the snow-capped Tien Shan looming to the east, we were excited by the imminent prospect of leaving settled country for the solitary realm of the mountains.

4

The 'secret garden'

KYRGYZSTAN WAS EVEN MORE SPECTACULAR than we had expected. I have always regarded borders as fairly intangible concepts, but crossing the one between Uzbekistan and Kyrgyzstan dissolved all my preconceptions. As soon as we entered Kyrgyzstan, faces, climate and terrain changed instantly. Green fields, thickly covered with wild flowers, stretched out in front of us to the mountains running across the distant horizon, with their jagged edges silhouetted against the clear blue sky. Out of these mountains which were several layers deep, rose a snow-capped chain that seemed almost removed from the rest. This crest glittered in the sun like a crown on these sternly majestic peaks. Even at such a great distance their immensity overwhelmed us. Suddenly I felt the enormity and power of nature. Everything was bright and vibrant and we seemed to be viewing the world with a new vision that gave each object more definition and depth than before: the icily clear river that gushed through its banks with such vigour and the little droplets of sparkling water that appeared to dance on the surface; the luxuriant grass and the sea of vivid flowers; the people themselves, so fresh and healthy looking, with their rosy cheeks and dark hair. Here was a beauty more infinite than anything I had seen before in my life.

The Kyrgyz people originally came from the headwaters of the Yenesey river, between Lake Baikal and the Altai mountains, in southern Siberia. According to a contemporary Chinese account, until the ninth century, pure-blooded Yeneseyan Kyrgyz were fair-skinned, green-eyed and red-haired. But after the Mongol invasion in the tenth century they became the broad-faced people we met, distinguished from their Uzbek neighbours by more slanted eyes and darker colouring. As soon as we were on

Kyrgyz territory every man we encountered wore an *ak-kalpak*, a felt hat with black trimmings and tassels that sits jauntily on the back of the head.

We rode through Karavan, a relatively large town for this sparsely populated country. A lumbering monument to Lenin reminded us that even this seemingly wild mountain paradise was once devastated by Soviet collectivisation and political purges. Luckily, industrialisation was never realised and the natural beauty of the mountains and high pastures was spared.

Riding along the foot of the Chaktal range, part of the Tien Shan mountains, we felt a great sense of exhilaration. In 1919 a Russian aristocrat, Paul Nazarov, who had fled the Bolsheviks into Kyrgyzstan, wrote in his diary: 'The wondrous beauty of nature and the knowledge that my journey was taking me into the fastnesses of the mountains, far from Communist experiments, brought a profound sense of peace to my soul.' The magnitude, wildness and intense beauty of Kyrgyzstan engendered in me too a feeling of near religious awe that only such magnificent scenery is able to create.

As we crossed the border even the air cleared – instantly fresh from recent rains, in contrast to the sultry and motionless air of Uzbekistan. We camped among lime trees looking out on to the snow-capped mountains, which glowed a rosy pink in the setting sun. As darkness fell, shepherds passed us, fathers and sons riding two abreast.

I felt so happy that I wished this stage in our journey would never end. But Vadim completely shattered this complacency at supper, indifferently announcing two pieces of very bad news. First, we had apparently not been registered in Kyrgyzstan, which is obligatory within the first seventy-two hours of entering the country. As is always the case in the former USSR, this was supposed to have been organised for us in advance, but our request had been brushed under sheaves of paper on some bureaucrat's desk and forgotten. We would therefore have to travel nearly a hundred miles to Dzhlalabad, the regional capital, and register there, as well as later in the other three regions of Kyrgyzstan we were to pass through. Due to the primitive roads, we would have to allow a day just to get there, let alone to register our visas and return to the camp. The second piece of news was that Shamil had not been registered either, which for some mysterious reason bore much more serious consequences. Vadim warned us that if he had not been registered he would be obliged to leave us a few days later and return to Tashkent – a prison cell being the only alternative.

I repeatedly asked Vadim why Shamil should receive such different treatment from the rest of us – why could he not register with us the following day? But Vadim remained elusive and uninformative. He just repeated himself, saying that there was no option. We suspected some foul play: the last few weeks had witnessed a continual power struggle between Shamil and Vadim and, now that Dyadya Tolik had left, Shamil's forces were considerably depleted. Vadim knew very little about horses; his interest lay solely in getting us to the Chinese border. Shamil was insistent that we must follow a rigid routine with the horses, rest them at regular intervals, feed them three times a day and not ride them for an hour after each feed. Vadim, meanwhile, was quite happy to dispense with this routine if it meant we could get to China quicker. He seemed totally unaware, despite our endless explanations, that it would be slower in the long run if we abandoned the horses' rest days. They might be able to continue solidly for ten days or so but then they would collapse, as our Turkmen ponies had done.

Vadim and Shamil had fought daily about this, with Vadim trying to push Shamil to go further each day than we should. But beneath the arguments simmered another dispute, which made each of them become even more intransigent. Vadim was in charge of the camp, so Sacha and Igor were under his command. He also considered that Shamil should come under his authority, but Shamil immediately flouted this idea. He said he had been appointed by Zheniya to provide and look after the horses, and that he was independent from the rest of the back-up team. In theory the two could co-exist, Vadim managing the camp and Shamil the horses. There should have been no room for disagreements because the areas did not overlap, but in practice it was a hotbed of discord. Each morning Vadim would tell us how far he thought we should ride and where we should camp that evening. Shamil would invariably protest that it was too far and that Vadim had not taken into account the terrain. Ten miles over mountains are equivalent to at least twenty miles on the flat. Therefore Shamil maintained it was ridiculous for us to try and travel a regular twenty-five miles, irrespective of the terrain. To this, Vadim replied that it was his responsibility to choose the route with us, not Shamil's. Vadim was obstinate about his point but having a placid temperament, he never raised his voice. Shamil, however, was much more passionate and became quite heated. Sometimes I became involved – Mouse, Lucy and Wic could not because of the language barrier. I also become agitated very easily, so the morning would often begin with a row.

Our sympathies lay with Shamil, not only because his views seemed much more realistic and he had now been riding with us for over a month, but also because it was thanks to him that we had acquired proper horses suitable for such an arduous journey. If we had not found Shamil, we would probably have had to change horses every few weeks. By this time we had become extremely fond of our horses and felt that Shamil was championing their cause, while Vadim seemed to treat them simply as he would a car. If they became ill or too tired he would quite happily have dispensed with them, whereas we were extremely keen to continue with these horses to the Chinese border. They were very strong and under Shamil's regime had become extremely fit. Every day we walked and trotted in regular twenty-minute stints. Less regularly, we would canter, which we viewed as a great treat because it was so exhilarating to race through the valleys. *Risiyu* and *galopom*, meaning 'trot' and 'canter', were among the first Russian words the others learned because we were constantly pleading with Shamil to allow us to go faster. We knew that if we exchanged our horses for local Kyrgyz ponies, although they might be more agile on the mountain paths, they would never be able to go so fast.

We went to bed depressed and frustrated by the fact that there was nothing we could do. At five Mouse and I were woken by somebody undoing the zip of our tent. 'Sacha, Mouse, get up!' In Russian all Christian names have diminutives and I am known as 'Sacha'. It was Shamil, wanting our passports in order to begin the bureaucratic battle ahead of us as early as possible. He was as keen to stay with us as we were to retain him, so as soon as he had collected all four of our passports he set off back to Karavan to see if he could register us there.

Too anxious to go back to sleep we spent the morning restoring order to our camp after the torrential rains of the night before. Lucy, Mouse and I were preoccupied with washing our clothes, but Wic dedicated her spare hours to grooming her horse. She used a straw broom that Igor cleaned the truck with to give him a vigorous brushing and a piece of serrated metal to comb his mane and tail. After forty minutes, however, Black Pampers had had enough, expressing his displeasure with a violent kick, followed by a roll in the mud, and so undoing all of poor Wic's work. His final act of defiance was to munch his way through Igor's treasured broom.

Shamil returned by lunchtime with good news – we would not have to travel to Dzjhlalabad because he had managed to register us in Karavan. But unfortunately he had still not been able to register himself. He was told that as an Uzbek he should have registered in Tashkent. This process, which took fifteen days, was apparently a necessary part of the attempt to curb drug trafficking between Uzbekistan and Kyrgyzstan. Kyrgyzstan is the third biggest producer of marijuana in the world, most of which is transported to the West via the Ferghana valley in Uzbekistan. What did not seem right was that Vadim had not registered Shamil in Tashkent before his departure. Supposedly responsible for the back-up team, he had registered himself, Sacha and Igor – all also Uzbek citizens – in the correct way, so it seemed very suspicious that he had omitted Shamil from the list. We suspected he might have deliberately sabotaged Shamil's papers. That morning a Kyrgyz man, called Bazar-kul, had mysteriously appeared in our camp. At first we thought he was a local who had just strayed in out of curiosity, but then Vadim told us that Bazar-kul was to guide us through Kyrgyzstan and look after the horses. Our suspicions were heightened.

'What role will Shamil play?' I asked.

'Well, Bazar-kul is your horse guide now,' was Vadim's evasive reply.

'But we want Shamil to continue with us. He has looked after the horses so well and we don't want to risk a repetition of what happened in Turkmenistan.'

'Bazar-kul is very experienced with horses and there will be no problem.'

'But these horses aren't Kyrgyz ponies, they're Uzbek horses. Will we be able to continue with exactly the same routine of feeding them three times a day and resting every four days?'

'Well, Bazar-kul says we can't do that in the mountains and we won't always be able to feed them in the middle of the day.'

I translated for the others, who were as perturbed by this news as I was. Vadim seemed indifferent to my protests, so I resorted to a different tactic:

'Vadim, we're paying for the guides and horses and so we think it is our right to choose whether we have Shamil or not.'

'I am responsible for the camp and so it is up to me who works here.' This was the first occasion when Vadim had shown any visible anger, as well as the first clear intimation that the obstacles Shamil faced were not all bureaucratic.

'No, it's up to us and we want Shamil to stay with us until the Chinese border. Anyway, I thought you said he couldn't stay in Kyrgyzstan because of his visa, not because you don't want him here.' I said this with triumph because all our suspicions seemed to have been justified, but he tried to get his revenge by deflecting from the issue in hand.

'Are the horses the only reason you want Shamil to stay?' His question was thick with sarcasm.

I defensively replied, 'Of course,' but I could feel myself beginning to blush, so I turned around and stalked off back to my tent.

I consulted with the others. Mouse suggested that we should get Igor to take us back to Karavan, where there was a tiny post office from which we could telephone for help from our logistics company in Tashkent, as well as an English cotton company, in Tashkent too, where she had a contact. Vadim grudgingly consented to this idea but repeatedly said that there was nothing they would be able to do; Shamil's visa problem was strictly an official one.

We were not to be deterred. Mouse and I jumped into the truck and Igor drove the two of us, Bazar-kul and Vadim to Karavan. We found the post office, which consisted of a room with mud walls and a solitary table, inside which sat a couple of men, wearing *ak-kalpaks*. The telephone system still used switches, so it took at least twenty minutes to get a line to Tashkent and when we did it was incredibly fuzzy. I managed, after a lot of shouting, to explain to one Vladimir, at the logistics company, what had happened. I guessed that Vadim had already spoken to Vladimir that morning, because he had insisted on going to Karavan with Shamil, and I feared that he had simply told Vladimir that he did not want Shamil to continue with us. I asked Vladimir to clarify the problem, and explain exactly why Shamil had not been registered like everybody else. He either would not or could not answer these questions, and replied evasively, 'I'll see what I can do.'

'Well, we do not want to continue without Shamil and it's you or Vadim who has made the mistake, so we feel you should rectify it. Nobody warned us about this and we are not even sure whether to believe it.'

'Don't worry, Sacha, I'll do everything I can. Call me back in an hour.' I could tell he was desperate to get rid of me.

We then called Meredith-Jones, the cotton company in Tashkent. Mouse knew the owner Giles Meredith-Jones, because he lived near her home in north Wales. His company had been producing cotton in central Asia since before the Bolshevik Revolution, and Giles had given Mouse a lot of helpful advice before our departure, making her promise to contact him if we ever had a problem in Central Asia. He employed a former KGB agent in Tashkent called Boris, nicknamed the 'brown-faced snake' for his wily behaviour, to keep an eye on things in Uzbekistan. I asked to speak to Boris, assuming that he would be a fountain of knowledge on Shamil's visa problem. We were also told to call back later in order to receive the brown-faced snake's verdict.

Bazar-kul suggested we took a walk around the town while we were waiting, and he led us to a shop where they sold the distinctive *ak-kalpaks*. Made of white felt and lined with black velvet, these conical shaped hats have flat tops from which hang a black tassel. The front have a black symmetrical pattern embroidered on them and their bottom rims are turned upwards, to expose the black velvet lining. They are also seemingly completely waterproof. Every man and boy in Kyrgyzstan wears one in all weathers, pulling them down over their faces against wind and rain. Bazar-kul bought us each a hat and we felt rather ashamed that we had been so hostile to him. I remembered how that morning he had tried to help Wic with her horse and she had almost pushed him away, saying, ' I wish he'd just leave me alone.' He could not understand English, but it had been obvious from her tone and gestures what she was saying. It was not his fault that Vadim did not want Shamil to remain in our camp, and of course he was only too happy to have a job for the following six weeks.

When we returned to the post office we called Boris the Snake. But he had obviously received a very garbled message because he was under the impression that Shamil had been arrested and was sitting in a police cell. Our reverence for Boris's powers of omniscience received a great blow. He seemed to know nothing about the registration of Uzbek visas in Kyrgyzstan and was clearly no help, so we thanked him and went back to Vladimir at the logistics company. He sounded much more conciliatory than he had been earlier (perhaps under the influence of our threats to withhold our final payment), saying that he had managed to sort out Shamil's visa problem. I could hardly believe that after all this fuss and drama he had capitulated so easily. I was even more astonished that he was now making it blatantly obvious that Vadim's story about the visa registration had been fabricated. Relieved at not losing Shamil, I did not want to jeopardise this by probing further. We had won our battle and that was all that mattered. Shamil received no further stamp on his passport but Vadim retained his dignity by telling us, somewhat improbably, that Vladimir had registered the visa at lightning speed in Tashkent.

When Mouse and I told Lucy and Wic back in the camp that Shamil was staying, they were equally excited by our news. We quickly saddled up the horses. As we left the camp a small crowd of children gathered to see us off, breaking branches from the trees and stripping them to make us whips. We gave them a packet of biscuits in return, which the boys grabbed and ran off with, barefoot along the gravel road. The girls were left, wide-eyed, staring mournfully after them.

We wended our way slowly along the valley floor, towards the mountains. We were so elated to be back on our horses, with Shamil leading us, that we savoured the leisurely pace, drinking in every detail of our surroundings. The Kyrgyz people seem more gentle and passive than their Uzbek neighbours. They also appear to be less driven by national consciousness than the Uzbeks, their sense of identity conditioned more by the family unit than any kind of national one. The borders of Soviet Central Asia were created by Stalin after the Russian Revolution but, unlike the Turkmens and Uzbeks, the Kyrgyz have shown little enthusiasm for their new found national identity, following the break-up of the Soviet Union in 1991. Niyazov and Karimov, the current presidents of Turkmenistan and Uzbekistan, have done much to cultivate a feeling of nationalism in their countries since then, exploiting and manipulating history. The Uzbeks, for instance, have been taught to herald Tamerlane as the founder of their state. His world-renown makes a convenient peg on which to hang their origins and help create a sense of unity, but it is all historical myth. The modern Uzbeks, as well as the Kazakhs, originally came from southern Siberia, where they were ruled by the Uzbek khans, descendants of a grandson of Ghengis Khan. In the fourteenth century they converted to Islam and began to move south, reaching the north bank of the Syr Darya (Jaxartes), across which lay the declining Timurid (descended from Tamerlane) state. The Uzbeks then invaded and established control over the territory between the Syr-Darya and Amu-Darya, the land known by Ptolemy as Transoxiana and by Alexander the Great as Sogdiana, which is now Uzbekistan. Uzbeks are the largest Turkic group outside Turkey. Having made up the third largest ethnic group of the Soviet Union, today they are perceived as the political and military strongmen of Central Asia.

By contrast, the Kyrgyz are descended from about forty different clans, so they lack such a strong social or political hegemony. They also have a less militaristic history than the Uzbeks, having moved peacefully in the Middle Ages from Siberia to the Tien Shan. Lastly, and most importantly, it has often been suggested of Uzbekistan, the most islamicised of the ex-Soviet Central Asian states, that religion has been used here cynically to encourage a feeling of nationalism. The Kyrgyz, on the other hand, although nominally Muslims, often are not practising and, unlike in Uzbekistan, new mosques are not mushrooming up all over the Kyrgyz countryside.

There are very few cities in Kyrgyzstan (Bishkek, the capital, was built less than a century ago) for it is still a principally nomadic country and, because of the mountainous terrain, there is minimal infrastructure. In the sixteenth century the Uzbeks gradually adopted the sedentary agricultural life best suited to the fertile river valleys they occupied. This involved building cities, which entailed administration, literacy and learning, and consequently Uzbek society is coherent and solid, both physically and socially. The itinerant Kyrgyz, by contrast, living in their *yurts*, or felt tents, lack such cohesiveness.

We immediately noticed how friendly and open the Kyrgyz people are. In Uzbekistan we had had stones thrown at us and Shamil had been very wary about our horses being stolen, but here the people seemed always to be smiling, or simply curious. On this first day across the border the only traffic we met was donkeys, carrying anything from entire trees to sackfuls of corn on their backs, a cadaverous mullah on a docile stallion, and a horse caravan, consisting of two horses, four people and a dog. The father and eldest son took the best seats in front while the mother and younger son were led behind. The mother was the first woman we had seen on horseback since beginning our journey.

As Wic put it in her diary, 'On riding over the border two days ago I immediately felt as though I were entering my own secret garden and wishing that it could always remain so.' Everything in this country, from the vast mountains with their jagged edges to the rushing rivers, brightly coloured flowers and smiling Kyrgyz faces, seemed so untouched and unaffected by the modern world.

Some of our most enjoyable moments were when we passed through villages and were able to observe the details of everyday life. A typical village was Dzhoe Sai, not far from the border. Here we received the usual stares and questions, yet this time a number of warm smiles broke out across the villagers' broad faces. From the road, or rather rocky track, we could peer into the houses and gardens. The houses were simple white, one-storeyed buildings – Shamil told us that they are generally only used in winter, as in summer the families move to the higher pastures and live in *yurts*. The gardens were overflowing with flowers, and obviously great care was taken with them because I noticed that often little walkways had been built, covered in vines and flowers, leading to an outhouse. We saw women hard at work washing, beating out rugs, sweeping doorsteps and carrying water while the men ploughed the fields, repaired the houses or chopped wood. We could not understand where all the animals were or who was looking after them, until Shamil explained that although animals are owned by individuals one shepherd is usually put in charge of the village's entire livestock. At the beginning of the day the villagers hand over their sheep, goats and cattle to him and then collect them again at dusk. The responsibility of handing over the animals seems to fall on the children, who could be seen herding their reluctant charges home in the early evenings. Usually barefoot and brandishing a stick, the children looked so tiny next to the animals that it always amazed me that at the age of five or so they could already be this responsible and independent. In the West children of that age can barely dress themselves, let alone guide a herd of cows home alone.

After leaving Dzhoe Sai we continued along the valley bottom, flanked by smooth vertical walls of rock. We reached our camp around midday, which occupied a large patch of lush grass between a fast-flowing river and a spectacular waterfall that gushed down the valley side. We spent the rest of the day resting here and washing in the waterfall.

During the afternoon I suddenly heard Wic crying, 'Where's he going on my horse?' I thought somebody must have stolen Black Pampers. But I looked up only to see Bazar-kul trotting off on him down the road. Vadim told us he was going to buy fresh *kefir* and milk for us from the village a mile away. Wic was cross because Black Pampers had lost a shoe on the previous day and the road was very rocky. She paced up and down the camp, fuming and repeating, 'I can't believe he didn't even ask.' She was convinced that Bazar-kul would do Black Pampers lasting damage, but even Shamil, the previously sworn enemy of Bazar-kul, said there was nothing to worry about; they would be back in an hour. However, Wic refused to be pacified. Suddenly she grabbed a pair of binoculars and began climbing up the valley side in order to spy on Bazar-kul from the top.

Sacha, our cook, had told us earlier not to go off on our own in the mountains because he had had several bad experiences of people getting lost or hurt. Wic had protested volubly against this, 'Why can't they leave us alone and let us do what we want? We're not babies.' I knew she would become angrier if I said anything now, so I paid no attention as she marched off towards the rocks. Shamil looked at me and raised his eyebrows. Lucy and Mouse were also silent – they hate conflict and were very protective of Wic.

Wic having been left to vent her anger, after quarter of an hour the camp was calm once again. Shamil, Lucy, Mouse and I were playing cards when suddenly the sound of shouting shattered the peace. We looked up to see Wic stuck on a ledge, unable to move either up or down. Vadim gestured to her to climb up and across the cliff but she called back that it was too sheer for her to move. Before we could think, Igor was scaling up the rocks until he was just below Wic. She had not noticed him and it was only when she saw a pair of hands grasping at the rock below her, followed by a set of sparkling gold teeth, that she realised he was there. She told us afterwards that, having caught his breath, he mimed to her that he had been shaving when he heard her cries and quickly finished off the job with two decisive strokes, applied two squirts of aftershave (which he insisted on her smelling on his neck) and had shinned up the cliff. Wic laughed gratefully, calling him 'James Bond', which he clearly appreciated. He then managed to scale another overhanging rock face above her and, leaning back over it, offered her his hand. As Wic wrote that evening, 'On clutching each other's wrists and taking the strain I suddenly became terrified that Igor would not be able to take my weight and instead would be flung over my shoulders to the valley's bottom. Remarkably, he pulled me right up and we continued up to the top and then finally over and down.'

On reaching the camp Wic was relieved to see that Black Pampers had been returned unharmed. Everybody relaxed and she spent the afternoon helping Bazar-kul to reshoe her horse. Black Pampers had to be tied up with a series of ropes to prevent him kicking: one rope attached to the back leg being shod was held by Shamil at a safe distance, while Igor pulled on another rope that was tied around his two front legs and Wic held his head firmly, to stop him from rearing. Bazar-kul then undertook the hazardous job of actually fixing the shoes on to the hooves. At every blow of the hammer Black Pampers thrashed out, so that when the shoes were finally attached they were all slightly askew.

That night was Igor's last before he returned to his wife and family in Tashkent, so we toasted his departure and heroic stunt with vodka shots, sitting around a campfire. Weeks before, Shamil had nicknamed Igor the *polkovnik*, meaning 'colonel' in Russian, because he had served for several years in the Soviet–Afghan war. Wic had found the word difficult to pronounce, usually calling him '*polovnik*', which means 'soup ladle', much to the hysteria of the rest of the back-up team. Now Shamil explained

Igor's climbing prowess as the product of these years in the wild mountains of Afghanistan, partly, I think, to account for his own failure to reach Wic first.

We spent the next three days riding through Sary Chelek, a nature reserve nestling in the northern peaks of the Ferghana valley. In its centre lies a 3-mile long alpine lake, thought to have been created by an earthquake that caused a landslide over 800 years ago. The lower slopes are covered in groves of wild pistachio, walnuts and fruit trees, while each little valley boasts its own lake.

Bazar-kul replaced Shamil as our guide for these three days because this was his native territory and he knew all the paths like the back of his hand. Shamil reluctantly handed over Malish and joined the rest of the back-up team in the truck. In order to reach the park from our campsite, we rode through a small village called Arkit, which Bazar-kul told us was home to the park rangers, including himself and his family. On either side of the village street the rugs of Arkit were receiving a good airing, draped on the low wire fences that set the houses away from the road. Many of the houses had open top floors where sheepskins and hay were stored for winter.

Soon we left the village behind us, having stocked up our saddlebags with milk, *kefir* and large brown *lepyoshkas*, and started to climb steeply through the wooded hills, the ground covered with small purple violets, wild irises and miniature tulips. On every side were trees – wild apples, walnuts, pistachios, maples and poplars, all intermixed with evergreens. Mouse, who impressed us every day with her botanical knowledge, became the target of our relentless questioning as we asked her to identify the different species.

Having climbed for a while up the twisting paths, stooping below the branches and pulling our legs back to avoid large boulders we reached a small open grass plateau. We waited for a few minutes to allow Bazar-kul and Wic to catch up. Suddenly we heard a thundering of hooves, followed by Wic on Black Pampers crashing into our peaceful clearing. After galloping past us, Wic eventually came to a halt and explained their dramatic entrance. Climbing up the path, Black Pampers had gone up on to the verge to avoid the muddy and slippery path. He had then tried to squeeze through a hole in a thicket to avoid the path but had clearly chosen to forget Wic's existence. The hole could neatly accommodate him, but not Wic, and, as much as she tried, she could not bend down far enough to squeeze through with him. She was also carrying the video camera on her back and was terrified the branches would damage it. But the further Wic bent down, the more Black Pampers, following his *ulak* training, accelerated until finally she found herself prostrate on the ground with her shirt ripped across her back and the camera lying by her side. Bazar-kul, who was riding behind her, helped her up again, restoring some of his shattered credibility.

Not much later we arrived at our camp on the banks of a small dark lake in a wide valley enclosed on one side by a chain of snow-capped mountains and on the other by a low ridge, crowded with fir trees. We pitched our tents in a glade of mountain silver birches and led our horses down to the lake to drink. Then, Shamil, not content with simply watering our horses, stripped down to his shorts, jumped bareback on to Malish and plunged headlong into the lake. Bazar-kul, looking, as Lucy put it, 'less Adonis-like, more Sumo wrestler', swiftly followed. Soon the lake was filled with horses and riders.

It was now sadly time for Igor to return to Tashkent. We suddenly realised how much we had already seen and done in our eight short weeks together; our arrival in Merv seemed such a long time ago, almost impossible to recollect. Igor's gold grin had accompanied us through so many experiences and his fishing rod, extracted from the truck at every possible opportunity, had become an integral part of our camp life. Always cheerful, he had proved an excellent mediator between the two distinct camps that had evolved in the back-up team. We would really miss the 'colonel', as well as his distinctive yellow truck that we had grown so used to searching for on the horizon at the end of each day.

Shamil and I accompanied Igor for the first mile or two because Shamil wanted to make sure the truck got safely through a small river it had to cross. Having waved him goodbye, we walked slowly back through the grassy slopes, thick with clumps of peonies and tulips. The sun was sinking behind the mountains ahead of us, leaving a haze of pink that glowed on the snowy tips. Shamil took my hand and pulled me down beside a stream, where we sat and listened to the repetitive call of a cuckoo and the incessant croaking of the bullfrogs. It was wonderful to feel so far removed from the rest of civilisation, alone in this celestial corner of the world. We lay back in the grass, chatting and laughing for hours. It was difficult to tear ourselves away from this idyllic spot and return to the noisy camp.

That night, having managed to sleep an unusual ten hours, we woke up to find that Shamil had touchingly picked us bunches of the glorious mountain flowers and lain them outside our tents. We had decided to spend our rest day walking with Vadim to the central lake, so after breakfast we set off over the hills, feeling oddly liberated without our horses. The heat and gradient quickly took their toll, however, and our respect for our horses escalated accordingly. As hill after hill hove into sight, each time we thought we were scaling the last one, but finally we glimpsed a chink of aquamarine water and a log cabin peeping through the pine trees. Having descended the last slope, Vadim opened his rucksack to produce a feast of *lepyoshkas*, salami, cheese, apricots and a bottle of bubbling *kefir* that exploded when we opened it. From the cabin we had a spectacular view of the lake, a deep slice of clear blue water cleft through the mountains, rising sharply to either side of it. The tiniest change of light, as a cloud moved across the sun, made the water dramatically change colour, reflecting and magnifying the sky. The lake became almost black within seconds of having been the lightest turquoise and the atmosphere changed accordingly: one moment it was threatening, the next peaceful.

We left the hills to walk back to camp along an easier path and arrived to find Sacha bearing a bucket of tiny fish, which he had caught in the lake. They belonged to the carp family but unfortunately their Kyrgyz origins did not make them any more palatable than their English brothers. They were too muddy-tasting, with a disproportionate number of bones, so we washed them down with vodka. After supper, Shamil suggested playing the ubiquitous Russian card game of, '*durak*', meaning 'fool'. Wic and Mouse were led through a laborious and seemingly illogical explanation of its rules. However, they finally mastered it and went on to beat their teacher, much to his dismay.

In the middle of the night, on a trip to the lavatory, Mouse and I were surprised by unfamiliar voices. We darted back to our tent and lay there silently in our sleeping bags, too scared to move, until suddenly we heard a booming voice right outside the tent. '*Dobriy dyen*' – 'Good Day', it shouted, rather inappropriately, considering it was well beyond midnight. I cautiously shone my torch through the tent entrance to find a man's face grinning at me.

'Who are you?'

'Sergei.'

'Sergei who?'

'Sergei the driver.'

'Oh, it's our new driver, Mouse.' Relieved, I ran to wake Vadim. In the moonlight I saw our new truck; sadly, it was not the bright yellow of Igor's truck we had grown so used to, but it looked solid and reliable enough.

The next day we left the national park, winding our way up to the top of the Sary Chelek range on a small rocky path, ducking to avoid being speared by low-slung hawthorn branches. The smell of blossom was intoxicating – cherries, apples, pears, seringa and hawthorn all lent their sweet scents to the air. Occasionally the rocky path led us out into glorious meadows filled with flowers.

We picnicked in a silver birch grove before leaving the reserve and descending once again into Bazar-kul's village of Arkit. The village took us back to early geography lessons at school where year after year it was drummed into us that when man became 'civilised' he settled along rivers. This was a classic example – the village was made up of a long, thin string of self-built houses, all jostling for a plot next to the cascading torrent. We wound our way back and forth over the river before finding our camp several miles down stream.

Usually we arrived at our camp spot to find some kind of order. The back-up team would drive ahead to a site agreed with us in the morning (which always had to be near water), and Vadim would then unload the tents, bags, hay and food from the truck while Sacha would start cooking. When we arrived we would tether our horses to stakes, far enough apart from each other so they could not fight, and after an hour or so first watered and then fed them. Three times a day they would have seven pounds of oats each, mixed with vitamins that Shamil had brought from Tashkent and at night they ate hay, if Vadim had been able to find any along the road. Having put up our tents, we would eat supper and write our diaries, read or play cards. We usually did not arrive at the camp until around six in the evening and went to bed around ten, even earlier when it was cold. Going to bed quickly became a rigid routine – we would lay out our mats, sleeping bags, torches and books before supper, always in the same arrangement, with Mouse and I sharing one tent and Lucy and Wic the other. I slept on the right side of the tent and Mouse on the left, like an old married couple.

But on this day we found mayhem. The cab of the truck was tipped forward and Sergei was fiddling around with the engine. Belongings and food were spilling out of the door and Bazar-kul, Vadim and Sacha were sitting on the ground nearby with some Kyrgyz men.

'What's happened?' Shamil asked.

'We've only just arrived because the truck kept breaking down,' Vadim replied.

This seemed credible until we realised they were all blind drunk and could barely stand up. We took charge, set up camp, dining on a simple but delicious supper of honey, fresh cream, *kefir* and bread, while the back-up team drank some more, fought and passed out.

As we left the village, the valley became wider and the river more winding. On the flat ridges that extended like steps up the valley sides we saw a number of horses dragging ploughs back and forth. As we were riding along the road we heard a loud blast behind us from a lorry's horn. When the lorry drew up beside us we saw it was our old back-up truck with the 'colonel' at the wheel. We stopped and Igor jumped out. 'Verreee gooood!' he cackled in his familiar tones as he approached us with his arms outstretched. We thought he would have been back in Uzbekistan by now but apparently he too had had a problem with his engine.

For the last week the weather had been perfect: sunny, with clear blue skies but not too hot. We had been riding in T-shirts and had turned brown from the sun. But the next morning we were woken by an unremitting patter of rain on the tents. Wrapped up in full-length waterproof chaps, hats and coats, we set off in a crocodile, winding up a track into the hills. Mist, fog and rain intermittently obscured our path, lifting at one point to reveal a barking dog, guarding a village of *yurts*, damp and lonely on the edge of the hill.

Our path zig-zagged down the mountain, branches of rain-laden hawthorn swinging back into our faces. Soon, though, it picked up a stream, tumbling down the valley, and we traced its rushing course downwards through groves of walnut trees. Their huge leaves sagged with droplets of rain, swaying gently in the wind. As we trotted through this beautiful wilderness we passed a small, grizzled man, dressed in trousers and a waistcoat, with bare muscular arms. Beckoning us towards his house, he brought out a huge bowl of milk and a pile of *lepyoshkas*.

'Who are you?'

'We're riding the Silk Road.'

'She's a Tolstoy,' Shamil suddenly interjected, pointing at me. He loved telling people this, although most rural Uzbeks and Kyrgyz have never heard of Leo Tolstoy. However, this woodcutter, as he turned out to be, was Russian and had lived in Tula, a city not far from Tolstoy's estate, for ten years. It seemed incredible that he had moved from such a big, European city to this distant corner of Kyrgyzstan. But he seemed very happy with his wife and two small children, who shyly handed us bowls of milk and hunks of bread.

The rain continued unabated for the next few days. As soon as we had pitched our tents the campsite would become a mud bath. It was impossible to keep anything clean or dry and the horses looked more and more bedraggled each day. We had good waterproof clothes, but the rain still managed to trickle down our necks and soak through our boots. The sheepskins on our saddles, which had become sodden and matted, had begun to exude a pungent smell of sheep fat.

It was during these days that a saga began which was to dominate the rest of our time in Kyrgyzstan. It affected the tone of the camp and created fissures throughout our group, which lasted months even after the saga itself had come to an end. Everybody was involved, including the back-up team, and nobody was exempted from heightened emotions or unhappiness.

It all began with a bald saddle sore that Black Pampers had developed on his side. Wic spotted it and asked Shamil to treat it, but he told her it was normal and not to worry. This situation continued for a few days, with Wic protesting to Shamil every morning. Then one morning Wic decided it had gone far enough. She wrote in her diary, 'So far I have put all my faith in Shamil, despite my own beliefs, but as of today I could stand it no more.' She asked me to tell Shamil that she wanted to walk and lead Black Pampers for the next couple of days in order to give his wound a chance to heal.

'It's impossible,' replied Shamil adamantly. 'We've got to go a long way and we'll need to trot and canter, so she won't keep up.'

Wic could not understand why Shamil thought her request was so unreasonable, and how he refused to consider it even as a possibility. She looked and sounded cross, but became even more so when I protested angrily, 'But, Wic, he's right, you'll get left behind.' She shouted at me, 'You would say that because you're always against me and on Shamil's side!' Perhaps Wic had a point: I did indeed feel more sympathetic towards Shamil and the tone of my translating no doubt reflected this bias. I found it an extremely demanding task and impossible to remain impartial in arguments, often becoming very heated.

After that I walked off and refused to translate anymore, leaving them to fight it out alone. Somehow Shamil managed to tell Wic that it was not lack of treatment that was making the wound worse, but her riding technique. (She was hurt that he immediately pointed the finger at her riding and ignored other possible causes. One of the latter could have been the saddle, which Shamil had made himself, and so might have been too proud to blame.) However, Wic agreed that for the next few days Shamil would ride Black Pampers and she would ride Malish.

Wic now discovered that not only had Shamil dressed the sore with wound powder but he had also placed an extra folded quilt under the saddle. 'I can't imagine why he never let me do this. It is actions such as this that make it extremely hard to trust his judgements, despite his otherwise pleasing nature. Nevertheless I let him get on with it as I still hoped his riding would aid the wound's recovery.' Shamil was adamant that he had done nothing different from usual, and that all our horses always had folded quilts under their saddles. Mouse and Lucy were more sympathetic to Wic than to Shamil, which was ironic because it had been they who had been so insistent that we should reach the Chinese border as soon as possible. The previous night they had proposed that we should aim to reach the border a week earlier than we had originally planned because they were worried we did not have enough rest days planned in China. Wic and I did not see why it mattered if we finished the expedition a few days late, whereas it seemed very sad to lose a week's riding in what was proving to be the most beautiful section of our journey. It would also have meant that we had to travel faster, so reducing Black Pampers's chances of recovery.

'Why does it matter if we arrive a week later at the end than we had planned?'

'Because we'll have to pay the guides more and we don't have the money,' replied Mouse.

'I'm sure you're worrying about nothing, and anyway I think we should vote to see who wants to get there earlier.'

Occasionally I felt irritated because it seemed in some ways that the Silk Road expedition was a means to an end for Mouse, and it was the achievement rather than the journey itself that was important to her. She appeared highly concerned about the image we presented and eager to portray us as the toughest and most intrepid of travellers. She told us not to mention our back-up truck or cook back at home and events tended to be reported with an exaggerated sense of danger. This pressure to prove something more than the reality, as well as a sense of being hurried on, served to exacerbate a tense situation.

She and Lucy were perhaps acting more responsibly than I was but I was upset afterwards to find that they had sent a message to our Chinese logistics company in Kashgar, asking whether our permits could be activated for a week earlier than we had planned. Fortunately for Wic and me the answer was 'no', because the permits had been organised long before and it was too late to change them.

We set off from the camp that morning with Shamil and Wic on each other's horses. The other three rode ahead while Shamil and I rode together at the back. It was obvious that a division had begun to settle in our group, although superficially we seemed quite amicable. I felt the others were over-reacting and Shamil had been so kind to us, helping at every opportunity and always trying to make things fun, that I felt hurt for him. He was also obviously far more experienced with horses than us and so it seemed illogical that we should tell him how to look after them. I fear it was clear where my sympathies lay.

The afternoon became even more tense. Vadim had told us to take a short cut over the mountains and cut down towards Toktagul lake, a long and narrow body of water. He had shown Shamil the route on the map which involved following a small path over the peaks. The going soon became tough and we were forced to dismount in order to guide our horses over loose scree slopes and down rocky cliff faces. Here Wic wrote:

> Rather than stick to the smooth mountain ridges, Shamil decided to follow the overgrown and untrodden ravine. As much as I admire Shamil, he can be so stubborn. For example, when I suggested an alternative route, to avoid a two-metre drop that Mouse and Big Ben had just fallen down, Shamil simply insisted that it was a bad idea because it was covered with huge boulders and that I should stick right behind him. I couldn't see these huge boulders and decided to take my proposed route. It proved to be ten times quicker and less complicated. I am by no means saying my 'guiding skills' are better than his, only that I wish he wasn't so proud.

After a couple of hours we had only advanced half a mile down the mountain and were having huge problems with our horses. My horse, Ginger Lion, in trying to scramble up a vertical rock face did not quite reach the top and flipped over backwards. Luckily he managed to twist himself round in the air, like a cat, and landed on his hooves. His leading rope was wrenched out of my hands, leaving them covered in burns. He had landed safely, but this incident made Wic more upset. Meanwhile, Mouse was battling with Big Ben on a ridge. If Big Ben was clumsy on a flat surface, he was hopeless on the scree and rocks. He had slipped, skidded and stopped inches from the cliff edge, and now stood quaking with fear, refusing to move either forwards or backwards. Wic left Malish where she had been standing with him and clambered up towards Mouse. Together, they managed to move Big Ben a few steps forward by picking up each of his legs in turn and placing it in front of the others. The next move was to get him across the scree slope, which consisted of large slabs of slate and boulders. Wic and Mouse edged him slowly forwards until they were halfway across, when Shamil climbed towards them, yelling, '*Tempo, tempo*!' He grabbed the leading rope from Mouse and dragged Big Ben across the remains of the scree, frightened that Big Ben would lose his nerve and slip down the mountainside if he did not get across quickly. Wic observed, 'It was terrifying to witness, for his right hind leg suddenly became trapped between two large rocks. Shamil, who hadn't seen this, continued to drag Big Ben across until two abrupt screams stopped him. His hoof was released although it did little for his confidence.'

This incident perhaps highlighted the root of Shamil and Wic's conflict. Shamil's theory was that horses need to be strictly disciplined in order to perform – he would always blame us if our horse stumbled or misbehaved, saying that the rider is responsible for the horse's every action. He loved horses more than anything in the world and felt that the kindest and safest way to treat them was to show authority, like a parent with a child. Wic also loved horses enormously but she was more indulgent, allowing them greater freedom. Shamil's experience lay in making horses work and perform. Wic, on the other hand, had owned ponies as pets rather than as working animals. These conflicting approaches were aggravated by their personalities. Shamil has a very forceful and proud character. Always boisterous, he did not hesitate to say what he thought, even if he knew it would upset Wic. Incredibly good-natured, he never got in a bad mood – which almost made matters worse, because Wic felt he did not take things seriously and made her own concern look excessive. Wic has a very gentle character and never sought to impose any kind of control on the group, but she expressed her opinions about the horses in an intractable manner and that automatically made Shamil defensive.

Finally, after seven hours we reached the bottom. Shamil had run up and down the mountain helping each of us. It was not his fault that we had taken this path – on the map it had looked perfectly safe – but Lucy and Wic were furious, saying it was ridiculous to have attempted this descent on our horses. Wic rode up to Shamil and shouted in his face, 'You are so stupid, you *churka*,' waving her fist at him.

'Why does it matter if we're safe now and nothing happened?' I asked.

'Because we put our horses in such danger,' replied Lucy.

'Do you think Peter Fleming cried every time he encountered a sandstorm? I don't know why you bother coming on an expedition like this if you can't endure some danger and hardship,' I muttered.

This absolutely enraged Lucy, who would not talk to me for the rest of the day.

We eventually arrived in our camp, on the edge of Toktagul lake, in darkness at 9.30 pm. The others did not talk to me for the rest of the evening and we ate our supper in an awkward silence. The next morning I tried to apologise to Lucy. But she was still very angry, telling me it was not fair of me to criticise their behaviour when they had worked so hard to get here. It is true that she, Mouse and Wic had raised the vast majority of the sponsorship for the expedition – I had only found various bits of equipment. They spent six months writing to sponsors, giving presentations and raising sponsorship while I was in Moscow, organising the logistics for Central Asia. I knew that they all felt I had not contributed enough. During the last month before we had set off from England, I had gone on holiday for ten days as well as spending a couple of weekends away, leaving them to work and attend the medical training course without me. In retrospect I can see this was a very selfish thing to do. Every bit of help was needed and I had left everything to them. Understandably, this provoked some resentment on their part. Another unfortunate factor was that I spoke Russian, which meant that I exerted a certain power in the group. They were to some extent unavoidably beholden to me, since I became the spokesman for our team, while they were unable to conduct arguments with the guides without my assistance.

I now became homesick for the first time. I suddenly felt unsure that there was any point to what we were doing and that I should have been spending my time more profitably. I also dreaded reaching China, when we would leave Shamil and it seemed that I would be alone with the other three against me. I remember crying for a whole night, seriously considering whether to leave the others on the Chinese border and return to England alone. But I wrote to my parents, via e-mail, who reassured me that what we were doing was definitely worthwhile and that I would always regret it if I did not complete the expedition.

The next morning we circumnavigated Toktagul lake, riding through clumps of marijuana plants growing wild. Where the plains met the edges of the lake they became marsh and we saw Kyrgyz men paddling their canoes through the reeds.

In the afternoon the sun came out, but a strong wind sent clouds scudding across its rays, throwing huge shadows over the plain. Together with the wind, they swept across the open landscape, casting great grey shapes which disappeared to reveal the mountains ablaze in the dazzling sunlight.

We emerged from the plain into the city of Toktagul, the roadside dotted with *chai-khanas* covered with colourful awnings. Lorries were parked on the edge of the road as their drivers sat cross-legged on cushions, drinking bowls of tea. We begged Shamil to let us stop and join them but we were not allowed to because such places are forbidden to women. In the cities this was not such a problem, but in the countryside people's habits are more conservative, and we had to respect them. There were also small stalls selling cake, fizzy drinks and Russian biscuits. Rudimentary signs indicated the presence of fish or honey for sale. Shamil stopped to buy *kefir* and fresh strawberries, and we rode down the poplar-lined avenue feasting on them.

For the next few days we followed the course of the Chuchkan river, which cleaves its way through the Susamir-Too range of mountains. We spent our rest day at the foot of a mountain pass, in a glade of birches. Bazar-kul told us the Kyrgyz believe it is important to sacrifice a sheep before crossing a difficult pass, so he walked to a local bazaar, returning with a black sheep in tow. He left the sheep to graze for a while in order to allow it to relax, then began the process of slaughtering, skinning and gutting the animal. Bazar-kul followed a precise set of procedures, performing them with such speed and ease that it seemed the simplest operation. First, in the Muslim way, he slit the sheep's neck with a knife, allowing its blood to pour out. The animal thrashed around a little but it soon became still, then Bazar-kul began to skin it. Starting from the neck, he ripped the skin back to reveal the pink, warm flesh. This was done so delicately, yet so quickly, that he never once made a tear in the skin and within ten minutes or so the whole sheepskin was lying splayed out on the grass. Finally, the sheep was hung on a tree, cut up into parts and its guts removed. Bazar-kul told us that in Kyrgyzstan the back legs of the sheep are valued far more highly as meat than the front legs, with the trunk of the body being regarded as the least valuable. If a young man is able to rip cleanly off one of the back legs of a sheep, he is permitted to take the hand of the daughter of the sheep's owner in marriage.

Finally, the meat was cut up into small chunks and made into *shashlik*, or kebabs, skewered on twigs. Mouse and Shamil eagerly divided up the liver between them, the rest of us most willing to forego this delicacy.

In the middle of the river near our campsite there was a small island on which we had left the horses to roam free for the day. Shamil had built a campfire in the middle of this island and now we waded through the river's icy water, carrying *lepyoshkas*, tomatoes, onions and the *shashlik*. The horses stood nearby as we were eating, swishing their tails to keep away the flies and nibbling each other. At one point the peace was disturbed by Ginger Lion savagely biting Big Ben, but later he received his retribution when he erupted in another allergic reaction to fly bites, this time thankfully only around his eyes and stomach.

We were sad to leave our idyllic campsite the next day. After half an hour of plodding up a gravel track leading to the mountain pass, we were passed by a pick-up truck, in the back of which were huddled a Kyrgyz family, the women dressed in bright reds and blues and wearing headscarves and the men wearing their *ak-kalpak* hats. They were all seated, surrounded by bags, on thick quilts and blankets. In the middle stood a small calf and several chickens.

A couple of hours later we passed them again. This time they had stopped and were assembling their *yurt* on the grassy hillside. The men were erecting the inner layer, which consisted of a wooden trellis, and the women were boiling pots of water and organising their belongings into piles. Meanwhile the children, who seemed exempted from any duties, were playing with the donkeys and horses that stood tethered and hobbled nearby.

We continued on our way, only stopping for Shamil to buy a bowl of fermented mare's milk, or *kumiz*, from a stall. The latter was manned by a small boy whose only other ware was bunches of spring onions, which did not tempt us. We reached our camp, at 9,000 feet, just in the nick of time before a low storm cloud engulfed the mountain opposite and moments later reached us, dropping large flakes of snow on its way. The freezing air forced us to retire to our tents earlier than usual, where we lay huddled in our sleeping bags, reading by torchlight.

The next morning we crossed the Ala Bel pass, at about 8,700 feet. We had hoped to cross by a more remote pass, but were diverted because of late snows and now were keeping roughly to the only road that connects Bishkek and Osh, the capitals of northern and southern Kyrgyzstan. Kyrgyztan is the size of Austria and Hungary put together, but it has all of ten or so principal roads. Consequently this road was full of lorries, delivering goods between the two cities.

The road lay directly over the pass, just below the snowline. Once over the shallow ridge, it began to descend with the mountains drawing away and the plains opening up. Now we left the highway to follow a small trickle of water, dribbling over marsh and bog, which Shamil told us was the source of the Susamir river. Further on, the trickle became a stream and we galloped along beside it. Lucy's horse, Gay Donkey, had lost a shoe on the road earlier that morning, which did nothing to temper his mulish manner. Seeing the open plains ahead of him, he could think of nothing but losing his rider, so he and Lucy hopped and bucked towards the horizon.

Having spent the whole afternoon cantering across the plain, we suddenly spied our camp. Surrounded on all sides by snow-capped mountains it was divided from us by the Susamir river, by now about ten feet wide. We forded the river, climbed up its banks of dark green heather sprinkled with bright blue forget-me-nots and rode towards the truck. Here we were met by a Czech cyclist, Jan, whom Vadim had invited to stay the night in our camp. Jan had stuck a large sign on his back, saying 'FRAGILE,' in an attempt to deter lorry drivers from driving into him.

5

In the mountains

WE HAD EXPECTED JUNE to bring more clement weather. The last week of May had become icily cold after a mostly warm and sunny beginning to the month. But on the first day of June we were still astonished to wake up and find our tents covered in snow. Jan had slept in our mess tent and as we ate our breakfast of porridge and tea he was busy warming his chilblained feet over a naked flame. Jan was probably about fifty, with a greying beard, but he told us in broken English that he was cycling roughly sixty miles a day. The year before he had spent two months cycling from Lake Baikal, in Siberia, to his home in the Czech Republic and he planned to slowly make his way around the world in this solitary fashion.

He produced a crumpled magazine article he had written for a Czech magazine about his trip around Lake Baikal. He told us that he usually stayed each night with local families, in their *yurts*, who were always very intrigued by this article, begging him to feature them in his next. While we were saddling up our horses, Jan emerged from the tent in a cocoon of plastic layers to resume his lonely journey.

The snow slowly melted as we followed further the meandering path of the Susamir, leaving the road well behind us. As we cantered through the open plain, we were pursued by a herd of wild horses with a fiery stallion at its head. Luckily we were able to outpace them, galloping as fast as we could. The only other form of wildlife we encountered were some yellow birds, similar to wagtails. In the afternoon we passed several *yurts*, stopping at one to ask the way. Outside it a pole had been suspended across two stones with slabs of fresh mutton hung from it, drying for winter use in the elusive sun. The *yurt* was set apart from its fellows by two intricately painted wooden doors, one slightly ajar, revealing a pile of luxurious-looking floral quilts.

We gradually descended from the mountains, their peaks shrinking into the horizon and the grassy plateau contorting into hillocks crowned with copses of hawthorn and willow. As we rounded a bend in the river, a sheer slope rose in front of us, so we dismounted and struggled up on foot until we found a path to follow. Having remounted, we could look back to see a panoramic view of the Susamir river snaking its way down from its origins in the Tien Shan towards its namesake town. Then, passing several shepherds wearing the standard Kyrgyz garb of a suit and *ak-kalpak*, we cantered around a corner to find our camp lapping up the last rays of a rosy sunset.

We were to spend a rest day here. The next morning Shamil told me that there was a big problem with Black Pampers. He had found a large sack of pus on his withers, although not connected to the saddle sore. For the last three days Wic had been riding Black Pampers again, using a blanket with a hole cut around the sore, but she had not noticed this new development on his withers. We were all shocked and worried by Shamil's revelation, especially when he told us that the sore needed to be lanced as soon as possible. Black Pampers stood looking rather dejected as we discussed his fate. Two schools of thought quickly emerged. Bazar-kul was of the opinion, and had been since all these problems began, that Black Pampers should be exchanged for another horse – he was convinced that his condition would not improve without complete rest. (He also used the opportunity to tell us that all our horses were useless and should be exchanged.) The other school of thought headed by Shamil but closely seconded by Wic, was that Black Pampers should be retained. They both displayed such conviction that Bazar-kul retired somewhat. Although the situation was bad it was redeemed a little by the fact that Shamil and Wic were once again united in their wishes. Finally, a compromise was settled upon. Because Black Pampers was otherwise perfectly healthy, it was decided that he should stay with us, we would rent a horse for a week or so and lead Black Pampers in order to give his withers time to recover.

As if by divine intervention, a horse and rider appeared out of the scrub. The horse was a dark bay stallion and his rider a young Kyrgyz man, grinning from ear to ear. Bazar-kul immediately proposed our idea to him. It was accepted and the bartering began. While the young Kyrgyz and Bazar-kul were bargaining, Shamil tested the new horse. He leaped on to the saddle, spun its head round and pelted at full gallop up an almost vertical hill bordering one side of our camp. The poor horse was obviously unused to such dramatic bouts of exercise and Shamil returned, shaking his finger in disapproval: he was not substituting Black Pampers for this panting, unfit animal. But we managed to persuade Shamil that on no account did we intend to exchange the horses permanently; we just wanted to rent this new horse for as long as it took Black Pampers to recover. The horse's owner would travel in our back-up truck and ride back home at the end of the rental period. Shamil was somewhat placated by this, although we could not understand why he so vehemently objected to what we felt was a very sensible idea. I suspect it arose from the immense pride he felt in our horses – any injury or slight they suffered was considered a reflection on him.

Our Kyrgyz friend agreed to return the next morning from his village, a few miles away, at half past seven precisely. But before he departed, he needed to avenge his horse's honour. This duel took the form of a race up the mountainside; the first one back to the camp would be the winner. Shamil and the Kyrgyz took their positions on the starting line and Vadim counted to three. Within seconds they were off at a gallop and the Kyrgyz was speeding straight up the hill, not glancing to left or right. Shamil, meanwhile, was experiencing difficulties: Malish had careered off in the opposite direction and Shamil was unable to restrain him. We laughed and laughed as the Kyrgyz sped back towards us while Shamil was still turning circles at the opposite end of the camp. Our new horse had proved himself.

But Shamil's pride and appetite for competition were not satisfied. Unable to revenge himself on his former opponent, he challenged Bazar-kul to a horseback wrestling match. Bazar-kul accepted the challenge and Shamil suggested he borrow Ginger Lion. This was perhaps a slightly misguided choice, because as soon as they started wrestling Ginger Lion followed suit and began biting poor Malish. Shamil and Bazar-kul were locked with their arms around each other's shoulders when Shamil suddenly swung his body around Malish's neck, pulling Bazar-kul with him. Bazar-kul was unable to keep in his saddle and fell to the ground with a thud. The triumphant Shamil responded to Mouse and Lucy's cries of 'More, more!' by suggesting a Kyrgyz game, played by a girl and boy. I was chosen as his accomplice and was told to get on Ginger Lion. Shamil explained the rules to me. I was to ride as fast as I could towards the camp while Shamil chased me, trying to kiss me. In retaliation I was allowed to whip him. After a count of three we began. I kicked Ginger Lion on but Shamil caught up almost immediately and managed to wrap his arm around my shoulders and kiss my cheek. To screams of laughter from Wic, Lucy and Mouse, I clouted him on the leg with my whip and managed to release myself.

In the early evening Shamil rode to the local village, in search of a vet. But he found nobody; he would just have to do his best alone. He decided not to lance the wound immediately but to wait for a few days in order to see if it would cure itself naturally. He produced a small jam jar of a black, tarry substance which he applied to the swelling, telling us that it should draw out the pus.

By eight o'clock the next morning we were scanning the horizon, in expectation of the bay stallion. But after an hour of waiting we realised that our Kyrgyz friend was not planning to keep his side of the bargain. We had no option but to ride to the village and hope that we could hire another horse there.

We quizzed the first man we came across. He seemed very eager to do business with us and motioned to his wife to bring us *kefir*. A well-rounded woman with a headscarf, she waddled towards us with a large bucket of the white, creamy liquid which she slopped into bowls. Then, noticing her neighbour's turkeys entering her garden, she abandoned the *kefir* and returned to her house, brandishing a long wooden stick above her head and screeching abuse until she had ushered the turkeys back into the next-door patch. Moments later there was a thunder of hooves behind us and two small boys, presumably the sons of the man who was helping us, approached on two fiery ponies. They jumped to the ground and proudly exhibited their animals. The first was a dark grey whose initial energy was apparently deceptive. Although he could clearly gallop at an impressive speed up and down the village, Shamil declared that his legs would not cope with eight hours of riding every day. The second pony seemed more capable and despite his diminutive size – Wic declared she had seen bigger donkeys – appeared strong and healthy. However, after a closer inspection Shamil noticed a large lump on his near front leg. The owner said it was a result of being hobbled; Shamil said it was an old injury. Bazar-kul and the back-up team, who had arrived soon after our discussion began, took the owner's side. Before we knew it, a full-scale argument had ensued. To make matters worse, the owner said he did not want to hire out the pony, only exchange it for Black Pampers, which was plainly unacceptable to us. By this point everybody was becoming involved, yelling and gesticulating. When the commotion finally subsided, Vadim told us that we had greatly insulted the owner of the pony by refusing his offer. Embarrassed at having caused offence, we apologised profusely. But Shamil consoled us later by telling us that the worst horses are always brought out first, so we would have appeared idiots if we had made an exchange.

We set off as quickly as possible, down a straight dusty road into the hills. Wic was still riding Black Pampers, but without a saddle, so no pressure would be applied to his withers. Instead, Shamil had tied a girth around a thick blanket, attaching stirrups to the girth. In this way, we hoped the swelling would subside naturally.

During the afternoon we left the road for a track that meandered through the hills. At one point it ran near a river where we encountered some fishermen holding a large catch of fish. When Shamil asked, 'Can we buy some?', there was silence, then suddenly without a word the fishermen thrust their entire catch into our saddlebags. 'How much do we owe you?' Shamil began feeling in his pocket for some money, but still no response. 'How much do we owe you?' he repeated. The men looked at each other in confusion, then all at once leaped into a small Lada parked nearby and accelerated off down the track. We were very surprised, but Shamil enlightened us.

'They were fishing out of season and so were probably frightened that we might report them.'

I was astonished that in this sparsely populated, wild country such rules had been introduced, let alone complied with.

We counted eight *osman* – a type of mountain trout – which the men must have spent hours catching with their improvised fishing rods: we would eat well tonight.

We arrived in camp after sunset, around nine o' clock, having ridden thirty-five miles – a relatively long day. This meant we had to feed and water the horses in the pitch dark.

The next morning, after breakfast, we found Wic struggling to raise Black Pampers from his sleep. The night before we had not been able to see where we had been tethering the horses, but now in the light of day we found them surrounded by thick clumps of marijuana. Black Pampers was lying prostrate on the ground, surrounded by beheaded, chewed plants. Unsurprisingly for the rest of the day he was more sleepy than usual.

We spent the day riding between sheer cliff faces. Rising up to either side of us, they were gradated in varying shades of red and orange, representing a stark contrast to the verdant green and blue landscape of the previous days. They boasted almost no vegetation. At one point we emerged from the dusty track that wound between them on to an open plain, dry and featureless except for yellowing stalks.

Towards the end of the afternoon we left the cliffs and descended along the path into a small village sitting on the edge of a green plain. We spotted our back-up truck in the middle of this plain and headed towards it. But as we approached, Shamil exclaimed, 'they're stuck!' The back wheels of the truck were indeed deep in mud. We could hear the engine revving as Sergei tried to extricate himself. Suddenly Shamil, who was slightly ahead of us, shouted, 'Stop, stop!' and I saw Malish floundering up to his knees in mud. There was obviously a large bog which was not visible until you were right in it. We waited until Malish had safely removed himself before carefully circling the bog and choosing a safe spot for our camp among clumps of small wild irises.

Three local farmers had come from the village to help Bazar-kul, Vadim and Sacha push the truck out of the bog. Finally, after an hour, Sergei was able to drive free. We set up camp while Bazar-kul and Sergei thanked the farmers for their help by sharing a bottle of vodka with them. They became noisier and noisier and before long Bazar-kul came staggering towards me. Placing his hand on my shoulder to steady himself, he said slowly,

'Sacha, do you want to keep your horses in the farmer's field tonight?'

'Why?' I asked.

We were surrounded by rich grazing, so his suggestion seemed a little strange.

'Well, they'll be safer there.'

Shamil, who had been listening to our conversation, interrupted at this point, 'Sacha, it's better if they stay here.'

'Why?'

Without Bazar-kul seeing, he signalled that he would tell me later.

'Thanks, Bazar-kul, but I think we'll keep them here with us.'

As Bazar-kul lurched back I turned to Shamil. 'Why do they want to look after the horses?'

'Because they want to use them to cover their mares, so that they can introduce new blood into the herd.'

Kyrgyz horses are on the whole much smaller than our Uzbek stallions, so the attraction was understandable.

The farmers did not seem to be offended that we had declined their hospitality and continued drinking with Bazar-kul and Sergei. After a couple of hours, before it had become dark, we saw Bazar-kul stand up and totter towards his tent, where he collapsed, his feet protruding through the entrance. Half an hour later, as we were feeding our horses, we heard loud shouting and turned around to see Sergei flinging the table, vodka, glasses and all, up into the air and trying to punch one of the Kyrgyz farmers in the face. Shamil and Vadim managed to push Sergei into the cabin of his truck and lock the door. For a while he banged on the window, swearing and making wild threats, but they took no notice and eventually he too collapsed into sleep. This scene appeared quite normal to the rest of the back-up team.

'Were they fighting about something?' I asked.

'No, Sergei just has a small problem with drink,' Vadim replied laconically.

The Kyrgyz farmers said goodbye, looking equally unperturbed, and we ate our supper against the backdrop of a magnificent sunset.

Shamil had still not been able to find a vet to lance the wound on Black Pampers' withers. He had been covering the wound with his tarry medicine every day, but so far no pus had emerged, so Wic continued to ride without a saddle. Luckily the tension seemed to have subsided between Shamil and Wic, with both of them now only concerned about curing Black Pampers.

We rode further down the valley, leaving the horseshoe-shaped mountains behind us. On our right was a range of peaks divided into three distinct layers, with brown, scrubby scree at the bottom and snowy rocks at the top, sandwiching a hidden pastoral paradise of green in the middle. We passed through a village and then turned to follow a footpath, which led through more treacherous marshes. Clumps of higher grass were the only clue as to their whereabouts, which only become apparent when you fell into them. But, aided by the directions of a tiny shepherd boy, we negotiated our way safely through them and stopped for lunch. A dramatic and thankfully short thunderstorm sent us on our way, down to the banks of the Kirkirmeren river, which we crossed and re-crossed all afternoon, meeting countless Kyrgyz men on horseback along the way. We came to the conclusion that we had definitely encountered more horses than cars in Kyrgyzstan. Even in the villages there were hardly any motorised vehicles. Occasionally we would see a primitive wooden wagon being pulled by a horse, but otherwise the men jigged along on their long-maned ponies supported by saddles that had not changed since Tamerlane's time. These were made of wood and leather, with high pommels and basic iron stirrups. The rider usually sat on a couple of folded quilts and carried a leather whip known as a *kamcha*. Shamil was very dismissive of this style of riding: sitting far back in the saddle, the rider would flap his legs and arms if he wanted to go faster, certainly not following the European principle of shoulders, hips and heels being aligned.

Our next rest day was again dominated by the plight of poor Black Pampers. Shamil decided it was time to attack the swelling. He told Wic to lather the infected area with hot water and soap, in order to make the skin supple and more pliable. He then began to squeeze the lump as hard as he could. Black Pampers seemed at first to be in great discomfort, bucking and twisting his body, but he soon calmed down and stood still as Wic stroked his head. Pus began to ooze out, bloody and bubbling as it edged its way out of the sore. It was horrifying to see this extraneous lump producing such a vast amount of fluid and Wic obviously found it very upsetting to see her horse in such discomfort. Having cleansed as much pus as possible, Shamil applied more tar, then stuck a lump of cotton wool over the wound.

All day our camp had been plagued by visitors. Men arrived at a gallop on their horses, often carrying bottles of *kefir* which they nonchalantly presented to us. They then proceeded to loll around our tents, talking to Bazarkul and pretending not to watch us. Sometimes they would jump back on their horses and gallop wildly round the camp, only to dismount and sit down again. Then, that evening, during a particularly delicious supper of homemade chips, a group of children gathered on the brow of a hill that lay on the fringes of our camp. They began wrestling like young bullocks, throwing each other to the ground. One of them had brought a large hoop that he spun with a stick, running along beside it. We could hear bursts of laughter, and then suddenly they all disappeared, back over the hill.

The weather changed dramatically over the next few days. Scorching sun turned to pouring rain, which completely transformed our lives. It is easy and pleasurable to live outside in a temperate climate, but every little chore becomes a herculean task in the wet. Saddling up the horses was one of our most onerous duties: each horse stood with his head drooping and his hindquarters facing towards the oncoming rain. Placing rugs on their backs became almost impossible; as soon as you had turned around to pick up the saddle, their wet and slippery coats made the rug fall to the ground. If you were lucky enough to position the rug, just as you were about to place the saddle on top of it, it would invariably be blown off. Next we had to tighten the girths, rigid and inflexible from the wet. The bridles and stirrups were similarly stiff, making it extremely uncomfortable to grip the reins without gloves. But perhaps the worst aspect of riding in the wet was having to sit on the sodden sheepskins that soaked through to our jodhpurs, despite full-length chaps.

Sometimes the rain would clear dramatically, the clouds evaporating to reveal the clearest and most bright of blue skies. It was wonderfully invigorating to see the sun shining on the windswept grasses, glistening with drops of rain, and to bask in its warm rays. But our joy proved short-lived. Soon the dark clouds came looming back over the horizon, moving at great speed as the wind swept them along, and carrying pillars of rain.

We now rode through some of the most spectacular scenery of our journey: great sweeping valleys encircled by the jagged peaks of the Tien Shan. Each set of valleys and peaks in Kyrgystan was uniquely beautiful. Some were small and friendly, with rolling hills and flower-covered slopes, while others were imposing and dramatic, with sheer inaccessible cliffs and vast open valleys which seemed to stretch on forever. Now we were entering a region where the landscape was wilder and the mountains seemed to loom over us, in contrast to our former more gentle surroundings. There was less vegetation and the slopes to either side rose up in strata of multi-coloured rock, which glowed with different hues depending on the light. Each mountain might stay with us for a day or more so we had time to study its precipices and ridges, rock formations, corries and valleys.

From this point until the Chinese border we passed through very few villages; the people in this remote and often extreme landscape were principally nomadic, living in *yurts*. We were nearing the western tip of Lake Issyk-Kul when we rode through the last village we would see for a couple of weeks. The women drew water from a communal pump while young girls hugged each other as they giggled shyly at us. One child of not more than two years, barely able to walk, was being dragged along by a cow on a rope. Her older sister, dressed in a garish velvet dressing-gown, pulled a mangy foal and returned our stares. We were repeatedly asked the question, 'Where are you going?', to which we replied simply, 'China'. This inevitably produced a torrent of further questions, which I left the others to answer. Wic and Mouse's interpretation of the word 'hello' in Russian, *zdrastviytye*, had somehow evolved into 'rasputin' so the ensuing conversation was, as Lucy put it, 'amusing but not enlightening'.

We broke away across the fields to meet the Naryn road, which heads south towards China. Shamil shouted at us not to take the short cut we had chosen, riding one side of a triangle instead of two, but we ignored him, determined to show him for once that we could be right. Everything was going swimmingly; our route looked half the distance of Shamil's and we were trotting along, laughing at how annoyed he would be when we arrived first, when suddenly a major obstacle presented itself, in the form of a narrow canal at which the horses took immense fright. However, we were resolved not to give up. Wic and I finally managed to cross the canal by dismounting, jumping over it ourselves, then pulling Black Pampers and Ginger Lion behind us. But Mouse and Lucy were completely stuck. No amount of pushing, pulling or coaxing would make Big Ben or Gay Donkey move. We could see Shamil getting nearer and nearer to the road, with a big grin covering his face. We began laughing, too. The more we laughed, though, the more helpless we became and the more the horses refused to budge. Finally, Shamil had the triumphant satifaction of rescuing us. He rode up to us and within minutes forced Big Ben and Gay Donkey over the canal.

We spent the next couple of days resting and deciding on our route for the next few weeks. Originally we had intended to ride along the southern shore of Lake Issyk-Kul to Barskoon, then turn south through the eastern Tien Shan mountains. But Vadim had discovered that late snows had made the passes in these high mountains inaccessible, so we needed to make new plans. We studied our maps and agreed with Vadim that the only feasible alternative route was via Naryn, a small town directly to our south. The passes along this route were lower, so we could ride through forests and valleys beneath the snowline.

On our first rest day we made futile attempts to read our books, only to be disturbed by Shamil's insatiable desire to chat and tease. I agreed to darn his jodhpurs while he reconstructed Wic's saddle. He began by shaving slivers off the wooden skeleton, so heightening the spine of the saddle. He then tended to the wound on Black Pamper's withers itself. First, he cut two square inches of skin off the surface of the swelling, revealing a red open wound pitted with pockets of yellow pus. These he tweezered out, then applied antiseptic as Black Pampers understandably flinched with the pain. Next, Shamil sprinkled wound powder over the whole wound and finally shrouded Black Pampers in a floral quilt and tethered him under a line of lime trees with the rest of the horses.

When it came to feeding time we found that Bazar-kul had attached bits of string to the horses' buckets, so that they could be suspended from their heads, like nose bags. This piece of initiative provoked great disdain from Shamil: '*Churka!*' He was delighted when Ginger Lion and Gay Donkey began to headbutt each other with their buckets, while poor Bazar-kul looked on rather bashfully.

That evening was to be Sacha and Vadim's last with us before they too returned to Tashkent. The following day two new guides were to arrive, bringing with them two English friends of ours who were to ride with us for the next couple of weeks. We asked Bazar-kul if he could ride back to the village and buy some vodka for the evening's festivities, which he agreed to do with alacrity.

Sacha and Vadim went to great trouble making a special supper for us – a huge bowl of *plov* and salads of aubergine and tomato. At eight o' clock we all assembled in the mess tent where Bazar-kul produced not only vodka, but also some exotic-looking bottles of Russian peach champagne. The toasts began, first to happiness, then to women, success, our friendship, and in fact anything that gave an excuse for another shot of vodka. Then came a lull while we began eating the *plov*. Mouse decided to dispel the silence by asking Sergei some questions, using me as her interpreter.

'Sergei, are you married?'

'No.'

'Are you married to marijuana?'

Sergei had shown a great interest in the wild marijuana, along with Black Pampers, and we were always suspicious that this accounted for his general sleepiness. He hardly ever spoke but if he did, it was always in very lethargic tones.

Now, perhaps under the influence of the alcohol, he suddenly came to life. 'Right, I'm really offended, that's my personal business.'

He jumped to his feet, but Vadim pulled him back down into his chair. I apologised profusely, but the damage had been done. Suddenly the table and all its contents were kicked to the ground and Sergei collapsed on the floor. Vadim deftly rolled him under the edge of the tent, from where he frog-marched him to the lorry. But Sergei soon reappeared. After a brief attempt at conversation he slumped against the table once more. We quickly became oblivious to his somnolent presence until he again suddenly lunged at the table, provoking Vadim to the same vigorous measures. After some scuffling and muffled shouting Vadim reappeared to resume our toasts. By this time Bazar-kul was giving us a bird-like rendition of a Kyrgyz song, with his arm firmly clamped around Lucy's reluctant neck.

'Looooooooooosy, you are my favourite!'

'Why's that?'

'Because we've got the same hair – short and black!'

Since we had christened Bazar-kul '*yozhik*', or 'hedgehog' in Russian, this was not entirely flattering. He had thick, shiny black hair that stuck out all over his head, like many Kyrgyz men, and we were constantly marvelling at the abnormally large size of his head, which sat like an enormous football on his body. But he then admitted that his soft spot for Lucy went further than her hair-do: 'No, she's so kind, you can see that straightaway.'

Meanwhile Sacha was ranting in his incomprehensible Russian, while Shamil was fuming because Vadim had dared to sit next to me. Shamil then retired to his tent to avoid punching Vadim and so our celebratory evening ended in true Russian fashion – everybody having fought with everybody else.

We woke up the next morning in great excitement because our two friends were due to arrive that day and ride with us until the Chinese border. We had known Rachel and Charty since university and Charty had accompanied Mouse on her reconnaissance trip to China the year before. In gratitude for her help, Mouse had invited her and Rachel to join us for a couple of weeks on the expedition. We had arranged that we would meet them on the junction of the Naryn and Issyk-Kul roads on 10 June. We spent the whole day in anticipation, gazing down the road, elated by the thought of this novel break to our repetitive routine.

Finally, we spied a white van bumping its way towards us on the distant horizon. 'Hellooooooooooooooo!'

English voices reached us before we could see whether it was indeed our friends. Then we spotted two familiar faces craning out of the back window of the van. 'Charty! Rachel!' we screamed. It seemed so extraordinary to see people from faraway England in this remote and windswept corner of Central Asia. In our excitement we were hardly able to greet Max and Zula, our replacements for Vadim and Sacha, who had also arrived in the van.

The rest of the day was spent animatedly catching up on news and reading letters and newspapers from England. We sent Bazar-kul back to the village once more to find two horses for Charty and Rachel: our plan was to hire them for the following two weeks, taking their owners along in the back-up truck. The next morning, we were pleasantly surprised to wake up and see two horses being led towards our campsite by some Kyrgyz boys. But it was all a bit too good to be true. As they came closer, we realised the horses were tiny and extremely weak-looking. Vadim and Sacha had already left for Tashkent early that morning, in the van, so Max was faced with the difficult task of solving the horse problem and fending off six girls single-handedly in his first hours as our guide. I was relieved to find that he spoke English so that I was released from having to translate for the others.

Mouse intervened, keen as always to avoid conflict and yet find a solution to the problem. 'Max, do you think it would be possible to continue looking for new horses as we're riding along?'

'OK, we'll go ahead in the truck and try and find bigger horses for them, then we'll find you during the day and tell you what success we've had.'

This seemed a sensible option, so we saddled up and set off in bleak weather, rain clouds bursting open just as we stopped for lunch. As we were sitting, huddled under the blankets from beneath our horses' saddles, the truck suddenly appeared around the corner of our narrow valley. It slowed down on approaching us, and Max jumped down from the cabin.

'I'm sorry but we haven't been able to find any new horses yet, but we'll continue to look.'

'While you're here, Max, could Bazar-kul re-shoe Black Pampers?' (Black Pampers' back shoes were loose and wearing very thin so Wic was keen for them to be replaced.)

'He'll do it later,' answered Max, having consulted with Bazar-kul, who looked reluctant to brave the rain.

'No, I want them done now.'

Max looked quite taken aback. After a rather lengthy discussion, Bazar-kul was bundled out of the truck with his shoeing tools. Wic described the incident herself in her diary:

> One shoe was fixed, although without his usual care. Bazar-kul then left Black Pampers with one 'platform' shoe and one 'pump'. When I asked him to do the other hoof he said he'd do it this evening. WHAT? WHY? I just couldn't understand the logic behind Hedgehog's thinking. We had a long afternoon's riding in front of us and all I was trying to do was prevent a further injury down the line. After a heavy debate, Bazar-kul agreed to shoe the other hoof. I leaned over him and directed his actions with a fussy finger.

Maybe Wic did not appreciate that he was doing his best, with inferior tools and knowledge. Very few horses are even shod in Kyrgyzstan – it was only because we were travelling so far and over such rocky terrain that it was felt necessary ours should be shod at all. Thus, Bazar-kul's skills were unusual in the context and we were lucky to have any kind of shoeing. Strangely, Shamil chose not to become involved in either this incident or the one in the morning, over Rachel and Charty's horses. Both afforded the perfect opportunity for him to denounce Bazar-kul's abilities, as he had been so eager to do before. We set off from our lunch spot as Charty issued Max with a fearsome ultimatum: 'If you don't find new horses you'll suffer six nagging women for the next two weeks.'

By now we were riding in the Naryn region of Kyrgyzstan, an area that is host to winter for seven months of the year. During this time valleys and mountains are submerged beneath six feet of snow. We were passing through in mid-June, when evidence of spring was only just beginning to show. It was incredible to think back to our time in mid-May, just over the border of Uzbekistan, where flowers had been blooming and we rode in T-shirts. Now we wore several layers, scarves and hats and the landscape was empty and barren. During the Soviet era those who worked in the valleys here as shepherds had received double wages, as recompense for what was perceived as a hardship posting. Their brief summer is spent collecting hay to store for the winter, when they are able to do nothing except keep warm in their *yurts*.

On our second day of riding with Rachel and Charty we approached the 11,000-foot Djalpak-Bel pass. Again we spent lunch huddled up in sheepskins, saddles and coats, shielding ourselves against the wind and rain. While we were eating our bread and cheese, a lorry with two small black heads poking out of it hurtled past us on the road. We guessed they might be the new horses. A break in the clouds saw us make a hasty departure from our riverside resting place as once more we braved the storm.

Half an hour later we were hailed by the lorry driver on his way back.

'Where's Shamil?' he asked.

We pointed behind us to the celebrated Shamil. The two men talked for a while, then Shamil imparted the welcome news that Charty and Rachel's new horses were indeed grazing in the next valley, watched over by Bazar-kul.

The lorry driver then revved his engine and accelerated forwards quite suddenly. Both Big Ben, who was standing with his flanks flush to the lorry, and Mouse, who was fumbling in her saddlebags, were startled and Big

The four of us in the Tien Shan mountains

Our camel train outside Jiayugan fort

The only other camel train we saw in China

Ben lunged forwards in my direction. I had dismounted to pick my hat up off the ground and had Ginger Lion's reins looped around one arm. There was no love lost between the two horses and Ginger Lion must have perceived this as a sign of attack. He reared up, one of his front hooves striking my arm as he crashed back to the ground, and flung himself at Big Ben, trying to bite his neck. Big Ben reared up in an attempt to avoid Ginger Lion's long teeth, and both let out shrieking whinnies. I rushed to grab Ginger Lion's rope, but he swung round and galloped off up the hill behind us, becoming hidden behind a rock. Shamil arrived on the scene, but too late: the Lion reappeared and headed down the hill towards a herd of mares. He hurled himself into their midst, attempting to mount one after the other, as they whinnied in terror and reared up, trying to avoid his advances. But the stallion of the herd had sought him out within seconds and a fierce duel began, the two horses rearing and biting, encircled by the frightened mares. The dramatic backdrop of the mountains, and these two animals fighting for control of the herd provided a primordial drama. However, human intervention prevented us from witnessing a bloody conclusion to this Darwinian scene; Shamil darted between the mares on Malish and finally, having avoided several kicks, managed to catch the recalcitrant Ginger Lion and drag him back unscathed.

Round a bend in the valley we were confronted by the two new little black horses, deposited in the middle of nowhere. Bazar-kul was sitting astride one that looked as if it might be pregnant, and was holding a rope attached to the other, who was similar but thinner. As we approached this rather comical spectacle, Big Ben became more and more excited by the presence of fresh blood among the horses, rushing and stumbling forwards over the rocky plain to reach them. Crossing a shallow river and rushing up the bank on the other side, I was shocked to see Big Ben come up beside me, riderless. Lucy and Wic turned back to see what had happened, to find Mouse lying on her side, immobile, with Charty cradling her head. They desperately tried to remember everything they had learned on the wilderness medical training course as Bazar-kul came running up behind them. As he grasped Mouse's right arm, to feel her pulse, she winced in pain but she was able to explain what had happened.

Apparently, Big Ben, in his anxiety to cross the river, had stumbled on a rock and caught his front leg. Falling to his knees and throwing Mouse to the ground, he had crushed her right shoulder, arm and leg with his body. She had been unfortunate enough to land with her head on a rock and had lost consciousness for a few seconds. We were very worried that she had broken a bone or damaged her head, because she lay completely rigid and spoke very slowly. But after a few minutes she began to recover from the shock and dizziness and shakily stood up, clinging to Charty's arm.

We found Max, Zula and Sergei waiting for us at the camp, pitched in a bleakly open spot where the winds swept past, buffeting the tents mercilessly. Exhausted by our eventful day, we crouched in our mess tent, its sides being flapped incessantly up and down by the wind and the rain as we tried to warm ourselves with large quantities of *plov*, washed down by sachets of hot chocolate and boiling water.

The next morning we found the snow on the hills had encroached into our camp and voluminous clouds on the horizon were threatening more later. The temperature had dropped to -10°C and Mouse's contact lenses had frozen overnight. The horses had worn perfectly symmetrical muddy circles around their tethering posts during the night, as they searched for grass beneath the snow. Charty and Rachel exchanged their rented ponies for the sleek little black horses Max had bought in the bazaar, and the two Kyrgyz boys rode slowly off home.

As we set off further up into the mountains, three shepherds on horseback came jogging up beside us.

'Where are you going?'

'China.'

They looked at each other in bemusement.

'Where are you from?'

'England.'

I could not help wondering whether vodka was not the principal staple of their diet, for after this peremptory introduction they asked me without further ado if any of us was willing to be purchased for 1,000 yaks. They thought Rachel, Charty, Mouse and I looked far too young for such a profitable deal but they were greatly taken by Wic and Lucy. Their wish for such a bargain was based on a smattering of American films, which had given them some unusual preconceptions about Western women.

'You all get married at forty don't you?'

'No, it depends.'

'Everyone has sex whenever they want, don't they?'

'No, definitely not!'

'Women in the West are better because they're civilised – they don't snore.'

'I'm sure some do.'

They looked rather crestfallen to have this unromantic vision dispelled so quickly, but it did not lessen their desire to buy either Lucy or Wic. One of our inquisitors had bright blue eyes, unusual in the depths of Kyrgyzstan, so I asked him how this came about.

'Once a Russian came to stay the night when my father was away and I appeared nine months later.'

'How many brothers and sisters do you have?'

'Eighteen.'

'Are they all from the same father?'

'Only Allah knows ... and my mother!'

At this point Shamil rode up and severely reprimanded me for talking to the shepherds. He said they were very drunk and would follow us all the way to camp if we encouraged them. So we trotted off in the falling snow, passing grazing yaks, their shaggy coats specked with snowflakes.

The following day we edged our way over the pass itself, the horses' hooves accumulating snow, which we had to dismount to remove every half an hour. As we climbed higher, so the views became more spectacular. Vast snow-covered peaks towered over our diminutive party, casting huge dark shadows over their neighbours. The path wound its way up and over the mountains, often losing itself in the new falls of snow. From the summit we looked out over layer after layer of glistening peaks, outlined against the cerulean sky. As we descended the other side the snow abruptly disappeared, to reveal verdant grass and clumps of primulas and buttercups. Below us stretched an expansive valley, a horseshoe of snow-peaked mountains enclosing its gentle slopes and a river, the Kichi Naryn, carving its way through the middle. When we reached the valley floor we galloped as fast as we could, exhilarated to find ourselves in this wild open space. As we raced across its grassy folds, an unforeseen dip would reveal a *yurt* surrounded by its flock of sheep and goats. Less frequently, we came across herds of mares, each one protected by a stallion, who rounded up his harem and steered them to fresh grasses by cantering around them, head down, tail up. I was thankful for their infrequency because each time we encountered one I had a struggle to pull back Ginger Lion.

We followed the Kichi Naryn out of the valley. Ahead lay more snow-tipped peaks and our camp, bathed in an exquisite golden evening light, on the banks of the river. On the other side of the river, directly opposite us, was pitched a *yurt* so we untacked our horses under the curious stares of a Kyrgyz family and their mares.

Bazar-kul walked over the nearby bridge to the *yurt* the next day and gained an invitation for all of us to visit. When we arrived, accompanied by Bazar-kul and Shamil,we were greeted by a young couple, recently married. They ushered us into their home and seated us around a low table placed in the centre of the *yurt*. Also present was an old man, the father of the groom, a younger brother in his late twenties and an even younger brother of about twelve. Later another brother arrived with two small children. Within that modest space sixteen people fitted quite comfortably.

On sitting down we were immediately presented with small bowls of milky tea and large wedges of freshly baked unleavened bread. The young hostess served us in silence, then continued with her domestic chores, perhaps to impress her husband, who looked on favourably from the other side of the *yurt*. We were keen to ask hundreds of questions about their lives and so began a three-way interrogation: I translated from English into Russian and Bazar-kul from Russian into Kyrgyz. The answers filtered their way back, sometimes, I suspected, coloured by Bazar-kul's own interpretations.

The *yurt*, like *yurts* all over Kyrgyzstan, was made up of three parts: the male section, the female section and the guest section. On the left as one entered was the male section, which contained saddles, whips and knives. On the right was the female section, dedicated to domesticity and containing the precious vessel made of horse-leather, sewn together with plaited horsehair that is used to ferment the *kumiz*. Finally, in the centre of the *yurt*, was the guest section, containing a low table and cushions.

More questioning revealed that our hosts produced eighty pints of milk per day from eight mares, which the young wife milked five times a day. In order that the mares could be free to graze yet not stray, all their foals had been tethered to a line of rope stretched out just outside the *yurt*. The other animals they kept included a flock of more than 200 sheep, a couple of wolf-like dogs, a small cat and a black lamb that had been orphaned and spent most of its time being dragged out of the kitchen cupboard.

From the age of about ten the children are sent out to the summer pastures to look after the animals. Despite having adopted more settled lifestyles since Soviet times, in the summer months many Kyrgyz shepherds still move to higher pastures, or *jayloo*. Traditionally a family would move around with one *yurt,* but nowadays they often use two. Our family had one for living and eating, and another nearby for sleeping. When Wic asked what time they woke up, the answer was 'With the light – five o'clock in the summer months.' Likewise, they went to bed when the light disappeared, around nine o'clock.

Soon our timid hostess scooped out several bowls of *kumiz* from a large bucket and handed them to us, accompanied by more bread, *kaimak* (thick yellow cream) and *sary-may* (melted butter). Bazar-kul told us discreetly that it was considered good manners to drink the *kumiz* all in one, so we braced ourselves and gulped it down. It was not as strange as we had anticipated, but had an unusual pungent fizziness. The bread, cream and butter presented no such difficulties. We had consumed great quantities before Shamil hinted that perhaps we should leave some for our hosts. Bazar-kul suggested we give the family a huge bag of sweets and chocolates we had in our back-up truck. We also gave the 12-year-old boy one of the T-shirts we had had printed before we left England, with 'The Silk Road' emblazoned across it. He took it shyly, then hid behind his elder brother. Bazar-kul laughed and told him to say 'Thank you', which he suddenly did in perfect English.

Back at camp we noticed Ginger Lion pawing the ground, then prancing about on the spot, clearly trying to attract the attention of our neighbours' mares that grazed a tantalisingly short distance away across the river. Shamil tightened his rope around the tethering post, but minutes later we were interrupted by a piercing whinny, to see the Lion charging through the river, undeterred by its foaming waters. Shamil chased after him on Malish, but he had to go round by the bridge we had used earlier. He arrived too late: Ginger Lion was already in the middle of the herd, brawling with the stallion. Having caught him, Shamil gave him a sound whipping and dragged him back to the camp. We were very embarrassed, particularly after all the hospitality shown to us that morning. When the same thing happened later in the evening, with our hosts having to fight off Ginger Lion while Shamil came running over on foot, the Lion received a very severe beating, which I watched wincingly from the opposite bank.

The next day we said goodbye to our Kyrgyz neighbours and set off to follow the course of the Kichi Naryn along the valley it has carved through the Tien Shan. The valley, roughly half a mile wide, housed one metal caravan behind which was hiding a Kyrgyz family engaged in the initial stages of erecting their summer *yurt*, belongings scattered everywhere. We waved good morning to them and they responded with an offer of tea, which we sadly had to decline.

Soon the riverbanks became too steep to follow and we left the valley to continue our journey over the hills. All morning a light drizzle hung over us, the clouds sitting low and grey in the sky. At rare moments a brilliant shaft of light would shine through, illuminating the grass to a vivid green, dotted with blue patches of forget-me-nots. Our route was leading us deeper into the steep mountains, whose precipitous slopes were covered in fir trees; the further we went the lower the forest encroached, so by the time our path crossed another river the trees were all around us. We camped in the only clearing we could find, buffeted by fierce winds and dampened by the continual drizzle.

The next day, descending from the clematis-draped forests, we followed the Kichi Naryn to its confluence with the Naryn river. Ceaseless morning rain now cleared to allow the sun to shine for the rest of the day. As we came down, we saw figures squatting in the shallow waters of the Kichi Naryn, scouring the riverbed for gold. They looked up suspiciously as we passed, wary because of the strict laws outlawing unauthorised gold-digging.

We came to a small village where Shamil wanted to buy some vodka. Mouse and I accompanied him down the main street to look for a shop and found an unemployed shepherd, who escorted us to an ordinary-looking house. Shamil and I were ushered into the main room, where we were invited to sit down. A plastic bottle of 'BonAqua' was brought in, containing some home-brewed 'spirit'. Shamil was handed a glass, but before he sampled it he insisted on testing its authenticity by igniting it with a match. Having verified its alcoholic content, he downed the shot. The Kyrgyz sellers were very impressed because 'spirit' contains ninety per cent alcohol and the usual custom is to dilute it with water. We left bearing the bottle of vodka and a huge *lepyoshka*, which they gave us.

The next day we began to follow the sister river of the Kichi Naryn. We were able to gallop through the valleys, their floors neatly grazed by flocks of sheep. Every so often we were taken unawares by a stream hiding in a fold of the valley and we would come to an abrupt halt before plunging down its muddy slopes into the bed below. We ended up skirting the pebbled shore of the great Naryn river itself, Big Ben slipping, sliding and tripping in a desperate attempt to stay in line.

After lunch, we followed the road through villages where the streets were lined with sleeping calves and lambs. Each house boasted a neat wooden fence decorated with diamond patterns, sometimes painted. Small children ran around, chasing makeshift hoops with sticks. At one point we were joined by a rider who told us he had found an orphaned fawn, only one week old, and wondered whether we would be interested in purchasing it. He came back carrying the fawn, with its tiny body and long awkward legs, completely unperturbed by all this attention, blinking thoughtfully at us with its large black eyes and flicking its delicate ears.

That night we camped three miles away from the town of Naryn, where we would take a rest day. Wic had been begging Max for the last week to find a vet for Black Pampers' wound, which had not shown much improvement, despite both Shamil and Wic's solicitous attentions. Every morning and evening they had been cleaning the wound of pus then applying the black tar. This had prevented further infection but there was still a gaping three-inch hole in Black Pampers' withers, revealing naked bone where the flesh had been eaten away. It was a grotesque sight, but luckily seemed to cause Black Pampers no pain unless pressure was directly applied to the area. Shamil's adjustment of Wic's saddle meant that she no longer had to ride bareback, and she was not worried about trotting or cantering. Max had promised to try and find a vet in Naryn, as well as new medicines for the wound, which Shamil thought should be available in a chemist. Mouse was also very anxious to find a blacksmith to file down Big Ben's hooves, particularly after her recent fall. (Bazar-kul did not possess a sufficiently powerful rasp.)

Early in the morning Max set off with Shamil to search for a vet, blacksmith and chemist in Naryn. By lunch they had returned to inform us that there were no blacksmith or vet to be found and that the chemist would only be open the following day. The next morning we were told by Max that the truck battery had failed and that it needed to be left overnight in Naryn being re-charged. This news did not cause us much dismay because it meant we had another rest day and we could investigate the bazaar in Naryn, famed throughout Kyrgyzstan for its felt carpets, or *shyr-daks*.

At the bazaar, we found several rows of stalls selling sweets, *lepyoshkas*, clothes pegs, batteries, *ak-kalpaks*, soap, grains, shellsuits, vodka and wine. At one end I found a solitary *shyr-dak*, made in the traditional manner of several layers of different coloured felt cut in swirling patterns to produce a simple, bright design. This one was red, green and white and, like all *shyr-daks*, had been made for a *yurt*. Kyrgyz shepherds make felt each winter by burying rolls of tightly compacted sheep's wool in the ground.

The pressure of the earth above causes the wool to become matted together, creating felt, which is then cut up and sewn into carpets. Extremely resilient against the biting mountain winds, these are hung inside the *yurt* trellis to shut out any drafts, creating an unrivalled atmosphere of warmth and cosiness. We were all keen to buy carpets, so Shamil organised with the seller, a stout Kyrgyz woman, for us to return the following day and view a larger selection.

Next we made our way to the animal, or *skotniy*, bazaar, which, having opened at dawn, was now finishing its activities for the day. We found two ponies and twelve sheep tied to a fence, looking forlornly at the empty stalls where healthier animals had presumably stood. We had come in search of leather and red wood whips, like one I had been given in Uzbekistan, but again we were told to return the next day. Shamil found the chemist, where he bought some more wound powder for Black Pampers, but still no vet.

Early the following morning, we revisited the bazaars of Naryn. We found a selection of new *shyr-daks*, sadly much more gaudy than the original red, white and green one. Luckily this was still hanging resplendently on the fence, so we struck a deal and Shamil rolled it up into a tube, which he attached to the back of Ginger Lion's saddle. Mouse and I stocked up on our favourite dairy products: milk, *kefir*, cream and butter, while Shamil found me a very rare *ak-kalpak*, in red and brown as opposed to the usual black and white. We then trotted through the streets back to the animal bazaar in search of whips. Only one very flimsy-looking whip was produced and there were five potential buyers, leaving all but Charty disappointed. Finally, we left Naryn, the carpet bouncing around on Ginger Lion's back.

We climbed up through the hills, of a very distinctive terracotta clay, apparently used to make bricks. When Shamil enquired at a *yurt* about taking a short cut, the owner proposed drinking the ubiquitous *kumiz*. He gazed very animatedly at Charty and, despite the presence of his wife, asked if he could buy her. Shamil guffawed loudly and prolonged the joke all afternoon.

As we cantered through the hills, Charty performed her trick for us, flapping her arms and legs Kyrgyz style to make her horse, now re-christened Bullet, shoot off ahead of us at a gallop. It never failed to amuse us.

6

Goodbye to the mountains

A COUPLE OF DAYS later, another incident with the horses occurred which was to cause a major rift in the camp. Shamil woke me at 6.30 am one morning to tell me that there was a serious problem with Charty's horse. I found Bullet standing in a muddy puddle, looking miserable.

'What's happened to him?'

'He must have been allowed to drink without resting yesterday, because his lower legs are completely swollen.'

By this time the others had emerged. Charty maintained that she had definitely not allowed Bullet to drink, which mystified Shamil, but by now a vet had been summoned from the local village. First he stood Bullet in a canal that ran along the edge of the camp and strapped him up in a makeshift harness of ropes to prevent him from eating or drinking. (The water was apparently meant to cool his legs and reduce the swelling.) Then, after three hours, the vet prodded Bullet's ankles and, finding them still swollen, made little nicks with a knife to release the excess fluid. Next, he galloped Bullet up and down the road for half an hour to ensure the blood supply was still flowing healthily around his small black body. Finally, the vet instructed Shamil to tie Bullet to the truck so that he could not lie down. He explained it was imperative that Bullet remained standing, because otherwise the blood supply would not get to his legs and he would die a slow and painful death.

We thanked the vet and retired to our mess tent. Bullet constantly shifted his weight from one leg to another, trying to relieve the pain. However, at one point he somehow managed to stretch his rope and sink to the ground, where he lay looking forlorn. Shamil noticed and ran over to pull him up, tightening his rope firmly to prevent it happening again. But an hour later

Bullet was once again lying on the ground. Shamil pulled at his rope and kicked him in the ribs to raise him. Charty, on seeing this unpleasant but necessary action, ran over to remonstrate with Shamil.

'Stop being so cruel!' she shouted.

Shamil called me over to translate.'Bullet mustn't lie down because his blood supply will get cut off from his legs if he does.'

'You're just so cruel!' she reiterated bitterly.

At this point I intervened. 'Charty, what do you propose doing instead?'

'Why can't they do something kinder than slitting his legs and forcing him to stand up?'

Shamil explained that if he had had the means he would rather have given Bullet injections, but in such a remote spot there was no chance of getting hold of any. I relayed this to Charty, who by now was crying.

'Charty, there's really no choice.'

'That's not true – I've ridden all my life and when horses get problems we never treat them in this way. They're just so unfeeling and cruel.' With this stinging condemnation she walked back to her tent, where she lay sobbing on the ground for the rest of the afternoon. Nothing anybody said could console her.

Shamil asked me why Charty was so distraught, and I explained that she thought Bullet's treatment was too harsh.

'But does she understand what the choice was?'

'Of course, but don't worry, English people tend to get very emotional about animals.'

The astounded Shamil asked me several times if Charty had really understood that there had been no alternative for poor Bullet. When he realised that she had indeed, he looked very hurt, saying, 'I can't believe she's accusing me of cruelty. I've spent over twenty years working with horses and I wouldn't have done so if I didn't love them because it's such hard and badly paid work.'

Shamil's twenty years experience was gained training as a show jumper to international level, followed by running a state horse farm in Uzbekistan. Here he was responsible for breaking in young horses, as well as retraining horses that had become uncontrollable. He also spent two years studying the physiology and anatomy of horses. The Soviet Union may have been poor in terms of resources, but its citizens were educated to a level I have not encountered in any Western country. Whether scientists, artists or mountaineers, they invariably exhibit a degree of expertise and skill that, even with all our material advantages, we struggle to attain in the West. I have travelled several times since with Shamil, and am constantly awed by his incredible knowledge of horses, nature and wildlife. It seemed strange that Charty could feel confident of superior expertise, but she was no doubt behaving irrationally because she was extremely upset about Bullet, and far from home. However, it was also perhaps indicative of the attitude adopted by some English people after centuries of imperialism. Travelling in Central Asia, I found it interesting to observe how differently the Russians are perceived from their English counterparts in former African or Indian colonies. There is no resentment displayed by the indigenous peoples towards their colonisers. In fact, the opposite sentiment exists, with Uzbeks, Kazakhs, Turkmens and Kyrgyz frequently eager not to lose their Russian populations.

Ironically, it was Shamil who stayed up all night watching Bullet to check that he did not lie down or that the swellings did not increase. Mouse had made the sensible suggestion of crushing painkillers and feeding them to Bullet concealed in a handful of oats, which seemed to alleviate his pain, but Charty still refused to speak to Shamil and continued to accuse him of being unkind to the horses. Unfortunately, Max exacerbated this delicate situation by dogmatically insisting that Bullet would be better in the morning and that Charty should continue to ride him. Shamil would not voice an opinion as to whether Bullet would be fit to ride but Bazar-kul also maintained that his recovery would occur overnight. Understandably, Charty warned Max that she would refuse to ride Bullet unless something miraculous had happened and that he should begin to look for another horse. Max told her to 'wait and see', so we tried to distract ourselves by playing cards and drinking vodka.

The next morning Shamil told us Bullet was better, but definitely not ready to be ridden. Max had already set off for the nearby village in search of a replacement horse. It appeared after breakfast in the form of a very white grey gelding, which immediately attracted the attention of Big Ben. Its owner was to look after Bullet in the meantime.

We set off, relieved that the drama of the previous day was over, though not without some lingering tension. The division in our group had reappeared, but this time exacerbated by the presence of two extra people, Charty and Rachel. Wic and Lucy's previous antipathy to Shamil meant they took Charty's side, while for the opposite reason I sympathised with Shamil. Mouse and Rachel endeavoured to remain impartial, but because they did not speak Russian and were old friends, they inevitably tended to support Charty.

The highlight of the morning's riding was a horse carcass strewn across our path. The cause of death was, according to Shamil, wolves and as we approached a dog slunk off across the plain, deprived of his feast. At the same time we spotted a host of large, dark objects rise slowly from the hill before us. We saw the forms of giant eagles, spreading their vast wings to reveal striped underbodies and counted at least twenty birds darkening the sky. We trotted on, eager to avoid their piercing eyes, as they came to rest on an adjacent hill. But I was curious to see how large they really were and whether they would attack us, as they seemed to threaten. I turned Ginger Lion's head towards their hunched bodies and galloped as fast as I could up the hillside. Once again, they rose up into the air, hovering above me with their wings outstretched. Their wingspan was wider than Ginger Lion was long and the sky darkened as they closed in above my head. I could not get down fast enough.

We ate lunch on the banks of the Tash Rabat river, two hundred yards upstream from where we could see that our truck was stranded. Sergei was bent over one of the wheels. We had not taken much to eat in our saddle-bags, so Charty decided to take advantage of the proximity of the truck and, jumping on to the grey gelding, she cantered off to bring back more food.

'Stop, don't canter!' shouted Shamil.

Charty either ignored his instructions, or did not hear his cries. When she returned with some bread, Shamil told her that we would now have to wait another hour for her horse to cool down before we could water him, although ours were ready.

'Why?' asked Charty truculently.

'Because it's dangerous to water horses when they're hot, and I don't want the same thing happening to him as happened to Bullet yesterday,' replied Shamil.

As I translated, Charty raised her eyes to heaven. 'Why does he always have to criticise everything we do?' she protested to the others. They gathered sympathetically around her, loudly lamenting Shamil's lack of gratitude for the bread, while I sat alone with him, silently. I felt so hurt for Shamil that I could barely speak to the others for the rest of the day.

These small dramas assumed exaggerated gravity at the time, although in retrospect they appear amusingly trivial. We all were and are good friends and it seems ridiculous that we became so distressed about such petty issues. However, in the artificial isolation of our camp life it was probably inevitable, especially being six girls!

The afternoon took us up the Tash Rabat valley, towards its famous Silk Road caravanserai. Stopping a couple of miles from our goal, by a bend in the river, we dismounted and unsaddled our horses. Just as we had put up our tents, clouds covered the sun and pelted down huge hailstones, the size of marbles. Perhaps Malish had never encountered hail in his short life, because he was terrified, flattening his ears back against his head and kicking his back legs high up into the air.

The following morning we rode up to the caravanserai itself, far up in the At-Bashinski (appropriately meaning 'head of the horse') range of the Tien Shan mountains. Opinions as to when the caravanserai was built vary from the tenth century, according to one guidebook, to the seventeenth century, according to some locals we met outside. Situated at the foot of the Tash Rabat pass, it was a stopping point for caravans on their passage along the Silk Road, from China to Central Asia, or vice versa. The caravanserai was built and owned by one man, who, in return for a fee, would house the merchants for the night, taking full responsibility for their goods and lives. The camels and horses were kept outside, protected by a band of guards and dogs.

The caravanserai is dominated by one large, domed room where the merchants ate and socialised. The dome has four square apertures in it, as in a Mongolian *yurt*, through which the sunlight shines on to the floor. From these it is possible to tell the time. On each side of this principal room are two long, rectangular-shaped rooms lined with stone benches, on which the merchants slept. There are also several small rooms, which could be rented individually and used to store goods. If the latter were particularly precious they could be hidden in a 'treasure chest', a large hole in the ground covered by a huge slab of stone, on which the owner slept. Vulnerable to bandits, the caravanserai had several underground passages leading out to the hills, through which its occupants could escape in times of emergency. Shamil led Charty, Rachel and me into a lightless circular room where, luckily, we all clung on to a central wooden pole: when he lit a match it proved I had all but stepped into a hole leading to one of these underground passages.

Unfortunately, the Tash Rabat pass itself, which we had planned to take, had not yet opened this year, due to late snow. Shamil and I decided to ride up and take a look anyway. Cantering up the valley, we followed the clear Tash Rabat river, encountering a herd of yaks, and clambered up the hills that mark the foot of the pass. Here we saw countless marmots, but came to a halt as we found ourselves face to face with the forbidding snow-tipped mountains over which the sinuous path crosses into China. Winding its way around a vast mass of rock it climbs up across a bed of shale, then over the snow to the other side. It was breathtaking to think that hundreds of camel caravans had once made their perilous way along this route.

That morning there had been another battle in the camp. Max had told us before breakfast that we could not cross over the pass, as planned, but Wic and Lucy thought he was making excuses because he could not be bothered to find a local guide.

Max's principal fault lay in tactlessness rather than malice, illustrated by his reply to this request.

'Well, Shamil says that even if we find a guide he's only prepared to take responsibility for Sacha and Mouse riding over the pass.'

'Why?'

'Because he says that the last time you rode over a complicated pass at Toktagul you and Lucy were frightened and became really angry with him. He says you're cowards.'

I winced in my tent, anticipating Wic and Lucy's fury.

'You can tell him he's the coward!' they yelled.

I never found out whether Shamil had really called Wic and Lucy cowards; he always denied it, but the damage was done and they were very upset. I was dismayed by all these arguments. There was so much criticism of the guides which I felt was unjust. Perhaps I was unsympathetic, but it seemed so inappropriate in this beautiful landscape to be absorbed by such triviality. I was amazed that none of the others wanted to join Shamil and me in going to look at the pass, after their argument with Max.

I was relieved to spend the afternoon alone with Shamil, away from all this tension. But when we rode back into the camp Mouse and Lucy drew me to one side. They were angry because they felt I was behaving unfeelingly and being too protective of Shamil, which was causing division in the camp. I defended myself, by saying I found it embarrassing when they were rude to the guides, criticising them and shouting at them.

'But you must understand, Wic is very stressed and it's just because she loves Black Pampers so much.' I had never seen Mouse angry before, but now she had really lost her patience.

'I still don't think there's any excuse for being rude, especially to Shamil, who has done so much to help Black Pampers. One of the reasons he doesn't want us to go over the steep pass is because of the wound.'

'I don't care, you've just got to get on with each other because I'm sick of this tension.'

With these words they left me to join the others.

Luckily, that evening Max and Zula made a large supper and bought several bottles of vodka from the shepherds at the caravanserai. We all sat down together and the frictions of the day diminished with each new toast. Suddenly all our differences seemed unimportant. We had achieved so much together, and were naturally very fond of each other, but at times it was impossible for things not to get distorted out of proportion in our enclosed world. I only wish I had known Wic better before the expedition, because I would have made more allowance for her behaviour. At the time I was unaware how out of character she was acting, which Mouse and Lucy appreciated, having known her well for years. But as I grew to know her properly I realised that she had only acted as she did because she was so upset about her horse. Now I see her as one of my kindest, most sensitive of friends and realise that I was judging her too harshly at the time.

The next morning Shamil suggested we all return to the foot of the Tash Rabat pass, before continuing on our way towards the Chinese border. Mouse was keen to hurry on, but Shamil persuaded her it would be a great pity not to see the pass's magnificent slopes. Big Ben, whose admiration for Charty's grey horse had been increasing daily, had lunged at Lucy's back with his teeth when she had happened to ride between them. Since this frightening incident Shamil had been insistent that Charty ride at the back of the line, out of Big Ben's sight. But Charty found this tedious and was often to be found jogging along beside us, despite Shamil's repeated warnings. On the way back, Shamil on Malish happened to come between Charty and Mouse when we were forced to suddenly return to single file. Big Ben, enraged by this apparent rival, flew at Shamil and ferociously bit his forearm. Shamil, understandably furious, leapt off Malish and gestured to Mouse to dismount. She refused. He grabbed her bridle and administered a few sharp strokes of his whip to Big Ben's haunches. Mouse protested, saying she had already punished Big Ben, but Shamil replied that he was doing it for Big Ben's sake because if he continued to behave like this he would have to be put down. He then jumped back on Malish and, in obvious pain, rode silently off ahead. I cantered after him, sympathising with his anger.

The afternoon took us over three rocky passes punctuated by flower-studded valleys, enticing us towards the next range of mountains. We cantered over irises, flax, speedwell and buttercups and along streams of icy, crystal water. At the top of one of the passes we spotted a pair of large orange marmots standing at the entrances of their adjacent burrows, erect and sizing up to each other. A short boxing match followed. Then, noticing our presence as we drew nearer, they froze momentarily before retreating down their holes.

Towards the end of the day we reached the main road that runs between Naryn and China. A temporarily deserted checkpoint was the only sign of life as we galloped up the wide valley to find our camp hidden in a gully in the hills to our left. That night was Max's birthday, so yet more vodka was produced and we sat up until late, celebrating.

We were now coming horribly close to the end of our time in Central Asia and the prospect of entering China was becoming more and more depressing. Soon we would be restricted to the monotonous sands and heat of the dreaded Taklamakan desert, leaving behind everything that had grown familiar to us in Central Asia.

It had also suddenly become extremely cold again, which had caused an old break in Mouse's ankle to give her great pain. This had happened each time the temperature had dropped dramatically. Shamil had offered some relief by massaging her ankle with a Russian cream, but I think she was looking forward to the heat of the desert, where the pain should disappear altogether. On the other hand, Wic and I were particularly anxious about the heat so we relished these last days of cold and wetness.

Our final day of riding in Central Asia was very sad. We tried to savour every last moment of the valleys, stopping for lunch to prolong the day. Some border guards joined us, using the opportunity as an excuse to get drunk. During the ensuing conversation I found out that Russian is generally better spoken in Kyrgyzstan than in Uzbekistan. This is because when the Soviet Union collapsed a decade earlier, the Russian military presence immediately withdrew from Uzbekistan but remained in Kyrgyzstan. The border guards also said that they regretted the departure of ordinary Russians: now the Kyrgyz were left with very few teachers, doctors or other professionals.

We said goodbye before we were forced to join them in their vodka-drinking session and rode on to our final campsite. Trotting past bunkers built in the time of tense Sino-Soviet relations during the 1960s, we found it on an open plain at the foot of the Torugart pass, which divides Kyrgyzstan from China.

The following morning we had twenty-four hours left before we crossed the Chinese border. It was, as Mouse said, 'like the end of an era'; the next five months of our journey would be different in every way. The weather would no longer be variable, only relentless heat and sun. Mountains and valleys would be replaced by flat, unchanging desert and our beloved horses by camels. Nor would we be able to communicate directly with anyone. While I had acted as translator in Central Asia, none of us spoke Chinese. But most of all I feared my imminent parting from Shamil. I could not bear the thought of leaving him.

While we were writing numerous letters home, in anticipation of Rachel and Charty's return to England, Max and Shamil were scouring the road for a truck to take the horses back to Bishkek, where they were to be sold. Eventually they found a rickety blue lorry and we were given a couple of hours to say goodbye to our horses. After three months and 1,700 miles, this was a difficult moment. Not only upset that we would never see them again, we were also concerned about their future, because while Shamil had wanted to take them back to Tashkent with him Max was insistent that they should be sold in Bishkek. Wic was worried about Black Pampers remaining in Kyrgyzstan because he seemed to find it difficult breathing at these high altitudes, and we were all keen that Shamil, whom we trusted, should find them new homes. He had been up all the previous night, waiting on the edge of the road in the hope of finding a lorry willing to go to all the way to Tashkent, but to no avail. Nobody wanted to drive the horses that far.

Our horses were tethered separately, still deeply hostile towards each other, despite three months spent in close proximity. They seemed to sense the imminent separation and stood looking forlorn, their heads hanging down. It was difficult for me to show Ginger Lion much affection because he persisted in trying to bite me as soon as I drew near him, but he had been so strong and reliable that, in spite of his rather unappealing character, I had become very attached to him. Wic was particularly upset to be parted from Black Pampers, because she had devoted so much love and attention to him. His wound had given him a vulnerability that had only strengthened the link between them. As a child, Wic had lived in the country, where she had kept a pony that she adored. Later, her parents had been forced to move to the city but Wic missed the countryside terribly. I will always remember Wic telling me that the happiest times of her life had been spent riding and perhaps Black Pampers had catalysed the nostalgia she felt for her own country childhood.

Shamil suggested to me a final ride before the horses left. We took Ginger Lion and Malish for a gallop along the banks of Chatyr-Kul lake, slightly to the north of our camp. Shamil challenged me to a race and we flew along, side by side, until the horses tired. I tried hard to enjoy every moment to its utmost but it was impossible not to feel some of the despondency that would inevitably follow.

The final moment arrived. Each of the horses was coaxed into the open truck, via a precarious ramp balanced on a high bank. But when it came to Black Pampers' turn he refused to place one hoof on the ramp, rearing and bucking to one side. His terror only seemed to increase with each attempt. Eventually, Shamil jumped on his back and, kicking him on, persuaded him to trot over the ramp and into the truck. Next, the horses' heads and legs were secured firmly so that they would not bite or kick each other on the long journey ahead. As we looked up at them they rolled their eyes at us, seemingly reproaching us for our disloyalty.

The truck moved off, throwing the horses from left to right and unbalancing the ungainly Big Ben. We stood watching as it threw up clouds of dust and diminished into the distance. The last we saw of our loyal steeds was their bemused heads looking out over the back of the truck. We retreated in silence to the mess tent. Wic and Mouse were in tears. While the rest of us felt exhausted by the day's events, Shamil, who had been equally fond of Malish, was soon laughing and telling jokes, philosophical as ever.

Our unhappiness, however, was diverted by the appearance in the camp of two handsome Swiss boys, Christian and Mario, who were cycling through Kyrgyzstan on to India, via China. Max had found them on the road and invited them to spend the night in our camp. They had no permits to travel across the Torugart pass into China, so Max had promised to help them acquire them the next day. The others were all immediately entranced, inviting them to join us in games of backgammon and cards. The Swiss boys produced bottles of vodka from their saddlebags, which were cracked open immediately, and we did not stir from the mess tent for the rest of the afternoon.

That evening Zula prepared a feast of *plov*, fried slices of aubergines, salads and soup to mark our last night in Central Asia. Our group was now thirteen, including the Swiss boys, so we only just managed to squeeze around our camping table together. The toasts began immediately with some home-brewed vodka that Max had bought from one of the lorry drivers. Shamil toasted each of us, raising his plastic cup of vodka successively to Lucy's 'kindness' and her position as his 'number one friend', Mouse's 'tactfulness' and Wic's 'beauty'. To me he raised his cup last, 'and finally to my fighting friend'! During the past couple of weeks we had had several blazing rows, usually sparked by his jealousy. If I spoke to Max, Bazar-kul or Sergei he would reprimand me for flirting, even though the conversations were generally centred on such unromantic topics as tent pegs. Nothing I said could dissuade him from his suspicions, and he would sometimes ignore me for whole afternoons. I must have looked rather dismayed by this toast because Shamil lifted his cup again and, suddenly becoming very serious, said, 'To you. There's nothing more I can say ...' This produced a moment's silence, but the noise was quickly resumed and more toasts followed. Wic had brought one precious tape with her, stored carefully in her rucksack, which she now unearthed and asked Sergei to play on the stereo in his truck. He quickly acquiesced and the incongruous strains of Boney M were soon to be heard floating out across the moonlit plain. As everybody began dancing, I remember feeling an incredible rush of exhilaration and freedom, as if nothing could restrain us in this wild, open landscape.

One by one we peeled off to our tents, exhausted from all the emotions of the day, and the vodka. We woke up the next morning with splitting headaches, hardly able to move. But we had no choice; we needed to sort out all our belongings, ready for the border crossing later that afternoon. We knew that on the following day we would already be sweltering in the heat of the Taklamakan. But we could not dispose of our winter clothes, because in September it would become cold again, so we packed them up, ready to be stored in our new truck. We sifted through everything, from cooking utensils to medicine, giving anything superfluous to Rachel and Charty. Finally, we collected all the bags into a large heap and sat down on top of them, waiting for the truck that would carry us across the border.

On certain days in the week vehicles with special permits are permitted to cross the Kyrgyz–Chinese border. If you do not travel in one of these it is extremely complicated to enter China so, together with the Swiss boys, we were waiting for one of these appointed trucks. Max was to accompany us and make sure we crossed the border safely, but we would say goodbye to everybody else in the camp.

I dreaded the arrival of the truck because that would mean leaving Shamil. When I saw it appear on the horizon I began to cry. He was silent but held my hand tightly. We had done and seen so much together that I could not bear the thought of continuing without him. I have never felt so happy as I was at that time with Shamil. I have met nobody like him before or since: not only good-looking and intelligent, he exuded such strength of character and confidence, without a trace of arrogance, that every situation became fun and infused with his enthusiasm. He introduced a feeling of vitality to everything. Unaware of his appeal, he possessed a rare and enticing ingenuousness.

By the time the truck drew up I was sobbing uncontrollably. I could hardly say goodbye to Charty and Rachel, let alone Zula, Sergei and Bazarkul. I felt very guilty towards Rachel and Charty, both close friends of mine, because they had made such an effort to come and join the expedition and I had been so preoccupied by Shamil during their time with us. But Max was very firm. As I was hugging Shamil he pulled me on to the bus and told the driver to move on. I watched through the window as Shamil waved mournfully at me, not moving until he had lost sight of us.

As I burst into yet more floods of tears, Wic did her best to console me. The truck was full of middle-aged French climbers who were also making the crossing. Seeing my distress, one of them looked at me curiously and said in a very loud voice, 'Do you have sunstroke?' Wic shot a look of scorn at her, adding caustically, 'No, it's been snowing for the last few days here.'

At the border post Max spent the next couple of hours chasing after us as we wandered in different directions, searching for lavatories, customs forms, pens and chocolate. When he finally herded us into a corner, a customs official beckoned us into his office. We squeezed ourselves onto a narrow bench, our eyes at the level of the top of his desk. Max remained by the door, twitching nervously. Apart from the portly official peering down at us from his desk, there were several other younger guards who stood silently behind him. For the first five minutes there was complete silence as the seated bureaucrat perused our documents. Eventually, there came a raucous shriek of laughter. The official swung round in his seat to share the unintelligible joke with his colleagues. He then picked up a stamp and brought it down arbitrarily on our passports. Then to the next checkpoint (a man in a small wooden box), out of a door and onto a bus, joining the French group again. We never said goodbye to the Swiss boys, who were one step behind us, but we hoped to see them again at the next checkpoint.

A well-worn road now led us through no man's land, in the direction of China. The bus came to a stop under an imposing arch where we had arranged by e-mail to meet Mr Jin, our Chinese logistics co-ordinator, whom Mouse had met the previous year on her reconnaissance trip. After an anxious wait of forty-five minutes a huge jeep screeched to a halt on the other side of the arch. Out jumped a large Chinese man, sporting a particularly bright pair of tracksuit bottoms, shimmering purple with pink diamonds cascading down the outer leg. Bearing an enormous grin, he bounded towards us, arms outstretched, yelling 'Sophia!'[Mouse's real name] at the top of his voice.

As we waited for the arrival of our new back-up lorry, we unloaded our numerous bags from the border truck. We were half expecting a clapped-out Lada to chug around the corner, so we could hardly believe our eyes when a relatively large lorry appeared in the distance. Despite its tiny wheels, more suited to a pram, it appeared just about up to the job. But this was no ordinary lorry. Draped over both sides was a large sheet of red silk with a map of China painted in yellow (we noted the patriotic colour scheme) across it. Marked on the map was our route, and above it were emblazoned the following words, in both Chinese and English scripts: '99 British Ancient Silk Road Camel Riding Tour'. To the left of the map were printed the statistics, '5000 km/161 days' and finally, along the bottom, 'Italian Makopolo in the Ancient Times' and 'British Girls on Today'. Later we were to discover that in the Chinese script they had included Mouse's name, so that for the following five months we were chased through villages by shouts of 'Sophia, Sophia!'

When we thought our surprises had run out, Mr Jin pointed out with enormous pride his shower invention. He had designed and built a large water tank that sat on the roof of the lorry. The outside had been painted black in order to heat the water during the day and out of the back of the tank passed a hose with a shower head attached to the end. Sadly, this ingenious contraption was to be used only once during our time in China, there rarely being enough water for either the camels or us to drink, let alone shower.

We all piled into Mr Jin's jeep and sped off to our first Chinese customs checkpoint, where we encountered a small army of teenage soldiers who eagerly gathered around us as if we were the first group to cross the border that year. We were summoned into a small room one by one and ordered to empty our pockets on to the wooden desk that sat in the middle. This seemed to generate tremendous interest – they fingered my lipsalve with particular curiosity. Having been pushed back and forth under a metal detector I was released and the next victim sent in. The guards only appeared to be content once the metal detector had beeped. Perhaps all this served to heighten the illusion of top-rate security.

Our next obstacle was a very young official who had obviously watched far too many prisoner-of-war films and rather fancied himself as an interrogator. After thumbing through our passports he stood up straight, raising his chin as if to gain some height over us (difficult given his diminutive stature) and pronounced the ominous words, 'Visa, no valid.' The corners of his mouth slowly turned upwards as he waited for our response.

'Yes, they are,' we all retorted in unison.

'Where you get visa?'

'Ashgabad.'

'I repeat, where you get visa?'

'Turkmenistan.'

'Where?'

'TURKMENISTAN.'

He looked down again, the soldiers crowding around him obviously asking what answer we had given. Finally he muttered, 'Turkmasan', and they were thrown into equal confusion. He changed tack.

'How much you pay visa?' he bellowed.

Three of us simultaneously replied, 'Seventy dollars', while Lucy answered with the figure of eighty.

'How much?'

Frightened of showing any disparity, Wic, Mouse and I replied, 'Eighty dollars,' and Lucy switched to 'Seventy dollars'.

'Arrrrrrh.' His grin broadened. 'You say seventy dollars, you say eighty dollars. Why you say seventy, why you say eighty?'

The smile quickly evaporated. It was pointless trying to explain that Lucy, our treasurer, was responsible for dishing out the money, so only she could remember the price correctly. Having answered the same question at least thirty more times, it became obvious to us that the situation was not progressing. Thankfully, he suddenly decided that even he had had enough. Looking rather smug, he asked, 'Why buy visa in Bishkek and no England?'

We drew deep breaths. 'We didn't buy them in Bishkek, we bought them in Ashgabad. We weren't allowed to buy them in England because the visas have to be used within two months of being issued,' replied Lucy with exaggerated patience.

'I say you,' he cried, pointing a threatening finger at us, 'why you no buy visa in Bishkek?'

We wondered whether he did in fact want to catch us out or whether his motive really lay in showing off to his colleagues both his command of English and his authority. We could tolerate this no longer. Mouse summoned Mr Jin to take over while we marched off to supervise the search taking place in our lorry. Our carefully packed rucksacks had been tipped upside down on to the tarmac and everything, from dirty laundry to suncream, was being inspected minutely. To our horror, the big blue bag that contained our illegal satellite telephone had also been thrown to the ground. The telephone was discovered, but luckily lack of training prevented its confiscation. We were simply told to declare it at customs, the next and final checkpoint. 'Absolutely,' we nodded as we walked back to the jeep, Lucy carrying the offending telephone. She stuffed it under the passenger seat where it remained, unnoticed, until we were safely over the border. We collapsed on the back seat of the jeep, hoping Mr Jin would be able to solve the visa problem.

Now we heard screams of 'Sophia, Sophia!' from afar. The intransigent official had lighted on Mouse's name, inscribed on the side of the lorry, and was demanding her presence. After a disturbingly long period of time she was released. Apparently the same questions had been asked and the same answers given. Finally, our foe marched up to the car and bellowed, as if addressing a fleet of tanks, 'Open fer dar!' We wound down the window instead. Our passports were handed to us and we were told to leave. We did so swiftly.

The last checkpoint was customs, where it was a relief to be welcomed by smirking officials who seemed more interested in our names and origins than our documents or possessions. We sailed through and breathed a collective sigh of relief.

It was not long before Mr Jin had driven us to our first campsite in China. There our camels were waiting: nine antediluvian-looking animals scattered among the poplar trees, chewing ponderously on the leaves. Unnervingly thin, they still had an air of majesty, their slow, languorous movements affording them great stateliness. Some of them had large clumps of fur hanging from their haunches. This did not detract from their dignity, although it made us worry about their state of health. However, Mr Jin assured us it was the moulting season which also, for some reason, affected their weight. We quickly christened them Sir David Moon Boot, Queenie, Punk Rocker, Merlin, DHL, Amec, Meredith-Jones, Neurotic and Frankincense, although it took us a while to remember which was which.

Next we were introduced to our two camel handlers, Rozi and Egem, two young Kyrgyz from south of Kashgar. Our cook, Mr He, seemed very enthusiastic, as did the lorry driver, Mr Lee. The latter was dressed in shorts, a T-shirt and a pair of white, nylon gloves that we found were never to be removed, even in the depths of the desert. Mouse described these two at the time as 'adorable' and 'sweet', epithets that were sadly later to prove completely misguided. Finally there was Sadiq, an English-speaking Uighur who was to accompany us to Kashgar. We all sat down to our first Chinese meal, a selection of stir-fried vegetables and rice, before erecting our tents. I lay awake for hours before going to sleep, reflecting upon Shamil and our time in Central Asia. Everything suddenly seemed so alien. I felt lost and homesick.

7

China, at last

CHINA, AT LAST. Although I was still missing Central Asia, it was strangely exciting to wake up in China where, despite being only a hundred miles or so from the Torugart pass and Kyrgyzstan, everything was completely different. Not least our breakfast of spicy vegetables and tomato and egg omelette, eaten with chopsticks and still washed down with the ubiquitous green tea. During this unfamiliar meal we said goodbye to Mr Jin, who was returning to Kashgar ahead of us.

As we cleared away our tents, the camels slowly moved around us like prehistoric monsters, calmly stripping the orchard in which we were camped. A crowd of children and adults had gathered around us, staring unashamedly, a habit that we were dismayed to find shared by all villagers in China. The girls were dressed in velour dresses, despite the heat, and all had pencilled a thick black line between their eyebrows like little werewolves. Apparently it is considered the height of beauty around here to have eyebrows that meet in the middle.

The dreaded moment came to mount the camels. Although Bactrian, and so significantly smaller than their Dromedarian cousins, they still looked ominously tall compared to our horses. Their saddles, precariously perched high up between the two humps, were made of striped canvas and stuffed with straw. Held together by thick branches on either side, bound with camel-hair ropes, they had two slits in them to allow the camel's humps to breathe. This type of saddle has been used along the Silk Road without adaptation for over 2,000 years.

Lucy's record of her first experience on a camel summed it up:

Camel on ground. Leg over. Shuffle into position. No problem. Then the camel lifted its head, stretched its two back legs and my whole weight was rushed forward towards the camel's neck. I floundered for the sticks securing the saddle to the camel's back and gripped tight as, getting up on to its front legs, I was thrown back again.

I was the next to go through this unnerving procedure and sat clinging to a tuft of hair growing on the front hump of my camel. Once all were installed, Rozi and Egem organised the animals into two chains. Each camel had a wooden nose-peg, to which was tied a rope secured to the saddle of the camel in front. In order for us to mount, the camels had each been forced to lie on the ground, their ungainly legs crumpled beneath their bodies, but Rozi and Egem deftly vaulted on to their saddles from the ground, shaming us all. They had taken the two front camels and, using the nose-peg ropes, guided them forwards on to the road. We later discovered that their artlessness was deceptive – this seemingly simple method of riding was in fact highly skilled. When Lucy and I once tried to take control of the front camels they eitheir refused to move or wandered round in circles.

The thirty miles to Kashgar lay along poplar-lined roads teeming with jeeps and trucks that raced past, horns blaring. The camels, unaccustomed to traffic, were understandably distressed and sidestepped nervously. This terrified me. Within five minutes I had forced Egem to stop our little caravan so that I could dismount. Walking all the way to Kashgar, I suffered two huge blisters and an insatiable thirst as a result. The others, who were braver, alternated walking with riding. At twelve o'clock we stopped for lunch in the shade – it was already a burning 30°C – and ate the apricots and rice cakes we had been carrying in our saddlebags. The camels were let free to graze when suddenly we heard a shrill cry as one of them, tangling its rope around a tree, accidentally wrenched the nose-peg out of another. A large pool of blood appeared on the ground. But Rozi and Egem, who were clearly inured to such scenes, calmly picked a twig from one of the trees and inserted it through the bleeding nose hole, in place of the broken peg.

By the time we had reached the outskirts of Kashgar, stopping off for a very welcome beer, Lucy and Wic had spent a whole six hours in the saddle and were unable to straighten their legs at first. Before reaching our hotel we encountered our back-up team, who had picked up a photographer from Beijing. He wanted us to ride our camels right up to the door of the hotel for a photo shoot. Reluctantly forced to remount, I rode my camel in terror along two extremely busy streets.

As we passed through the hotel gates we were met by an incredible sight. A large inflatable rainbow had been erected over our path and lined up around it stood the entire staff of the hotel applauding our entrance. We did not know where to look. Finally, we were permitted to dismount and enter the hotel. All we could think of was running water and having a shower, something we had been deprived of for over two months.

Having expelled a couple of cockroaches from our bathroom, we took full advantage of this luxury. Later, feeling different people and dressed up in almost clean clothes, we set out for John's Café, famed in Kashgar for its banana pancakes and fruit milkshakes. Just as we were settling down to our meal, however, the manager approached us. 'Are you the girls with the camels?' It was amazing that news could spread so quickly in such a large, busy city.

'Yes.'

'Going all the way to Xian?'

'Yes.'

'Via the Taklamakan?'

'Yes.'

'I drove that route once – it took four days.'

'Really?' We tried to feign interest.

'Nothing there.'

'Oh, right.'

'Yes, all desert, no trees, no bushes, no life. I said to the guy driving, "Let's get out of here. Close all the windows and lock the doors – let's go." Yes, nothing.'

Luckily, we were enjoying our pancakes too much to be upset by his foreboding words, which turned out to be all too accurate.

The next morning we woke up, excited to explore the city of Kashgar about which we had read so much. Kashgar is situated in Xinjiang (meaning 'far border'), formerly Eastern Turkestan, and its population is principally made up of Uighurs, a Turkic people said to be descended from the Huns.

In 138 BC, an adventurous young Chinese traveller called Chang Ch'ien set out from Ch'ang-an (modern Xian) on a secret mission on behalf of the Han emperor, Wu-ti, to explore the then remote and mysterious regions of the West. After thirteen years, Chang Ch'ien finally returned from his travels, bringing with him information that was to cause a sensation at the

Han court. From his emissary the Emperor learned not only of Xinjiang but of the rich and previously unknown kingdoms of Ferghana, Samarkand, Bukhara and Balkh. Also, for the first time the Chinese learned of the existence of Persia and of another distant land they called Li-jien (almost certainly Rome). For his efforts, the Emperor Wu-ti bestowed on his emissary the title 'Great Traveller'. Often described as the father of the Silk Road, Chang Ch'ien is still revered in China today, as it was he who laid the first tracks of the trail westwards towards Europe that was ultimately to link the two great powers of the day – Imperial China and Imperial Rome. It was not, however, until AD 73 that the region of Xinjiang was put under formal Chinese control, by a military hero called Ban Chao who used Kashgar as his headquarters.

After the Han, Kashgar fell under an assortment of different rulers, until it was reclaimed by the T'ang dynasty (618–907, the period during which the art and civilisation of the Silk Road was at its height), only to become one of Genghis Khan's first conquests in the early thirteenth century. It was not until the Ch'ing (1644–1911) that China once again took an interest in the territories to her north-west.

During the Great Game Kashgar played an interesting role. In 1865 the exiled Muslim ruler of Kashgar decided to recover his former territory from the Chinese, accompanied by a small force of armed men led by the adventurer Yakub Beg, who claimed to be a descendant of Tamerlane. Having managed to wrest Kashgar and Yarkand from the Chinese, Yakub Beg ruthlessly pushed aside his patron and declared himself the ruler of the newly formed region of Kashgaria. He continued to annex parts of Chinese Turkestan until his army was finally routed by the Chinese, and he was forced to flee to Kashgar, where he died in 1877.

Nearly all the more famous Silk Road travellers, including Marco Polo, Peter Fleming and Hsuan-tsang, the great Buddhist pilgrim explorer of the seventh century, passed through Kashgar.

Marco Polo wrote of the city:

> Cascar is a region lying between north-east and east and constituted a kingdom in former days, but now is subject to the Great Kaan. The people worship Mahommet. There are a good number of towns and villages, but the greatest and finest is Cascar itself ... From this country many merchants go forth about the world on trading journeys. The natives are a wretched niggardly set of people; they eat and drink in miserable fashion ...

This seemed a sadly accurate description of twentieth century Kashgar, too, after our hotel breakfast of pickled black eggs and puffs of stodgy unbaked bread. Sadiq came to collect us and we set out from the quietness of the hotel to find ourselves in streets reminiscent of the colourfulness, bustle and heat Kipling's Kim experienced along the 'Great Road': 'such a river of life as nowhere else exists in the world'. The principal traffic was donkey carts, but there were all sorts of animals everywhere, except for dogs, which apparently all had been killed in the previous year due to an outbreak of rabies. At every corner food was being sold, generally from round, clay ovens, and piles of melons lined the streets. The men appeared dressed just as their forbears would have been, in baggy trousers, long, unbuttoned coats tied at the waist with a sash, and Muslim skullcaps. The women wore dresses, often with a brown, woollen scarf covering their head and face. It was a shock to find ourselves in the midst of all this excitement, noise and heat after the solitude and calm of Kyrgyzstan.

We spent several hours that morning buying string, bags, mirrors, quilts and some light cotton material. We then visited a tailor where we had the material made up into trousers and shirts. He operated in a tiny room full of young girls sewing on old-fashioned Singer machines. Our next stop was at a Uighur doctor, whose family has been practising medicine for over four hundred years. Wic wanted to consult him about a rash on her arms that had appeared over the previous month. He claimed to recognise it immediately, saying it was caused by a toxin in the blood rising to the surface – telling her it should improve in a month, he gave her some sticky black medicine that was to be mixed with oil and rubbed on the rash.

Later that evening Sadiq took us to the night market – rows and rows of food stalls set along several streets, selling dumplings, kebabs and noodles. He had assured us that Marco Polo's derogatory description of Kashgarian food could only be applied to the Chinese dishes and that Uighur food was in an entirely different category. Eager to prove his point, he took us to a Uighur café where we ate vegetables and noodles. Typical of restaurants all over Xinjiang, it was very informal, with people eating either alone or together at small tables, but not talking. The owner was convinced that we had come in the day before – they find it as hard to distinguish between Europeans as we do between Asiatics.

While we were eating, Sadiq told us a little about Xinjiang politics. Unlike Central Asia, where many people regret the withdrawal of the Russian population, the Uighurs greatly resent the Chinese presence, despite there having been a much longer history of colonisation. He also told us that, like the Russians and indigenous Central Asians people, the Chinese and Uighurs rarely intermarry, and if they do it is always a Han Chinese man who marries a Uighur woman. The year before there had been several bombings in Xinjiang, perpetrated by the Uighurs against the Chinese, and Sadiq told us there was now a feeling of uncertainty in Kashgar and the other major cities of Xinjiang. He estimated that of the Uighur population 80 per cent resent Chinese rule but remain politically apathetic, 10 per cent benefit from the Communists and are therefore inactive, and the final 10 per cent support the bombings. He sympathised with the bombers, calling them 'the brave ones'.

Having finished our vegetables and noodles, which did indeed prove to be delicious, we moved on to a stall in the street where Sadiq ordered dumplings, kebabs and beer. We could hardly move after this feast and, despite Sadiq's entreaties to go to a Kashgar nightclub, we could only think of bed.

After a restorative night's sleep, despite the heat, we returned to the Uighur restaurant of the night before, where we ate surprisingly good spicy jellied vegetables and fried lumps of dough. By ten o'clock it was already 30°C – it seemed almost unbelievable that a few days before we had been sheltering in our tents from snowfalls. We had exchanged thick jodhpurs and coats for T-shirts and the loose trousers made for us by the Kashgar tailor. Sadiq now suggested we visit the Abakh Hoja mausoleum built in 1640 by Abakh, a famous Muslim leader, in honour of his father, which lay in blissful solitude away from the teeming city centre. We were among the first visitors to arrive that morning and, lingering at the gates, we found two Uighur women making silk under the shade of a mulberry tree. The first woman, clothed from head to toe in swathes of diamond-patterned silk, boiled about a hundred dried silk moth cocoons in a huge vat of water, in order to soften them and entice the minute threads of silk to unravel. These were then plucked out of the water and threaded through a square frame towards the second woman, who spun them on to a wheel and eventually on to a spool. By this time the silk had been so stretched, pulled and refined that it was ready to be dyed and spun on to a loom.

Sadiq pulled us away to show us the mausoleum itself, set in a patchwork of fields and graveyards. The domed building, covered in blue and green tiles, contains a group of unmarked tombs that occupy almost all the cool interior and are rumoured to hold a total of seventy-two bodies from five generations of political and religious leaders, among them Yakub Beg, whose uprising was crushed by the Chinese.

Now we left the serenity of the tombs for the market. Strategically placed at the convergence of the southern and northern Taklamakan routes to the east, and the Indian and Central Asian routes to the west, Kashgar is still a trading crossroads, as it has been since the days of the Silk Road. Its legendary Sunday bazaar, where everything from pendulous-bottomed sheep to fur hats is sold, was already a hive of activity by the time we reached it at midday. Getting there was a feat in itself, however. For miles around there was a throng of donkey carts, bicycles, barrows and cars piled high with produce. Animals were everywhere, some restrained by pieces of string, others kept in order by sticks. The noise of shouting, bleating, mooing and squealing music, in combination with the heat was almost overwhelming. Sadiq led us into an open arena flanked by food stalls. The central area was heaving with every type of animal – donkeys, sheep, goats, cows, bulls and chickens – each allocated separate sections where they were inspected and prodded by prospective buyers. At the far end a small ring had been cleared for testing horses, where we found a group of small grimy boys galloping up and down in the rising dust. Every now and then a man would enter the ring with a donkey to test out, which would invariably leave the ring abruptly, kicking, bucking and occasionally dislodging its rider.

We escaped to the relative cool of the covered market itself, which was laid out in a grid pattern under the shade of multi-coloured material draped loosely across the wooden stalls. We soon found ourselves bartering for lynx fur hats, towels, sacks, shampoo, dried figs and doughnut sticks, but after an hour Sadiq decided it was time to head for 'The Orchard', a Uighur restaurant set outside in the shade of some fruit trees. Having passed through tiny back streets to reach it, we found a group of tables clustered around a central stage filled with people: old men playing mah-jong, women chattering, young men drinking, and children running around among them all. Around two o'clock the stage burst into life, as a Uighur musician began to produce wailing strains and the crowds wove towards the dance floor, their hips circling in time to the music. We dined amid this swaying throng on kebabs and melon, accompanied by Sadiq's fiancée, a very pretty and demure-looking Uighur girl with dark eyes, her hair covered by a headscarf. In contrast to Sadiq, who was constantly talking and seemed very fond of beer, she sat in complete silence, smiling at us throughout the afternoon. Our time in Kashgar was coming to an end: the following day we would finally be braving the desert. When I repeatedly asked Sadiq how hot it would be, he replied evasively, 'Like here.'

'And when will it begin to get cooler?'

'Um, around the end of July.'

'Wow, that's excellent – we were told it wouldn't be until the end of September.'

In fact, the prognosis we had received in England was to prove far more accurate than Sadiq's. But, in retrospect, we were fortunate to be misled, because the thought of three months' intense heat ahead of us might have made us give up there and then.

After enjoying our last night in the hotel we mounted our camels in the courtyard, where they had been grazing all weekend. Rozi and Egem sat at the front of our two little caravans while we clung on nervously behind as we headed south out of Kashgar. What we had not anticipated was the two-hour detour we were led on before escaping the city. The photographer had reappeared with all sorts of grand ideas in mind. We only learned later that he had been hired by our cynical Chinese logistics company to acquire some shots of us for their next advertising campaign.

Our first stop was the main bazaar. Thankfully, it was not Sunday, although the traffic was still completely chaotic. Donkey carts, flocks of sheep and children were darting around everywhere, dodging between the camels' legs, and music blared from loudspeakers, sounding like some sort of warbling backed by an orchestra of wasps. The camels jogged along uneasily, yanking at each other's nose-pegs with every panicked jerk. Once again, I was terrified and begged Rozi to halt and let me dismount.

The situation became slightly less nervewracking, however, when the camels took an abrupt turn up a narrow side street, part of a network of tiny streets that ran through the old town. Here the houses became much more higgledy-piggledy, made mainly of clay or wood, often with small balconies that hung low over the street. Busy craftsmen – blacksmiths, metal workers, carpenters and tailors – all advertised their products by displaying them in the streets or hanging them from stalls.

Eventually we emerged from this maze of back streets at the Id Kah mosque, one of China's largest. Built in 1442, it suffered heavy damage during the Cultural Revolution but has now been restored to its former glory. Its warm, yellow-tiled exterior sat well against the deep blue sky behind and the photographer decided to take advantage of such a picturesque backdrop. An enormous crowd, which had by now gathered around the camels, watched with bemusement as Rozi and Egem steered them backwards and forwards for him, as well as a television cameraman who had also appeared, seemingly from nowhere.

Finally, we were allowed to continue our journey. As the hours rolled on and we headed further and further east, the traffic began to diminish, yet still occasionally a car would screech to a halt just in front of us, flinging the cameraman out of the back. The sun was strong and the thermometers on our watches showed a constant 34°C, so we were relieved to see our camp at the end of the day, after about twenty-two miles of riding.

Just as we had finished tethering the camels and were about to quench our thirst, the photographer appeared yet again and insisted that we ride on a further couple of miles, where there was, apparently, an ideal stage set of virgin dunes for us. We protested, but Sadiq had obviously been given strict instructions by Beijing. He persuaded us reluctantly to get back on our poor, tired camels and head for the dunes with Rozi and Egem. Meanwhile, Sadiq, Mr Li and Mr He re-packed the camp and followed us in the truck. We attracted a curious audience once again, who seemed to find our tents and sleeping bags quite extraordinary.

We set off again the next morning at eight o'clock along the same road, heading east into the Taklamakan. There is only one road that skirts this desert to the north, and one to the south. We had chosen to take the latter because nobody before us had retraced this branch of the Silk Road on camels. Our chosen road had begun as tarmac in Kashgar but quickly deteriorated into dust and stones as we travelled further east. Despite the shade provided by the poplar trees that lined the road, we soon realised that in a region where temperatures soar beyond 35°C for months on end the only way to make satisfactory progress was to get up before the sun rises. We vowed to introduce a new regime into the camp from the following morning, rising at daybreak and riding until lunch.

We felt our second pang of disquiet that day when we met some carts pulled by Bactrian camels. We had, until this moment, assumed our scrawny camels to be normal since Mr Jin had assured us several times that their bedraggled appearance was due to them being in moult. But on seeing these stocky, sleek, pert-humped animals, we felt deceived. Mr Jin had promised Mouse that our camels had been fattened up and resting for three months, but our emaciated animals, with their drooping humps, had obviously not grazed properly for a long time. Sadiq promised to telephone headquarters in Beijing from a village along the road. Unfortunately in China, where it is impossible to travel without using a government agency, we had been forced to buy our camels and hire our guides through a company, run by a Mr Ma, based in Beijing, over 3,000 miles away. Sadiq insisted that we were unable to make a decision about buying new animals without Mr Ma's approval. There was nothing more we could do, so we looked out impatiently for a village.

At eleven o'clock we reached some good grazing land and, worried about the camels' strength, we released them into the grass. Meanwhile, we sat down to feast on two honeydew melons Sadiq had been carrying in his saddlebags. Having rounded up the camels from their hiding places in the long stalks, at half-past twelve we were back on the road again. I had been forced to conquer my fear of riding the camels by the intensity of the heat. It became unbearable walking for more than an hour at a time: my head felt as though it would explode so I had no choice.

The early afternoon brought us towards Yengisar, famous for its knives, as we discovered when a smiling Uighur man in a cap rode up on a bicycle. We smiled back and he pronounced the word, 'Englia?' 'Yes, we're from England.' This was as far as our conversation could go, for at this point he removed a sheath from his belt, and from this a large knife, which he thrust towards a startled Lucy. When he said 'bazaar' we all breathed a sigh of relief – he was only trying to sell us the knife.

We rode through Yengisar, a collection of adobe houses with a dusty main street running between them and arrived on the other side to see a huge reservoir spanning the horizon. It shimmered in the heat as we approached and we eagerly asked Sadiq if it was possible to swim. 'No, it's dirty.' But we camped close to the water's edge, with the beginnings of the Kun Lun mountains rising to the south, although unfortunately our proximity to the water meant we attracted hordes of mosquitoes that plagued us all night.

The next morning we rose at half-past five. We had intended to start at six but our concern for the camels delayed us. One of them was painfully thin, and we had discovered great raw patches on his stomach where the saddle ropes had been rubbing. We asked Rozi and Egem to remove the saddle and store it in the truck, because it appeared inconceivable that we could ever ride him. Eventually, at seven we set off, although the morning was already very hot. In a village en route we were all invited into a local man's orchard to eat his apricots. We walked through his comfortable adobe house and courtyard, which was shaded by a vine trellis and had one side lined with large, square benches covered in quilts. The orchard at the back of the courtyard was small but the apricot trees grew densely and we stripped several branches bare of their succulent fruit. The old man was very disappointed when we told him we had to leave so quickly (because of the heat) as he would not have time to slay a sheep in our honour. Sadiq told us later that the old man was horrified by our clothes. He had apparently expected us to be dressed in gorgeous dresses, instead of which we were wearing dirty, ripped cotton trousers, T-shirts, and battered walking boots.

An hour or so later the sky thankfully clouded over and it actually began to rain. We wrapped ourselves up in the green quilts we rode on, and the dye came seeping out all over our clothes. In our camp we hid in the truck until the rain relented. It was a hugely welcome break from the inexorable rays of the sun but the heat itself did not really seem to abate. That evening we received our e-mails, including one from Charty and Rachel. They had successfully reached Tashkent, having driven all the way with Shamil, Sergei, Zula and Max. Rachel told me about Shamil and a tape I had given him on leaving: 'He is pining – he is desperately sad and is manically playing his Elvis tape whenever possible – in taxis, restaurants, etc ...' It made me cry and all evening I sat alone recollecting everything Shamil had ever said to me.

At half-past five the next morning we woke up to a dramatic pink light over the Kun Lun. As the sun rose, the mountains became a hazy yellow and we packed up our tents as quickly as possible in a race against the rising heat of the day. We began our trek alternating walking on foot with hours of riding on the camels, along the long, straight road to our next camp, with not so much as a rise or kink in it to enliven our journey. Only the intensity of the sun and the two lines of telegraph poles that flanked our road indicated that we and the day were moving on. After five hours the mountains on our right disappeared, and we found ourselves in a vast sea of grey sand that stretched out in every direction.

In camp melons and cups of green tea helped to quench our almost insatiable thirst as we lay, motionless, under a piece of cloth suspended on four sticks, waiting for sundown. Sadiq had managed to speak to Beijing about our camels. The news was not good. He had been told that they were not our responsibility, but Mr Ma's, and therefore we should simply wait until the unfortunate animals died. We decided we could do nothing until a new guide joined us, as he was due to do, in a couple of days' time.

That night, we had our first and last shower from the truck. Privacy was impossible, so we crouched behind the truck, enjoying the sun-warmed water, as the occasional truck driver drove past hooting at us. Then suddenly Lucy felt very ill, with excruciating stomach cramps. As she lay in her tent, with the doors open, Sadiq asked her a series of questions. 'When did you begin to feel ill?' 'What did you eat today?' 'Do you have runny dung?' We could not suppress our laughter at this point, but hoped it was not dysentery.

Although we had risen at daybreak that morning, we felt it was still not early enough because our final two hours of riding had been in the heat of the day. Therefore, we had reluctantly decided that from now on it was necessary to get up in the dark, enabling us to set off with first light. At four o'clock the next morning, we crawled out of our sleeping bags to pack up our tents and belongings by torchlight. Lucy had not slept a wink all night and was still feeling nauseous, so we decided she should sleep in the back-up trunk. We set off shortly after sunrise, around five o'clock, enjoying the first hour of breathable air and unsweaty clothes. However, by seven it was already hot, and by eight our vision had started to blur in the heat. The road continued straight towards the horizon. Occasionally a small black vibrating object would appear in the distance, its shape indiscernible in the waves of heat until it was only yards in front. I was convinced at one point that an approaching juggernaut was in fact another camel caravan.

The camels' swaying motion had become more familiar after a week of riding, its effect often soporific. Wic wrote, 'As the minutes and hours progress with little surrounding material to feed the imagination, I find it is almost too easy to close my eyes and, with the rhythmic rocking of the camel, drift off into a slumber. At times I simply rest my eyes by shutting them and on opening them feel suddenly unbalanced and disoriented.' Rozi and Egem were constantly having to turn round to check we had not fallen asleep.

Fortunately, in the late morning, we were treated to the sight of a large oasis containing the towns of Yarkand and Karghalik. The abrupt change from the grey broken stones of the desert to the green and fertile oasis was startling. It took only a murky river, no more than five feet wide, to act as the natural border between these two extremes. Poplar trees lined the road once more but, unlike those of Central Asia, there was no rustling among the branches. The air remained still and stifling.

Just off the road, in a shady opening, I noticed a spectacular carpet of bright orange apricots, which were being laid out meticulously by a number of men and women. Our truck overtook us and drew to a halt. In the front sat Lucy, who looked even worse than earlier. Her complexion had lost all its colour and dark circles had formed around her bloodshot eyes. Sadiq had decided to take her to hospital in Yarkand, a fifteen-minute drive from our camp.

We would visit Lucy later, but first we must meet our new guide. He looked very clean and fresh next to us. Straight out of university, Mamat-Jan, or Marmite Jam as he became known, was Uighur but spoke Chinese as well as English. We were quite shocked to discover that he was only twenty-one years old, the same age as my younger brother, but thought it best not to ask how much experience he had of travelling through the desert. Having introduced ourselves, we were driven by Mr Li to the hospital, a small building with several cell-like rooms leading off a narrow corridor. People lay prostrate on rickety beds as moans and infant screams echoed back and forth about the walls. We found Lucy asleep in a room, empty save two unoccupied beds. Although still obviously weak, she looked better. Soon, though, Mouse also started to feel ill and decided to lie down in one of the empty beds next to Lucy.

Meanwhile, the rest of us went off in search of noodles, returning later to find Mouse having taken a turn for the worse. She and Lucy were both presented with a box not much bigger than a matchbox and a small glass bottle and told to go off and bring back samples. An hour or so later, a solid nurse came crashing into the room carrying a tray of mediaeval-looking instruments. Picking up a cotton bud, she marched over to Lucy and started to pull her trousers down. Initially rather alarmed, Lucy burst into giggles as she made us look away while the delicate operation was performed. Several minutes later, the formidable nurse returned with a fresh cotton bud. Mouse turned even paler. As if the anticipated torture was not enough, the nurse slowly rotated her shoulders several times before carrying out the procedure for a second time.

By the afternoon, the eagerly awaited diagnosis was confirmed: 'Diarrhoea Number Two' was apparently the condition from which they were suffering. This information was only slightly reassuring. Just before Wic and I left the two invalids we witnessed them being wired up to a drip suspended from a lop-sided rusty pole. We asked how they would visit the lavatories. The drips were certainly not designed for mobility and the dung heap, to use Sadiq's terminology, was outside in the courtyard. Our answer was given in the form of a small plastic bowl sitting in the corner of the room.

Back at the camp we were greeted by what looked like the entire district's police force. Clearly dissatisfied by the lack of local crime, they informed us, through Mamat-Jan, that our camp needed to be under 24-hour surveillance. We watched in surprise as the policeman unfurled their sleeping bags within inches of our tent. This led to great embarrassment on poor Wic's part as, also now feeling unwell, she was making frequent trips throughout the night to the lavatory. In the morning Mamat-Jan approached us awkwardly.

'Umm …,'

'Yes, is something the matter?'

'Well, in future, maybe you should go to the lavatory in one place during the night.'

The policemen had obviously suffered an unpleasant enlightenment by the light of day.

Wic and I started out on the camels, feeling very strange not having Lucy and Mouse with us. But by seven o'clock her strength, too, was beginning to wane. We told Mamet-Jan that Wic needed to join the others in hospital, which she duly did, filling the second empty bed. She offered the nurse a sample of her 'dung' but it was refused on the grounds that it was the weekend and no doctors were at work.

Two minutes later a doctor walked in. He questioned Lucy minutely, through Sadiq, but took no notice of the others. Then, having satisfied himself that she was slightly improved from the day before, he left the room. Next to enter was Gulina, a 16-year-old Uighur girl who had taken it upon herself the previous night to fan Lucy and Mouse. Now she returned with an army of friends to show off the foreigners and her command of English (which was remarkably good). Throughout the day she came and went, never knocking or showing any embarrassment as Wic squatted in the corner for the hundredth time. The only other visitor was the cleaner, a dour-looking Uighur woman who washed the floor by pushing a grubby mop across it, using some very murky water.

I spent the rest of the day alone with Rozi and Egem, alternately riding and walking as usual. We covered about eighteen miles, passing out of the oasis of Yarkand and back into the scrub and solitude. Mamat-Jan told me excitedly that he had found a small inn where the camels and I could spend the night. The prospect of a break from my tent was most appealing, but my hopes were dispelled when I was shown my room. Without any windows or electric light, it looked like a small black hole. I descried a decrepit metal bed in one corner, and insects crawling over everything, including the bed. I decided to lay my camping mattress on the mud floor and sleep on that: at least I would be safe from the bed bugs.

Before I lay down, though, Mamat-Jan brought me a bucket of filthy water to wash in. I was so hot and sweaty that I took it, hoping it would at least cool me down. It felt strangely lonely without the others. The back-up team were sleeping in other rooms around the courtyard, but I was still frightened to leave the door open, after several men had stared curiously at me earlier in the evening. The airless room was stifling as I lay rigidly still in order to minimise the sweating. Despite my efforts to avoid the bugs, they seemed to swarm all over me. Then, just as I was finally falling asleep, there was a great banging on the door. I nervously opened it to find a small, withered old woman standing there. She forced her way past me, grabbed the bucket and left the room, not saying a word.

The next morning I found it almost impossible to rise. After seven days of waking up at four and not sleeping enough, I could hardly walk and spent most of the morning riding on Moon Boot, so-called because of his luxuriantly furry feet. As we rode out of the village he plucked with his long lips at every branch that hung across his path, often tripping as he did so.

By half-past eleven we had reached our camp on the outskirts of a settlement. We had covered another eighteen miles – our camels walked at a steady pace of three miles per hour, never less and never more. Approaching our camp, Rozi's roving eye had spied a girl on a bicycle taxi, who offered to give me a lift. She was the most extraordinary-looking person I had encountered on our travels yet. More like an Aborigine, with a wide mouth and coarse, wavy black hair, than either a Chinese or Uighur, she had covered her face in white powder. This stopped in an abrupt line at her neck. As our journey continued the powder began to dispel in the heat, but this did not quench Rozi's admiration. The girl left, returning with a bag of eggs for me while coyly leaving her orange apron on Rozi's quilt. Now the others returned from hospital in a taxi. They were feeling much better and we ate a delicious supper of homemade bread and noodles, delighted to be reunited after my lonely couple of days.

Sadiq entertained us that night by recounting the reaction of the hospital staff to our appearance. Apparently, our fairness and height had provoked great surprise, even horror. We were told that they thought Mouse and I, with our blonde hair and blue eyes, looked like ghosts, and any man would be scared to meet us on a dark night. The doctors had repeatedly asked Sadiq what Wic and Lucy ate to have grown as tall as men. The Uighurs have dark eyes and hair and are generally shorter than Europeans. This southern, rural part of Xinjiang had only just opened up to foreigners, so we were often the first the people had encountered. From this moment on I always felt very self-conscious walking through a Uighur village, seeing the villagers staring at me.

That evening, we said goodbye to Sadiq who had been very reluctant to leave us (this was good work for him), and had spent the previous few days criticising Mamat-Jan, in the hope of ousting him. Not only were we were sad to lose him and his amusing way of talking, but we were also rather nervous about Mamat-Jan. He had come with Mr Jin's high recommendation though, so, despite his young age, we felt we should trust him.

The next morning was almost cold with the sun shielded behind a thick blanket of clouds. Within a couple of hours, though, it had become intensely hot and stifling. The road took us through the lush oasis of Karghalik, past marshland, fields and rows of solicitously tended vegetables. As our camels padded past a cluster of flat-roofed adobe houses, from our elevated position we had a bird's eye view of this 'Uighur Roof Kingdom', in Mouse's words, where baskets, vines and even miniature kitchen gardens were to be found, above the dust of the streets.

As usual the local population was transfixed by our procession. The men put down their tools and stood, staring open-eyed at us, while the children screamed and the women peeped at us from under their headscarves. The passing traffic ranged from harnessed horses and some goats riding in the back of a donkey cart to women walking to work in the fields with wooden hoes and skull-capped men piled high on a tiny wagon.

The following day was to be our first rest day for almost two weeks, so that night we were to stay in the small but basic Mountaineering Hotel in Karghalik. It was blissful to wake up late the next morning and realise that we could lie in bed for as long as we liked. It was only here that we appreciated how tired we really were. We spent most of the day sleeping and reading, only leaving our rooms to eat in the hotel restaurant. Our waitress, delighted to have some customers to serve, hurried back and forth from the kitchen with an enormous grin stretching across her face. It was difficult to discern exactly what she served us because everything had been smothered in batter. However, we were able to identify battered aubergines, battered mutton and, worst of all, battered chips. Despite the copious quantities of grease we managed to consume the lot. We went to bed that night, dreading our four o'clock start.

The next day, 14 July, was my twenty-sixth birthday. The others mumbled their congratulations as we sleepily packed our stuff up and headed out of the hotel in the dark. By now we had developed a routine of walking the first six miles, which we could measure precisely using the mileposts that lined the road. Today, just as our six miles ran out, so did the oasis of Karghalik. One minute we were walking in the shade of some immensely tall poplars flanked by fields of maize and rice, the next the trees abruptly disappeared, the fields melted back into the oasis and we were confronted by a vast expanse of grey earthy sand. The contrast was startling.

The desert looked like a vast beach, with great flat expanses of sand instead of undulating dunes, the surface covered in tiny ripples where the wind had swept across it and nothing to break its grey mass except the road, stretching out into the horizon. Eventually we found ourselves in a windswept camp, where Mamat-Jan had erected our shelter in preparation for my birthday celebrations. It was 40°C and a wind had begun to stir up the sand, flinging it in gusts all over us and our belongings. I sat down eagerly on my quilt, as the others appeared from the back of the truck with some exciting-looking presents. I was very touched because they had obviously gone to great trouble, even finding paper to wrap them in. My first present was some striped canvas saddlebags for my camel, which sat like two huge envelopes over the saddle. The second was a pair of little gold earrings that Sadiq's girlfriend had suggested they buy, which I wore each time we stayed in a town. The final present was a huge bar of chocolate that had melted and quickly became covered in sand, but was still greatly appreciated. Mamat-Jan had bought a gaudily iced cake from a Kashgar baker, which we tucked into with gusto, although second bites were taken with more reserve. We drank it down with a bottle of sweet red wine and some beers, cooled in a wet sock suspended from the tent poles (a tip passed down to us by Mouse's grandfather, who had served in the desert in the Second World War). I was surprised to hear a ringing sound and looked around to see that Mouse had surreptitiously set up our satellite telephone. 'I think it's for you.'

'No? My family don't know the number, and who else could it be?'

'Go on, pick it up.'

I am notorious for my love of the telephone, so I had no problems following her instruction.

'Happy Birthday!'

'MUMMY!' I screamed in shock and happiness. Her voice sounded so close and clear, yet she could not have been further away from our windy spot of desert. I was delighted to speak to her and the rest of my family, and yet upset to think of them all cosily at home together while I spent my birthday far away in the middle of the Taklamakan desert.

That night a vicious sandstorm shook our tents, filling them with sand. We set off regardless, but all morning it continued, obstructing our vision and lashing our faces. Around midday it stopped, only for the temperature to become very hot once again. We had been campaigning with Mamat-Jan for the previous few days to exchange two particularly thin and weak camels for some others, but he could not persuade Beijing. Mamat-Jan was very likeable and friendly but not the most assertive person and we feared his powers of persuasion were limited. We were also not convinced that he had actually called Beijing, because we had not passed a telephone so far as we were aware, and he had never asked to use our satellite telephone. But on this day everything came to a head: after several hours of plodding through the sand and heat one of the two weak camels, Queenie, suddenly collapsed, refusing to move any further. Incredibly thin, with great concave gaps between his hind legs and ribs, he had been struggling at every step. Now his legs crumpled, ripping out the nose peg of the camel behind and setting off a loud wailing. Rozi and Egem managed to cajole the pathetic creature to its feet. The rest of our day's journey was very slow, only interrupted by a busload of Taiwanese tourists who suddenly appeared from nowhere and jumped out to take photographs.

One extremely tall man interrogated Lucy and me, 'No boys?'

'No.'

'You CRAZY!' and he pointed his finger at his head.

With which, they jumped back in to the bus and returned in the direction from which they had come.

Finally, drenched in sweat and covered in sand, we reached the tiny oasis of Pishan, our campsite for that night. We stayed in a small courtyard where we were able to wash in a bucket of water, after which we ate bowls of rice and vegetables, cooked by Mr He. Queenie collapsed on the ground once more and refused to eat, an ominous sign. We urged Mamat-Jan to leave him and the other weak camel, Punk Rocker, behind because it would be cruel to make them walk any further. At first Mamat-Jan was reluctant to agree, saying that he had received strict instructions from Beijing not to abandon any camel.

'But, Mamat-Jan, what's the point in forcing the camels to go on until they die?'

'Mr Ma says we have to.'

'That's not important. We paid for these camels and we can choose what to do with them.'

'But Mr Ma says we mustn't leave them.'

'Why does it make any difference whether we leave them or take them – we don't ride them anyway?'

Wic's clear reasoning threw Mamat-Jan for a minute or two before he replied, 'I don't know but Mr Ma says they must continue until they die.'

Mamat-Jan's lack of common sense and rigid obedience to Mr Ma's rules were to plague us for the next few months. Exasperating as he was, though, he never stopped smiling and by the end of our time with him even his way of thinking had endeared itself to us.

We managed to leave the next morning without the two ailing camels, however, leaving them with the hotel owners who had promised to feed them. Our point had not been won through the logic of our arguments but rather by force. Mamat-Jan was in a state of terror about what would happen to his career when Mr Ma found out about this rebellious decision, but we said we would take the blame. Sad as we felt to leave the two skeletal camels, it had become unbearable to watch them struggling at every stop, obviously in great pain. Our camel train was now down to seven animals, which left us with only one spare.

Unfortunately, Pishan oasis proved only a very brief respite from the desert proper. As the temperature continued to rise, our exhaustion increased proportionately, even though we covered shorter distances. For the last couple of weeks the oases had been fairly frequent, but now they were becoming rare and smaller. We were beginning to feel the oppression of the desert about which we had been warned so often in England. 'Taklamakan', whose name means 'he who enters never leaves' in Turkic, is one of the most arid deserts in the world, barely supporting any plant or animal life. Unlike the Sahara, it is not made of picturesque, undulating dunes but rather of flat, infinite stretches of *loess*, or stone smashed to smithereens by the relentless wind. This gives it its dull grey colour and ghostly, almost lunar appearance.

Having covered twenty-three miles in a day we thankfully reached another tiny oasis where we found Mamat-Jan shading himself under a tree. He leapt up to tell us that the camp was only half a mile further on – but it was almost half a mile too far. We all collapsed in the dust under the shade of a couple of spindly acacia trees, our heads pulsating, oblivious to the hundreds of tickling ants that crawled over us. Mouse and I were feeling particularly unwell and, although we drank as much water as possible, our heads were still throbbing when we went to bed.

I woke up the next morning feeling no better; the remorseless thumping in my head was now accompanied by an acute feeling of nausea. Wic guessed I had heatstroke, so we all agreed it was better if I rested for the day. My day was spent chasing the shadow of the truck and trying to sleep, in our new and completely shadeless camp, while the others continued on the camels. As Wic recorded:

> The hours passed slowly. I feel I have thought about and even discussed in great detail every topic under the sun. Every time I think of something different I relish the minutes they take up in thought. However, most of the time my thoughts centre around swimming-pools, ice-creams, power-showers, Arctic circles, fridges, freezers, snowmen and sprinklers in an English garden. I have also finally mastered the art of reading astride a camel, and this, I might add, is a wonderful means of escapism. I can now spend numerous hours fantasising about D'Artagnan, my new found hero from the *The Three Musketeers*.

Books were becoming an integral part of our lives, more important than food or even the distraction of oases. We were lucky enough to have been sponsored by Everyman and were carrying a small library of their classics and other books, ranging from *The Hobbit* to Evelyn Waugh's *War Trilogy* and Peter Hopkirk's *Foreign Devils on the Silk Route,* in the back of our truck. Although we had read in Central Asia, it was only in the monotony of the desert that the books assumed such importance. We deliberately read the same books one after each other so that we could discuss and analyse them afterwards, thereby increasing our enjoyment.

By the time the others arrived in the camp, Mouse was also feeling unwell, suffering, like me, from heat exhaustion. It was therefore decided that she and I should take a bus, accompanied by Mamat-Jan, to the next big oasis, Khotan, where we would stay for the following three days until the others reached us. As Wic recorded:

> Meanwhile, back at camp, Lucy and I noticed Rozi and Egem climbing out of their tents, looking like they were planning to hit the local nightclub. For the first time since they had been with us they were wearing different clothes. Rozi was in a beautifully ironed purple shirt very neatly tucked into some clean beige trousers, whilst Egem was in a boldly printed shirt, again tucked into a pair of clean trousers. They then spent a good five minutes each peering awkwardly in a mirror the size of a jam jar lid and combing their hair thoroughly. After all this preening an argument between the dashing duo broke out. Egem then changed straight back into his old clothes and reverted to drinking beer with his disgruntled companion. A most peculiar performance.

Mouse and I were installed in a reasonably clean hotel in Khotan, of a much higher standard than the other 'hotels' we had encountered on our journey. It even provided clean towels and an *en suite* shower. But at a cost, as we discovered when Mamat-Jan presented us with a bill for his room the next morning. When he graciously offered to stay with us until the others arrived, we quickly assured him it was not necessary and that he should resume his duties as camp manager. Reluctantly, he caught the next bus back to the camp, leaving Mouse and me to sleep and recover.

Mamat-Jan found Lucy and Wic already on the road, having survived a sandstorm or *buran*, as they are known locally. Lucy described it in her journal:

> By four o'clock, when we were meant to be waking, we hadn't yet been to sleep and suddenly our tent made a run for it. It had chosen its moment well as Wic sat up to get some water. Taking advantage of this momentary lack of pressure on her side of the tent it began to roll, tossing the pegs in the air, and for one moment, as our belongings flew in every direction, we thought we might arrive in Khotan a day early. Thrown upside down in our tent several feet from where we had pitched it, we took some time to decide on a course of action. We finally opted for tethering the tent to our water barrels and had a restless rest of the night as the wind kept up its relentless tirade.

Wic continued,

> We were trapped in our small ball of flapping canvas for another two and a

> half hours while the storm continued to attack. By seven o'clock we decided to brave it and, on looking out in our ski goggles, we staggered off into the howling sandstorm. Sand slithered across the road like strips of silk and all around us whirlwinds lifted the particles up into the hazy, dusty sky that hung extremely low before us.
>
> Despite the sand getting EVERYWHERE: in your ears, down your shirt, in your boots and in your hair, the whole experience was far from unpleasant. Temperatures had dropped, which made everything ten times more bearable, and so long as you kept your mouth closed, it was fine.

As Lucy and Wic grappled with sandstorms for two days, Mouse and I slept, only leaving our hotel room to buy bread and water. I was already beginning to feel better but poor Mouse had now been suffering from diarrhoea for over a week, as well as heat stroke. Her head had stopped hurting, but she was finding it difficult to keep food down. On my trip to buy fresh bread I also found a sweet melon, which Mouse persuaded me to eat in the bathroom to avoid any envy on her part.

Wic and Lucy arrived that evening, a day earlier than expected. Hot and grimy from the road, they were eager to jump in the bath. The next day, one of our precious rest days, Lucy and Wic were understandably keen to lie in bed for as long as possible, but by nine o'clock, five hours later than our usual rising time, they had already had enough and were ready to visit Khotan's bazaar in the old town. I felt well enough to go with them while Mouse stayed behind. The scene was reminiscent of Kashgar, but on a smaller scale. Donkey carts, horse carts, cars, buses, motor bikes and bicycles all fought their way along the narrow streets, creating as much noise as possible. Stallholders dashed out from behind their tables, brandishing their different wares and shouting, 'Hello, hello, hello!'

After several hours of haggling, we walked away with a few presents for Mouse (her birthday was coming up). On our return she looked no better. Lucy and Wic rooted around for our medical book and diagnosed her as suffering from salmonella, for which they prescribed antibiotics.

We woke up the following morning to find the weather had cooled slightly, with even a tiny drizzle. Mouse and I joined the caravan again and set off, excited to be back on the road. We wound our way through the back streets of Khotan as dawn appeared, passing traders sleeping in the open air in front of their stalls. Several ovens had already been started, fires blazing, with balls of dough waiting beside them to be baked into bread.

Wic and Mouse disappeared to return five minutes later with fresh bread and hot doughnut rings, which we guzzled as we walked. Before long we were travelling once more down a long poplar-lined road with mud brick houses nestling in the shade. Several had magnificent pumpkin plants rambling across trellises attached to the walls, their yellow flowers sitting in splendour amongst the deep green leaves. Hanging beneath were the pumpkins, already plump and ripening.

The poplars in these oases are grown in a way that maximises the daylong shade. Those closest to the road slope inwards so that when they are fully grown the tops almost meet and those furthest from the road slope outwards, while the trees in the middle grow upright. We walked in this corridor of shadows, enjoying the cool. But after twelve miles or so the oasis came to a stop, giving way to desert once again. A few newly-planted poplars separated us from the sand, but this time in single file. Mouse, who noticed that their branches had become distorted at the ends, told us that this had been caused by pollution. In support of her deduction, we soon passed a factory belting out billowing clouds of smog – the first sign of industry we had encountered since Kashgar.

As we left behind this last remnant of shade, we jumped up on to the camels, Rozi and Egem stopping to give us leg-ups. Lucy was eating a bread roll from her saddlebags when suddenly she felt a sharp sensation in her elbow. Looking down, she saw a large set of teeth gently nuzzling her arm. It was the youngest camel, behind her in the line and hoping for some crumbs. We had been worried for weeks about how little the camels were being fed and this seemed to confirm our fears. Each evening Rozi and Egem fed them a pile of maize balls, rolled out of maize, salt and water, but these seemed only to whet their appetites – they would lick the bowls for hours afterwards with their long, thick tongues. We supplemented their diet with bundles of grass that we carried on the top of the truck but this provided them with little energy. Wic and Mouse had suggested to Mamat-Jan that they be fed more but he, predictably, said he had received orders to feed them exactly ten maize balls each and no more. This made us furious because we had paid a lot of money yet Mr Ma was trying to economise at this petty level. We wasted a lot of time trying to reason with Mamat-Jan, eventually winning some kind of a victory through sheer persistence. He agreed that evening to feed the camels extra maize balls, although not as many as we would have liked. From then on Wic often monitored how much Rozi and Egem fed them.

By this point Rozi and Egem were gradually attempting to talk to us more, in their few words of English, as well as teach us Kyrgyz phrases. At first they had been very shy but now they were constantly swivelling around on their camels to point things out to us. The next morning they were particularly kind, helping us to pack up our tents and becoming very animated as we examined our map. Mamat-Jan told me that they could not calculate distances, and sometimes we were not sure whether they could even read properly, but they were in a way much more sensible and worldly than poor Mamat-Jan, who lacked their intuitive common sense. As they became more friendly and inquisitive, so Egem become more vain. Each morning and evening he spent hours staring in his mirror, doing press-ups, then punching the lorry's tyres. Slight, wiry men in their early twenties, both Egem and Rozi were already married, and Rozi even had a baby at home, south of Kashgar. Friends since childhood, they showed remarkable signs of affection towards one another, going so far as to hold hands at times.

That day Mamat-Jan had found a spot to camp among the undulating dunes. Now the clear evening light, highlighting the vivid green of the camels' grass, the stripes of the saddles and the yellow of the sand, made it all seem very picturesque. As we sat eating our rice and vegetables, a jeep drove up, out of which climbed a group of men. One introduced himself in Russian as the Kazakh ambassador to China. He told us he was driving around the Taklamakan, looking at the ancient cities uncovered by the famous archaeologist Sir Aurel Stein and others, as well as writing articles on relations between China and Kazakhstan.

'Come to Almaty [the capital of Kazakhstan] whenever you like,' he said. 'It's fate we've met because fate likes good things to happen and therefore we will meet again.' We were touched by this invitation, particularly as he also described our venture as 'heroic'.

Two days later, we reached Lai-Su, a typical oasis village of the southern Taklamakan, with clean streets and comfortable-looking houses. The people all seemed content and their animals well fed. In the early hours of the morning we found that some took advantage of the cool by getting up and working, while others continued sleeping until eight o'clock or so, lying on the ground outside their houses under blankets, possibly to take advantage of the fresh air. Many of the houses are clay structures, enclosed by clay walls, while others are created entirely of bamboo sheaves and surrounded by bamboo fences. They are divided into sections segregating animals from the owners. The smaller houses, however, are made of brick, generally with large carved wooden doors. Set between these well spaced houses and the road is usually an irrigation canal, giving water for cooking and watering the animals. The main tarmac road running through the oasis, which follows one of the ancient branches of the Silk Road, is intersected at regular intervals by narrow dusty tracks leading to glades of poplars and fields of melons. We would often wander down these inviting tracks on foot to investigate as the camels plodded on ahead.

One morning, Mamat-Jan told us about a lake, but his predictions were generally far from accurate, so we were pleasantly surprised when we did indeed arrive at a large expanse of water. It was also cleaner than we had expected and we were reassured to find a Chinese couple coarse fishing on its muddy banks. After a rather unsuccessful attempt to swim, during which we were attacked by a swarm of mosquitoes, we returned to our camp to doze in the shade until, as Wic said, 'we saw a couple of eager-looking Chinese girls heading our way, no doubt to ask us where we were from, what we were doing, why, how old we were, whether we were married, whether we had children, whether we would like to hear their life history etc.' Before they could reach us we had jumped up and darted back to the lake where we had a quick wash and a paddle. The temptation to swim was great but the fear of contracting some fatal skin disease even greater.

That night we fell asleep to the tortured sounds of camel wailings, as Rozi and Egem applied household fly spray to their raw noses. On discovering maggots swarming around the poor animals' open nose-peg holes, and rejecting our homeopathic horse ointments, they insisted that the only reliable treatment was fly spray. We objected repeatedly, but to no avail, so hid in our tents, praying that this brutal cure would at least be quick and effective.

By now we had had five consecutive overcast days – a joy that I could never have anticipated. In addition we spent two whole days riding through Lai-Su village and then the oasis of Keriya, which afforded additional shade from the poplars, walnut and mulberry trees that lined the road. Many of the rivers in the Taklamakan only flow in the summer when the glaciers of the Kun Lun mountain range, separating the desert from Tibet, melt. Most flow only to the edges of the desert, hence our decision to skirt this arid plain, rather than cross it. As Sir Aurel Stein observed, the Keriya river is 'the only river among those descending from the Kun Lun east of Khotan which, being fed by considerable glaciers, manages to penetrate far into the Taklamakan before it too dies away among high ridges of sand.' Consequently, Keriya is the largest oasis on the southern rim of the desert.

There the local women trotted along in their donkey carts, making a particularly intriguing sight. Dressed in the usual Uighur fashion of dress and headscarf, each had a tiny upturned black bowl, like an eggcup, perched on top of her head. It could not have served any practical function but every woman wore one. Meanwhile, the men wore tall, black or brown sheepskin hats, oblivious of the intense heat. We never again saw such hats outside Keriya and Niya, the next oasis, which shows how localised such traditions can be.

Our night in Keriya was spent camping in the large square yard of the local school, about a mile from the centre. The camels rested in a basketball court while we chose the cool of a classroom, pushing the desks together to make wooden beds above the dusty mud floor.

From Keriya to Niya took us three days through the desert, walking, riding our camels and occasionally hitching a lift on a donkey cart. As we left Keriya in the early morning we passed an imposing Chinese statue of Chairman Mao, smiling benevolently as his hand rested on the shoulder of a Uighur man. Famously short, Mao had been made to tower over the Uighur.

As I walked next to Egem, the hours crept on and he became more communicative, telling me about his life in a *yurt* with eight others.

'How many in your *yurt*, in England?'

'Umm, six.'

Having told me how his father kept yaks, sheep, goats and horses, he suddenly gestured at my face, saying, 'Good, good, you firty!'

'No, no, I'm twenty-six,' I protested.

'No, you firty,' he insisted.

'No, I'm twenty-six,' I reiterated firmly, dismayed to think that the desert sun had already made such a devastating impact on my skin. I finally gave up.

Later, as Lucy and I were chatting to him and Rozi, it suddenly dawned on us that 'firty' had the more flattering meaning of 'pretty' in their pidgin English.

In our first camp outside Keriya, Lucy and I decided to sleep outside, setting up our beds along one side of the truck on the sand. It was unbearably hot in the tents, so Mouse and Wic soon joined in us in the open. The only disadvantage of sleeping outside was that changing our clothes became a long and complicated process, as we tried to avoid the shameless stares of our back-up team. We were constantly begging Mamat-Jan to intervene on our behalf with the others, but even when, laughing with embarrassment, he translated our request they would continue to gape at us.

On that first evening without our tent, Rozi and Egem made up a double bed, out of sacks and camel blankets, very close to us, on the sand. 'We fight bandits.' Lucy and I lay down and started reading. Suddenly, in the torchlight, we noticed that Egem had left the bed and was lying in a sultry pose against the background of us in our sleeping bags. Rozi, meanwhile, was taking a picture of him with their camera. They then changed positions and the scene was re-enacted. No doubt their friends would be entertained by these curious pictures. This was only the second time they had used the camera: the first time being when they had recorded the two dying camels we had left behind.

We continued for the next two days through gravelly desert, overlain in parts by big ridges of drift sand. On the second day Mamat-Jan decided to accompany us with the camels, presumably bored of sandwiching himself between Mr He and Mr Li in the cramped cabin of the truck. He started off by marching confidently away from the road and southwards into the desert.

'I think it is good we take short cut.'

'How do you know it is a short cut?'

'I saw car lights over there last night,' he replied, gesturing in the direction of the Kun Lun mountains and Tibet. 'There is turn in road.'

Sceptical as we were, we followed him obediently into the dunes, gripping our water bottles tightly. The going was relatively easy and much more forgiving on the camels' feet than the tarmac road. The sand, although untouched, was still quite firm and consisted of heavy grains, while the dunes, which were low with gradual gradients, shimmered in the dawn light, creating the illusion of a silver blanket in the dips. Stretching out into the distant horizon, these thousands of dunes produced an eerie but magnificent effect. We could have been on a different planet, so alien and remote was this landscape. The air was still and the only sound to be heard was the crunching of sand beneath our camels' feet.

Miraculously, the road came into sight once more and we commended Mamat-Jan on his intuitive navigational skills. Once back on the road, we continued on our endless, bendless route, quizzing Mamat-Jan on his girlfriend to pass the time.

'Are you going to marry her?' asked Wic.

'Of course.'

'When?'

'After my brother.'

'When's he getting married?'

'When I go to Kashgar, after trip. They wait for me.'

'Do you like his fiancée?'

'Maybe.'

'Er, is she nice?'

'I don't know,' he said, shrugging his shoulders as if our question was quite ridiculous.

'Why not?'

'I never meet her, I only see photograph.'

'Ah, is she very beautiful?'

'So, so,' he replied, scrunching up his face and rotating his hand from side to side.

We discovered that the fiancée's parents, who were good friends of Mamat-Jan's parents, had sent a photograph of her to them, requesting Mamat-Jan's elder brother as a husband. Such an arranged marriage would have once been universal in this Muslim society and is still widely practised.

Our conversations generally took place before eleven o'clock in the morning, when the sun was already high in the sky and the heat precluded any further talking. A couple of hours later, we were met by the truck. Two irate Chinese men – Mr He and Mr Li – were waving their arms about wildly.

'OK,' Mamat-Jan began to translate, 'we can go twelve miles to Niya'. This represented six more miles than we had planned for that day, having already covered nearly fourteen. Six does not sound many, but when your mouth is dry, your bottom raw, your head throbbing and your clothes soaked in sweat, it feels like fifty. In fact, the very idea had an immediate weakening effect on us. We decided to cover only another three miles and save the remaining nine for the next day. Mr He and Mr Li consequently tore off in a rage, their hopes of spending the night in a hotel shattered.

We found the truck parked a mile or so further on. Mr Li had made no attempt to get off the road, informing us that there was nowhere to camp in the area. We looked around in astonishment at the vast expanse of flat desert. His pride was dented when we lighted on a gravel track leading off the road, a couple of yards ahead, and, to prove his point, he put on a dramatic, nail-biting performance of parking the truck. Leaning out of the window and keeping an eye on his back wheels, he shifted the vehicle up and down, moving only inches between each gear change.

Having finally set up our camp we sat enjoying a melon and watching the camels. Every evening we would separate them out and tether them individually by their nose ropes to boulders. We were amused on this occasion to see one of the two bigger camels, having spotted a lump of edible vegetation out of reach, and after several painful attempts at dragging his tether, pause for a moment's thought. Then, seeming to throw us a nervous glance, he picked up the rope in his teeth and dragged the stone along the ground.

The following morning, we quickly covered the remaining distance to Niya, reaching our hotel, a one-storey building set around a courtyard, at half-past eight in the morning. Our first step was to catch up on some sleep, so we did not emerge from our rooms until lunchtime. With Mamat-Jan, we made our way to a Uighur restaurant consisting of one long table lined with small bowls, which were soon filled with green tea. To enter we had passed through an outer room facing the street, which contained two fires for cooking. Ash was scattered all over the floor and a pail of dirty water stood in one corner, apparently the only means of washing anything. The small room behind, where we sat, was decorated in typical Uighur style, with large fading posters portraying fruit baskets piled high with exotic Caribbean fruits, simulated scenes of waterfalls and a lake seen from a vivid bed of tulips with a swan sitting squarely and most unnaturally in its centre. Our lunch of noodles with spicy vegetables and juicy kebabs, followed by large bowls of fermented yoghurt and fresh honey, was simple yet delicious. We particularly appreciated it after nine days of rice and rotting vegetables.

The last day of July was Mouse's birthday. We spent it visiting Niya's small bazaar, where we found the conical fur hats we had seen the men wearing in Keriya. As with many Uighur towns, Niya's old centre had been destroyed by the Chinese, the intricate streets replaced by one sweeping road, lined on either side by white-tiled buildings. The latter were always dilapidated, with missing tiles and broken windows. Completely characterless, it was impossible to distinguish one town from another by these central streets. Invariably empty and lifeless except for occasional shops selling an arbitrary assortment of goods, ranging from sweets to car tyres, they had an almost sinister atmosphere. The Chinese had built them unsuitably wide for desert oases, allowing great gusts of wind and sand to blow through. But luckily such attempts at modernisation had been limited and beyond these ugly scars generally still seethed a mass of winding, bustling Uighur streets. Among such streets we found Niya's bazaar. Mamat-Jan was always bemused when we asked to visit a market, telling us they were 'primitive' and that Chinese shops had much more to offer. His father was a successful official in the Xinjiang bureaucracy, so inevitably Mamat-Jan had been brought up with a great respect for the Communists and their 'reforms', despite his own Uighur heritage.

However, we found much to interest us in the bazaar and bought some 'papples' (a delicious cross between apples and pears), for which Niya has been famed since Marco Polo's day. We celebrated Mouse's birthday that evening in another Uighur restaurant. Shut in a back room, with no windows, it became stiflingly hot and we fanned ourselves with paper napkins. But the food was good and some tepid beer helped to cool us.

8

The Taklamakan

ON LEAVING NIYA we finally entered the desert proper. The tarmac road deteriorated once again, (or improved from our point of view – it was no longer hot and sticky) into a dusty track, with the sand often encroaching over its edges. The landscape varied from flat, bald expanses of sand to hillocks covered in scrub, and rare clumps of trees. Little has changed since our precursor, Sir Aurel Stein, wrote at the beginning of the twentieth century,

> Whether the traveller enters the Taklamakan from the edge of cultivated ground in the oases or from jungle belts along the river beds, he first passes through a zone with desert vegetation, mostly in the shape of tamarisks, wild poplars, or reeds, surviving amongst low drift sand. A very peculiar and interesting feature of this zone consists of 'tamarisk cones', hillocks of conical form and often closely packed together. The slow but constant accumulation of drift sand around tamarisk growth, at first quite low, has in the course of centuries built them up to heights reaching fifty feet or more.

It has traditionally been believed that the desert places of the Earth are features impressed on God's creation by sin. Out of this belief, men over the ages have conceived of the desert as the haunt of evil spirits. The horrors of the Taklamakan desert as experienced by Hsuan Tsang, the seventh-century Buddhist pilgrim, and by generations of merchants, were to shape the following invocation of the ancestral spirit:

> O Soul, go not to the West
> Where level wastes of sand stretch on and on

And demons rage, swine-headed, hairy-skinned
With bulging eyes;
Who in wild laughter gnash projecting fangs.
O Soul, go not to the West
Where many perils wait ...

Much later Marco Polo was to remark of the Taklamakan in his famous *Travels*:

> Beasts there are none; for there is nought for them to eat. But there is a marvellous thing related of this Desert, which is that when travellers are on the move by night, and one of them chances to lag behind or to fall asleep or the like, when he tries to gain his company again he will hear spirits talking, and will suppose them to be his comrades. Sometimes the spirits will call him by name; and thus shall a traveller oft-times be led astray so that he never finds his party. And in this way many have perished.

Essentially the desert is as wild and uninhabited now as it has been for century upon century. After Niya the oases only come every two hundred miles or so, the equivalent of ten days' riding. Between these rare patches of inhabitation we were to encounter barely any life on an empty road.

We set off from Niya in semi-darkness. As dawn emerged, the darkness withdrew to reveal a mist shrouding the tops of the last poplar trees. Every now and then an ox and cart appeared as if from nowhere, seemingly floating past us with its enormous load, only to disappear quickly into the mist again. Soon even these small signs of life stopped and we were left completely alone, surrounded by the silent mist and the gentle sound of the camels' padding feet. Sometimes we could perceive the outline of tamarisk bushes and wild rushes, but when the mist finally cleared by mid-morning we found that wind erosion had created thousands of waves in the encrusted sand. The weather became more and more oppressive as the day progressed. There was no sun, but instead a closeness that reduced all our clothes to sodden rags as the sky seemed to sit just above our heads. We each drained five pints of water in as many hours and began looking for a place where the camels could drink as well. Suddenly Rozi spied a flooded stream and steered Moon Boot, and the camels behind him, towards it. The bank looked deceptively sandy but as Moon Boot approached we realised it was in fact slippery mud. He slid gracefully towards the water as

Rozi leapt off just in time, his bare feet disappearing into the slime. Pulling Moon Boot to safety, we altered our path and decided to wait for a safer watering spot.

Eventually we found a small pool of water. We undid each of their ropes as they stood at the water's edge, noisily slurping at the muddy puddle and cooling themselves at the same time by raising their heads and flapping their lips together to produce a spray of water.

We camped next to a solitary governmental base in the middle of a scrubby expanse. Within minutes we were surrounded by 'officials' desperate to take our photographs. They did not seem to be the only inquisitive ones, however: herds of sheep, goats and donkeys took it in turns to nose around the camp. The camels were released without tethers for the first time to graze around a mosquito-infested pond. Seizing the moment, they shot off over the horizon.

As we entered the camp that afternoon Wic marched up to Mamat-Jan and reprimanded him because he had not given us enough water in the morning.

'Mamat-Jan, this isn't good enough.'

'But Mr He says you're not allowed more than three little bottles of water each.'

'That's ridiculous, we're in a desert; we've got to drink more than that.'

This had become an on-going battle between Mr He, who now joined the argument, desperate to economise and presumably pocket extra money, and us, frightened of contracting heat stroke again from dehydration. We tried to explain that it was dangerous for us not to drink at least eight pints of water a day, but Mr He was obdurate.

'It doesn't matter, we only agreed to provide twelve bottles each day.'

'This is ridiculous – we have paid so much money and you are refusing to give us more water.' Wic's voice was raised by now as Mamat-Jan looked on nervously.

'Can Mr He not boil extra water for us?' suggested Mouse.

'I'll ask him.' Mamat-Jan looked relieved to have found a solution.

Mr He snorted derisively, after which followed a series of sharp retorts between him and Mamat-Jan.

'He says there's nothing to put the boiled water in.'

'Don't be so stupid Mamat-Jan, we can use the old water bottles.' Wic's curt answer silenced him.

Meanwhile the government officials had surrounded us, imploring us to sit in a row as they snapped away with their cameras. As we sat down, I said, 'Poor Mamat-Jan, I feel quite sorry for him.'

'Why?' retorted Wic tersely.

'Because it's not really his fault – obviously he's terrified of Mr Ma and has been given these stupid instructions by him.'

'Well, that's not our problem and it's his responsibility.' Wic was angry.

'Actually, it's not fair, Alex,' intervened Lucy. 'Wic's perfectly entitled to be cross if she feels we're not getting what we're due.'

'OK, relax.'

'No, it's not fair – you think you're being so kind to Mamat-Jan, but he's useless and he should be able to sort this water problem out himself.'

Our voices had become raised, but we were restrained from further arguing by the presence of the officials, who were watching us curiously. Smiling grimly, we posed obediently for a few minutes. As soon as they had finished, I jumped up and ran to the other end of the camp, where I lay alone on the ground feeling miserable.

Longing to be at home with my family, I buried my head in the sand and began to cry. When I looked up, I saw Egem sitting beside me, smiling and holding my travelling chess set. He did not say anything but quietly began to arrange the pieces, ready for a game. I was touched by this gesture and grateful for the distraction.

After we had finished playing, I tried to read my book until Lucy approached me, looking uncharacteristically forbidding. She started to tell me that I was unfair to defend Mamat-Jan. I protested and she soon left me alone again to return to the others. I did not eat with them that evening, but made my bed on the other side of the truck alone, where I lay down early to sleep, disturbed by mosquitoes that had found their way from the water to our camp.

The next morning I woke to find that a mosquito had bitten one of my eyelids, causing it to swell into such a big red bulge that I could not open my eye. We ate our breakfast in an uncomfortable silence, my disfigured eye making me feel even more awkward. We set off, as usual, on foot, with me taking up the rear. However, after half an hour, I noticed that Lucy was waiting for me. Having discussed the events of the day before, eventually she said, 'This is stupid, we shouldn't be arguing because really we're such good friends.' And suddenly I felt a great sense of relief and happiness. Later I was to see this moment as marking a significant change in the relations of our group and any lingering tension that had been underlying our relationship since our time in Central Asia now suddenly evaporated.

Lucy and I continued walking together and chatting for the rest of the morning. On our return from the expedition to England we were interviewed by a magazine. One of the questions the journalist asked us was, 'Did you find that each of you assumed certain roles in the group?' Wic answered, 'Yes, Mouse was our nurse because she is so kind and Lucy is very organised and hard-working, so she was our treasurer.' Lucy continued, 'Wic did all the filming and Alex ... ' Here she faltered until, as if with a burst of inspiration, she said, 'If you were walking with Alex it was never boring because she always has something to talk about.' It was not perhaps the most commendable characteristic, but it did mean I could help to pass the monotonous hours more quickly. I found it particularly easy to chat with Lucy, as we had many common interests, including a fascination with history and literature.

By seven o'clock the wind had picked up. The blanket of clouds that had been protecting us from the sun had become a threatening black colour. A fine layer of sand shifted rapidly over the undulating dunes as the wind blew up into our faces a continual stream of dust that tickled our throats and irritated our eyes. Before long, we were enveloped in a large cloud of dust and could see not more than twenty feet in front of us. Often the camels would pass out of our vision and we would be left alone, feeling completely lost. The gale persisted for an hour or two before clearing, only to return at intervals during the course of the day. By the time we reached camp our faces were black, with two neat white circles around our eyes, where our goggles had been.

Even in camp, there was no escaping the wind. Our mess tent almost took off from its pegs, but there was little we could do. Eventually we managed to pin the sides of the mess tent into the moving sands, using stones to weigh down the pegs. Inside we lined up our water canisters as a blockade against the wind and slept huddled in a row with Rozi, Egem and Mamat-Jan. The wind became quieter as the night progressed, only to stir up again as dawn broke.

Except for the officials, we had not come across any human life since leaving Niya two days earlier. We continued along our straight dusty track, pummelled by the relentless wind. The flat horizon was broken only on occasion by tall reeds and, more rarely, a wild poplar with intensely green leaves.

We knew from our maps that roughly halfway between Niya and Charchan, the next significant oasis, lay a village, which we hoped might possess a well. The patch of water we had found near the governmental base had been filthy and Rozi and Egem had warned us against even touching it. Consequently, we had not washed for three days and, more importantly, the camels had not drunk. Our water canisters were running low, and they would not last until Charchan. That morning we had asked Mamat-Jan to go ahead in the truck in order to confirm whether there was indeed water in the village.

When we arrived in camp, we found Mamat-Jan with his feet up and his cap lying firmly across his face. It soon became clear that he had not been to the village.

'Why didn't you go ahead, as we asked you to?'

'Because Mr Li says he'll use up too much fuel going there and back.'

'What! That's ridiculous – we showed you on the map that it couldn't be more than thirteen miles ahead of us.'

We finally forced Mr Li and Mamat-Jan to drive to the village, water being more precious than petrol at this point. They did not seem to understand that if the camels collapsed from dehydration it would affect them as much as us. All they could think of was avoiding an extra chore.

Some time later we saw the truck appear, blowing up great clouds of dust. Mamat-Jan stepped down from the cab.

'There is not village in ten miles,' he announced.

'Sorry?'

'In ten miles from here there is nothing.'

'You mean, you went ten miles, saw nothing and turned back?' We were incredulous, having spent some time the previous night calculating how far away this village was and arriving at the distance of ten miles, give or take a few.

'Surely you carried on?'

'Yes – at tweleve miles from here there is a village.' He was clearly very proud to have proved our calculations inaccurate.

'Right,' we said, our eyes rolling, 'and is there a well or reservoir?'

'No, there is no water there.'

'Not even for the camels?'

'No, they could not drink from a well!'

'We mean a river – is there a river where they can drink?'

'Oh yes, I think so.'

We decided to wait until the following day to travel to the village and water the camels.

The sand continued to dance and swirl around our feet, so that cooking became almost impossible. In order to boil the kettle we had to hold our quilts around the gas stove so as to prevent the wind from extinguishing the flame. We poured the boiling water over some dried noodles and clambered into the back of the truck, shutting the doors and eating by torchlight.

Beside our camp were successive dips cut away in the crusty sand that helped prevent sand drifts from building up on the road. That night, we decided to bed down in our tents again, having barely slept for the previous two nights because of the sandstorm. Lucy and I chose to camp in one of these dips, hoping the extra protection would save our tent from destruction. Mouse and Wic, however, were bolder, erecting their tent on the wide, flat open expanse away from the road.

Suddenly, a large gust of wind blew from the west, which whipped Wic and Mouse's tent up into the air and carried it for almost a mile, pursued by its occupants. Large tamarisk cones stood in its path, but they only seemed to help the tent gain momentum. Finally, with the help of the back-up truck and Egem, the tent was recaptured and secured firmly in the dip next door to ours.

At two o'clock in the morning we were woken by Egem and Rozi squealing – it was pouring with rain and they had chosen to sleep outside. We went back to sleep, but woke again at four to hear the continued sound of rain pattering on our tents. It was actually cold and wet – a long-forgotten sensation – so we hunted out our waterproofs and set off, relishing every second of this novel feeling. After precisely twelve miles we met Mamat-Jan, looking very smug, in a tiny oasis village of a few scrubby bamboo and adobe houses and one restaurant, which we headed for, having watered the camels in the trickling river and tethered them in the courtyard behind. Typical of these oasis restaurants, it had an open front and a room inside with one long table lined with benches. We sat down to a delicious plate of noodles and vegetables. The rain had subsided, so, having eaten, we resumed our journey. By this time the skies were clearing and later our tents and camels, camped among clumps of bamboos, were illuminated by a radiant evening light.

Mamat-Jan had made friends with some locals and disappeared with them to slay one of their goats for our supper. He returned, even more proud than he had been that morning, carrying the corpse of a goat, skewered on a branch and roasted in a coating of maize flour. He hacked off pieces for us, and we ate it with some succulent chips cooked by Mr He.

The sandstorm did not return in the night, so we woke up to a fresh morning with a gentle breeze blowing through the bamboo stalks. However, the temperature quickly picked up and at nine o'clock we were glad to find ourselves in another tiny hamlet, Xu Tang. Mamat-Jan, Mr He and Mr Li emerged from the sole restaurant, built out of mud and bamboo, for the rare buses that pass through this remote part of the desert. Grinning broadly, Mamat-Jan explained, 'We stop here tonight.'

'Why?'

'Too big flood,' was his reply as he disappeared back to his noodles, the explanation apparently complete. Having also eaten a bowl of the predictable noodles, we summoned up the strength to enquire further about the 'flooding'.

Mamat-Jan gave a long and convoluted explanation, the gist of which seemed to be that a 'great' river ahead had burst its banks and washed away a bridge, covering the surrounding area and over twenty miles of road in twelve feet of water, making it impassable. Incredulous at the enormity of this deluge, when we had only experienced one day of light rain, we asked Mamat-Jan whether he had considered driving on to clarify this information. He carefully evaded this important question until Mouse frogmarched him and Mr Li to the truck. Her first objective was to check the fuel gauge. Mamat-Jan had given a number of excuses as to why they could not drive five miles to verify the extent of the flood damage, the weightiest being a lack of fuel. Mr Li removed the petrol cap and, looking at Mouse, gave the tank a hefty clout, as if to say, 'No fuel – told you so, you foreign devil.' However, the gauge showed that it was over half full. But still Mr Li stood obstinately beside the truck, refusing to drive. Mouse tried another tack. 'Mamat-Jan, if Mr Li doesn't want to drive there, maybe he should walk to check things out. After all, he is the only one who knows where the truck can or cannot go.' Mouse waited for the inevitable explosion. On cue, Mr Li thrust out his chin and let out a torrent of Chinese expletives. But Mouse had made her point. Mr Li tore opened the truck door, and shoved her and Mamat-Jan in beside him.

They drove off in stony silence towards the floods. Mouse told us afterwards that Mr Li's chin was 'jutting out so far in disgust, it almost reached the windscreen'. The flood did indeed prove to be worse than we could have ever envisaged. The desert on either side of the road was swollen with water and there was clearly no way that either our truck or camels could cross. It seemed ironic that our first setback in the desert should be due to flooding.

Mamat-Jan only chose to tell us now that every year, as the intense summer heat melts the glaciers in the Kun Lun mountains, the riverbeds of the Taklamakan swell with excess water and a combination of this and the recent storms had resulted in the worst floods in living memory. It could take up to a fortnight for the road to be opened again. Mamat-Jan looked delighted as he imparted this last piece of information, obviously relishing the thought of a break from our arduous life on the road. He eagerly suggested we stay in the village until the flood retreated. Although we were reluctant to give in, we had no choice but to agree with his idea. To move on before the flood had stopped would be crazy and put the camels and us at unnecessary risk. However, it did seem glaringly obvious that we needed a new truck if we were to reach Xian before the end of the year. It was another example of short-sighted economy that our truck, with its exceptionally low chassis, had been chosen by the back-up team for our expedition across the desert, for if it was not flood water blocking our path it would be sand. Having sent several e-mails to Beijing, we began to look for somewhere to install our camp in the village. The only place we could find was a dirty courtyard behind the restaurant. We spent the afternoon in the restaurant, eating, playing cards and reading until the early evening, when we returned to the courtyard and laid out our sleeping bags along one side of the truck. Mr He, Mr Li and Mamat-Jan had pitched their tents in one corner of the courtyard while Rozi and Egem slept outside with us, to keep an eye on the camels. There was an exceptionally clear sky that night and the Milky Way soared overhead in a great broad strip above our heads. As we lay in the dark talking and watching for shooting stars, our peace was interrupted only by a donkey that brayed regularly every hour. Falling asleep to the gentle noise of the camels' breathing, we were woken in the middle of the night by a heavily inebriated Mr Li. Stumbling across our feet, he tried, unsuccessfully, to open the door of the truck before slumping into bed, murmuring 'Mamat-Jan'.

The next morning we found Mr Li beginning to wake. Having drunk a whole bottle of rice wine the night before, he started to demand water from Mr He, who unwisely brought him tea instead. This error roused Mr Li into a state of fury. He started flinging empty beer bottles at the camels, as well as tearing down Mamat-Jan's tent. He then staggered into the lorry and tried to drive into the brick wall of the courtyard. Luckily, Mr He and Mamat-Jan managed to pull him out and pin him to the ground. He finally stormed off, with a little bag over his hunched shoulders and his arms flapping, only to return twenty seconds later to retrieve his wallet, which he had forgotten in his otherwise dignified departure.

Moments later we were informed by Mamat-Jan that Mr Li would no longer be working for us, although whether he had been fired or handed in his notice was hard to ascertain. His dignity received a further degradation, though, when he realised there was nowhere else for him to go. He was forced to join us in the restaurant, where he directed his fury at a kung-fu film that blared out from a fuzzy television set in the corner. The prospect of spending another day stranded in our one-donkey town now seemed rather attractive. We had done all we could and we could only rest and wait.

We woke up on our third day in Xu Tang to the now familiar surroundings of our courtyard. As each day passed it was becoming more fetid with the smell of the camels. We had not been able to wash since our time in Niya, a week earlier, and since temperatures were still in the high thirties and desert winds were coating everything in dust we were far from clean ourselves. Mamat-Jan joined us in the restaurant for breakfast, where he informed us that he had been talking to the village policeman.

'And what did he say?'

'There is flooding behind us too now, in the Niya Darya.'

'Oh.'

'Yes, and the policeman said that some lorries cannot move from the flood.'

It might be another week, according to the policeman's estimate, before we could move. However, since the policeman seemed also to be the owner of Xu Tang's restaurant, we suspected he might have an interest in exaggerating. Over the last couple of days more and more buses had arrived from Niya, and unable to continue further, were filling this tiny oasis well beyond its capabilities.

Although this influx of people was inconvenient, because the town's only public lavatory lay behind one of the low walls surrounding our courtyard, it at least gave us some form of distraction. Our new pastime was to sit in the restaurant all day, where although it was as hot as outside there was at least shade and we could escape the putrid smell that infested the courtyard air and all our belongings. The clientele were varied, ranging from Chinese students to Uighur families, as well as a man travelling with his daughter and grandson, who, like all babies in China, wore trousers with a wide split instead of a nappy. The grandfather spent much time dandling his grandson on his knee and attending to his every whim, while the daughter sat watching nearby.

As we laid out our quilts for another night beneath the stars, Mamat-Jan approached us with a piece of news.

'There is another forner in the town.'

'A forner?'

'Yes, a forner has arrived by the bus.'

I took the lead. 'What kind of forner?'

'A man,' answered Mamat-Jan, pausing for effect, 'maybe American, maybe German.'

'What did he look like?' asked Wic, as our interest increased by the second.

Mamat-Jan gave us a rather sketchy account of the 'forner's' appearance: tall, brown hair and wearing trousers. Since we were in a state of semi-undress and lying in our sleeping bags we sent Mamat-Jan off in search of the 'forner' with an invitation to visit us in the courtyard, among the beer bottles and ancient donkey carts.

Some time later he returned. 'The forner is go to the birch.'

'What?' we almost shouted. 'WHERE IS THE FORNER?'

'He is go to the birch,' said Mamat-Jan, a little surprised by our aggression.

'The bridge, the bridge!' shouted Wic.

'Why has he gone to the bridge? It's broken.'

'The bus has go to the birch to wait until the birch is mended.'

Suddenly our interest in the 'forner' evaporated at the news that people were going to the bridge. The thought that the 'birch' might soon be resurrected eclipsed all thoughts of 'forners' as we discussed the implications into the night.

Our fourth day in Xu Tang opened with our usual breakfast of steamed bread and jam, followed by onion bread. However, after this meal Lucy and Mouse made a radical break with routine by persuading the ever reluctant Mr Li and Mamat-Jan to drive to the bridge. Mr Li appeared to have been re-instated as our driver and, since we had no hope of finding a replacement, we asked no questions. They set off only to return with the depressing news that a lorry was stranded in the middle of the first patch of flooding and that fifty other buses and trucks were stuck between this and the 'birch', with the 'forner' unfortunately in one of them. We resigned ourselves to yet another day of stodgy noodles and lounging in the restaurant.

In the evening Mamat-Jan appeared again, beaming with pride at the two wonderful pieces of news he was bearing. The first was that chips were on the menu and the second was that we could escape Xu Tang on the following morning because the 'birch' had been miraculously mended. To celebrate, we begged Mr He, responsible for our budget, to let us stay in one of the restaurant's bedrooms. Although this would cost the equivalent of one dollar for all of us, our plea provoked sighs and scowls. We were told it was far too extravagant. After a lot of cajoling, he finally conceded and we were shown into two dusty bedrooms, one with no light. The restaurant owner/policeman and a waiter wrestled with the light bulb and after carefully inserting a new one, we revelled in the luxury of these dimly lit, uncomfortable bedrooms. Even better, though, we were offered a shower. It had the drawback of working on well water, which we had been warned was dirty, but we had become impervious to the risk of skin disease, and immediately accepted. The shower was of an original and ingenious design: a hosepipe hoisted across an empty room with an old coke can suspended from it. The can had been pierced all over with little holes and sprayed delicious jets of sun-warmed water over our grimy bodies.

The following day we set off fifteen minutes earlier than usual, thrilled to be on the move once again and desperate to get out of Xu Tang, if only to escape the noodles. The dust storm of the previous day had left a clear morning. We had arranged to meet Mamat-Jan at six o'clock at the first patch of flooding in case the truck was unable to pass. Predictably, six o'clock came and went, as did half-past six until eventually, at seven o'clock, Mamat-Jan sped up to us in a red taxi, screeched to a halt, said 'Hi' and moved off towards the flood. We looked at each other, bemused by this strange behaviour, and shouted after him, 'Mamat-Jan?' It was as if 'Hi' was a word that explained everything – the wait, our absent truck, the red taxi ...

We now saw the truck cruising through the desert towards us, with a scowling Mr Li at the wheel. It emerged that in the four and a half miles between the village and the flood the truck had got stuck in the sand twice. It was at this point that the taxi had rescued Mamat-Jan.

The main flood lay ahead of us. We crossed without any problems on the camels but for the truck it was more challenging. Mr He threw a few stones in the water, appearing to believe that this would save the truck from submersion. Then, taking a long speedy run up, Mr Li attacked the water, burning straight through it to arrive on dry land the other side in a matter of seconds. Opening the cab door and gesturing with his white-gloved hand, he allowed Mr He and Mamat-Jan to climb in before proudly accelerating off in a cloud of dust.

We followed at a more leisurely pace through the aftermath of the flood: patches of muddy desert broken by rushes, until twenty miles later we arrived at the 'birch'. We were a little disappointed. The twenty miles of flood reaching a magnificent twelve feet in height had shrunk to a mere two feet and measured not more than thirty feet across. A couple of workers sat eating onion bread on an island in the middle of the river, observing the makeshift bridge they had only recently finished constructing, out of wood, sand and tamarisk branches. Wic was riding Moon Boot, whose favourite food happened to be tamarisk branches. Making his way on to the bridge, he spied this gastronomic delight and, lowering his head, began to consume at a rapid pace the bridge that had taken so much time and energy to erect. The incredulous workers ceased eating and shouted at us. Moon Boot slowly raised his majestic head, tamarisk branches projecting from either side of his mouth, and proudly moved off.

The next day, having slept beneath the stars once again, we continued along the gravel track that led us through more of the same: crusty dunes dotted with reeds and shrubs. A disused road workers' shelter – three empty rooms, each carpeted with a thick layer of dust – could not have appeared at a more opportune moment, just as were looking for somewhere to camp. Everything was going well until I made the following suggestion: 'Mamat-Jan, maybe you should go ahead to Charchan tomorrow to investigate about the road to Charklik and Dunhuang and to check that the new truck will arrive soon.' To my astonishment he acquiesced and even said it was a 'good idea'. But as I was explaining the plan to the others, Mamat-Jan interrupted with a series of 'buts', finishing with the words, 'you said we would drive to small village with no phone in thirty-five miles.'

'Why would I ask you to go to a village with no phone?'

'Hmmm, I don't know.'

'Anyway, I said Charchan and you said it was a good idea.'

'Ah, I didn't understand you,' he said, as if that solved all our problems.

'Do you understand, Mamat-Jan?' asked Lucy, doubtfully.

'Er … yes,' he replied, which could really mean anything, 'but the Mr He and the Mr Li maybe no agree.'

'Well, why don't you speak to them?' we suggested patiently.

'Yes, but who will pay for petrol?'

'What?' we exclaimed.

'We do not have enough petrol for Charchan.'

Our minds momentarily jammed.

Someone finally spoke with firm decision: 'yes, you … do … have … enough … petrol … and … you … will … pay.'

'No, I don't think so,' was his breezy reply.

This battle regressed back to the old hospital bill saga. When the other three had been ill Mr He had paid for their 'treatment' but we had cancelled out our debt by allowing Mamat-Jan to use our satellite telephone in Xu Tang. We had owed 100 dollars for the hospital. He owed us 235 dollars for the use of the telephone. It did not take a mathematician to understand the logic here, but Mamat-Jan continued to pester us about the hospital bill. Lucy then tried to explain to Mamat-Jan that she needed the hospital bill for insurance purposes, to which his response was negative, as apparently Mr He also planned to claim back the money, having already demanded it from us. Poor Mamat-Jan was too naïve to realise that he was unwittingly revealing Mr He's dishonest intentions.

After an hour of arguing, we finally persuaded Mamat-Jan to promise us that he would get up at five the next morning, drive the forty-odd miles to Charchan, do some research and drive twenty miles back in time to set up camp. We stressed that the last point was particularly important because we could only carry a limited amount of water in our saddlebags.

This obstructive behaviour was to prove nothing to what followed. The next day was a logistical nightmare. Having woken up at four, we packed up our belongings, ate a quick breakfast and were preparing to go when we realised that none of the back-up team were up and dressed, despite our agreed plan of the night before.

'Mamat-Jan, time to wake up.'

'I am awake,' he replied, 'but we are not going.'

We gleaned that Mr Li had rebelled against the early start.

'You see,' continued Mamat-Jan, 'this is local time five o'clock which means Beijing time seven o'clock. Mr Li will not start work until Beijing time nine o'clock.'

'This is the DESERT!' Mouse shrieked. 'Surely you must understand that office hours do not apply? We have to wake up at four to avoid the midday heat and for you to get back from Charchan on time to meet us you must leave now.'

Mamat-Jan found this simple logic difficult to grasp. Mouse then demanded that Mamat-Jan translate directly to Mr Li, who was lying sprawled on the dusty floor. One of her principal arguments was to point out that Mr Li worked for no more than one hour per day, when he drove the truck from one camp to the next, after which he spent the rest of the day sleeping or throwing empty beer cans at the camels. This was not following office hours either and so we were entitled to demand he worked earlier rather than later. Hysterical cries came back from Mr Li, but eventually we left the camp, hoping that our ultimatums would have an effect on him. Sure enough, at seven o'clock, the truck drove past, a steely-faced Mr Li at the wheel, his knuckles clenched in their white gloves.

The road began to wind that day, making a welcome change. The dunes sloped gently down to meet it and occasionally we would find the road rising up above the sand, giving us a panoramic view of the desert ahead, vast and empty save for rare wild poplars.

After about twenty miles we expected to see our camp, but there was nothing in sight. Another two miles and we began to worry. The importance of our truck became more and more apparent as the midday heat consumed us and we yearned for water and shade. It was difficult to control a feeling of panic in this inescapable landscape. Our sunhats offered some protection, but my head still felt swollen and throbbing from the broiling rays of the sun. We lapsed into complete silence sitting motionless on the camels, unwilling to expend any superfluous energy.

At two o'clock, the stillness was interrupted by a swirl of dust on the horizon. We gladly discerned the shape of our truck. As it approached, so did our anxieties diminish, but our anger increase. Mamat-Jan, showing no remorse for being two hours late, seemed to have little comprehension of the danger he had exposed us to. When we slid off our saddles to the ground, we found we were barely able to stand after eight hours of walking and riding in the heat. However, I summoned up enough energy to shout at Mamat-Jan for at least five minutes. Still we received neither apology nor reassurance. In an attempt to placate us, however, Mamat-Jan produced a melon he had bought in Charchan. We sat eating it in silence, contemplating the back-up team's ineptitude.

The day closed with a final confrontation, over the unlikely issue of lavatory paper. Our meagre rations handed out by Mr He had come to an end and, finding a supply in the cab of the lorry, despite Mamat-Jan's assurance that there was none left, we had helped ourselves. This provoked a torrent of abuse from Mr Li, who accused us of stealing his personal supply, followed by a lengthy argument over who was responsible for buying our lavatory paper. Mamat-Jan told us it was our duty, while we were adamant it was that of Mr He, who was in charge of our pre-paid budget. It was not pleasant spending our days in these constant arguments that were more suited to eight-year-old girls, but they did have one beneficial side effect: our mutual antipathy towards the back-up team strengthened our own sense of loyalty towards one another.

The frustrations of the day, however, were more than atoned for by the tranquillity of the nights. The light had become beautifully clear over the last few days, producing magnificent sunrises and sunsets. The sun having set, in a glorious mesh of pinks and yellows, we lay awake for hours on the sand, looking up at the stars and the crescent moon, which shone with sparkling clarity against the black sky. I have not seen such pure skies before or since; there was no habitation to pollute them with street lighting and we never saw an aeroplane during our three months in the Taklamakan. The desert felt yet more infinite by night than by day, for it was only in the dark that one could feel the true magnitude of our isolation. But there was nothing frightening about this; in fact, it created a reassuring sensation of liberation and removal from the inanities of life. I will never forget the feeling of cosiness as the four of us lay in a row, talking and laughing until we dropped off to sleep.

But as the sun began to rise, reality intruded and we found ourselves plagued by the inexorable heat and dust once more. However, the desert did possess a raw beauty of its own. Everyday the landscape seemed to change, varying from flat, bald expanses of sand to mounds of wind-blown sand covered in tamarisk and clumps of wild poplars. We only came across habitation every sixty miles or so. The rest was as wild and inhospitable as in Marco Polo's time.

We reached Charchan later that day, four days and 100 miles after having left Xu Tang. Our morning's journey, however, had been interrupted by Rozi and Egem, who had discovered ticks all over the camels. They had been walking half a mile behind us and as the truck passed them we had noticed that it had stopped and Mr He, Mr Li and Mamat-Jan had all jumped out and clustered round the camels, while Rozi and Egem pointed at them. Mamat-Jan wielded a large stick, which was smeared in dark, glutinous blood at one end.

'What's happening, Mamat-Jan?'

'These animals are all over the camels.'

'Yes, they're ticks – all animals get them.'

'But the Rozi and the Egem say they're very dangerous and can kill the camels.'

'No, don't worry, you only need to remove them and the camels will be fine.'

'But the blood is so dark – they say it's dangerous.'

'Have Rozi and Egem ever seen ticks before?'

'Um, I think so:' Mamat-Jan's reply to every unanswerable question.

'Have Rozi and Egem ever seen them before?'

He reluctantly translated, then conceded that they had not, but had only heard rumours of such parasites. Mamat-Jan grabbed the stick and defiantly jabbed at one of the camel's armpits where a particularly monstrous tick had lodged itself. Its bloated body exploded and a trickle of the sticky, scarlet blood oozed down the camel's leg, while its head burrowed even more greedily into the flesh.

'No, Mamat-Jan!' cried Mouse, 'you must never do that. You should twist its head and pull it out, otherwise it can go septic.'

Mouse showed them deftly how it should be done. Soon she had removed most of the ticks, accumulating them in a pile on the ground, where we allowed Mamat-Jan to crush them with his stick.

We were amazed that Egem and Rozi, who came from a village and lived among sheep, dogs, goats, yaks, donkeys and horses, had never encountered these common parasites before.

Finally, we reached the outskirts of Charchan without further mishap. It was strange to pass through peopled streets once again, after the solitude of the desert. As the camels were not allowed to enter the oasis centre, we left them with Rozi and Egem to camp in a field, while we checked into the Muztagh hotel. Boasting the biggest piece of jade in the world in its dimly-lit lobby, the hotel was built for oil investors – southern Xinjiang is rich in this natural resource – and was rather more luxurious than those we had previously stayed in. However, because of the floods, the electricity was switched off when we arrived and our long-awaited showers had to be delayed for twenty-four hours. Instead, we found a small restaurant on the main street, distinguished from the monotonous white-tiled buildings by a carved green, wooden roof. Mamat-Jan had armed us with a list of our favourite foods, written in Uighur, and we eagerly pointed out kebabs, tomato salad, bread and yoghurt. They proved especially delicious after the interminable noodles of the past week.

The next day was intended to be a rest day, but we were unable to relax. Mr Li and Mamat-Jan's advance trip to Charchan a couple of days before had unfortunately proved futile. Mamat-Jan's enquiries about the road ahead, from Charchan to Dunhuang, had produced unnerving accounts of deep sand, so he had telephoned Mr Ma to request a new truck. But all he gained was an assurance that if an emergency occurred we would be sent a four-wheel drive vehicle. Bewildered as to what an emergency entailed if this was not one, we were forced to spend our rest day telephoning Mr Ma in a desperate attempt to secure such a truck for the rest of our journey. No more successful than Mamat-Jan, we finally found ourselves agreeing to continue with the same truck until it could literally move no further.

Mamat-Jan seemed very concerned that evening about the camel drivers. Apparently Rozi and Egem were plotting at this very moment to flee back to Karakol. 'What have you done to upset them?' asked Mouse. Back in Kashgar, we had already had to negotiate a pay rise for them because Sadiq had told us they were on the point of desertion.

'Nothing,' was the predictable reply. 'They have a wonderful place to camp – we found them the best places – water, grasslands. It is very nice – you will see tomorrow.' But Mamat-Jan's words did not reassure us. We bought a large box of cigarettes, hoping these would placate Rozi and Egem.

There were indeed both water and grasslands. As we approached the camels' resting place early the next morning, shrouded in mist, it seemed as if Mamat-Jan had done a good job. But, rounding the corner of a building, we were assaulted by a horrific stench. The building on further scrutiny proved to be a sheep abattoir, on the other side of which was a large square pit, from which the pungent smell emanated. We saw a man stride out of the building's tall iron gates, a bag of sheep's intestines hanging over his shoulder. He then stopped at the pit and emptied the sack's contents into its heart, hundreds of maggots writhing into action.

A few feet away our camel drivers were waking, their tent pitched in the shadow of the building. They looked understandably surly as they emerged.

'No wonder they want to go home, Mamat-Jan,' Mouse observed. 'This is disgusting. Two days here, isolated from the town, unable to get away from the camels. If you can't get someone to watch the camels for an hour or so we will do it. Egem and Rozi must have a break.' But

Mamat-Jan would not admit his mistake and refused to acknowledge the site's shortcomings.

Nauseated by the inescapable smell, we struck out ahead of the camels, following an old road out of Charchan. Mamat-Jan had discovered that the floods had not affected the road from Charchan to Charklik too seriously; only for the first twenty miles did we have to follow a diversion along an old road because a bridge had been swept away on the new one. On reaching a village, we turned off the tarmac up a dusty track, to be met by some other early risers passing us on motorbikes and donkey carts, amused by the unusual spectacle we presented. The mist hung low and the sun slowly rose above it, illuminating its layers.

Suddenly we rounded a bend in the road to find that there was flooding ahead, up to a foot deep. We foresaw trouble. Placing our camel quilts on the ground at the edge of the water we lay down and ate some melons and bread that Rozi produced from his saddlebags. Our breakfast finished and still no sign of the truck, we decided to pass the time by removing more ticks that had surfaced on the camels. All of them stood calmly except Frankincense, one of the smaller camels. They had begun to grow their winter coats now, even though it was mid-August, and Frankincense was particularly furry. But his cuddly appearance belied his character. Nothing would induce him to allow any of us near his hindquarters. He sat firmly on the ground with his legs buckled below him, making it impossible to remove the ticks that were concealed in the crevasses between his legs and stomach. Rozi and Egem tried to truss him up, binding his legs together and finally his jaw, to protect themselves from his potent spit. But Frankincense was too clever for us. With a few deft kicks from his back legs, he sent Egem flying and he struggled free from his nooses.

Several hours later the truck appeared, by which time the flood had fortunately diminished. However, more and more streams crossed our path, so we continued very slowly, waiting to check that the truck could get over. This was a very laborious process because each time Mr Li had to get out and dig away with his spade, while Mr He rolled up his trouser legs and, with a double tray of eggs held high in the air in one hand and his leather sandals in the other, waded carefully through the water. Then would follow Mr Li's triumphant splurge as he revved and depressed his accelerator, gearing up for a five-second dash across the water. Our triumphant cheers of 'hooray' were met by a terse nod as he climbed down from the cab – his one and only thought being to check his beloved carburettor.

Seven hours later, we had covered about three miles. Ahead of us lay a beautiful stretch of sand dunes, looking like a calm sea punctuated by thousands of ripples of sand. They glowed a golden red in the rays of the blazing sun, in contrast to the flat, grey monotony of the previous landscape. We continued for half a mile before the lorry met a small slope of sand that it could not climb, even after several attempts. Our endless predictions had finally been fulfilled. Mamat-Jan, however, saw no difficulties. 'Keep going,' he shouted, 'we'll catch you.' Our camels having slowly reached the top of the sand dune, we looked back to see the truck still struggling. Sceptical of Mamat-Jan's optimism, we sat down to wait once again in the overpowering heat, crouching in the shadows of the camels.

Suddenly we noticed a couple of figures appear on the horizon. Having spoken to Mamat-Jan, these two men then went off and returned with a tractor that tugged our truck across a couple of sand dunes. By this time it was about four o'clock (we had started at 5.00 am) and we still had another twelve miles to go. But nothing would deter Mamat-Jan. He chided us, saying, 'Carry on, why do you wait?' We headed slowly off into the dense mass of rolling sand dunes that seemed to us so obviously impenetrable.

After twenty minutes we heard a horn blast in the silence of the desert and halted warily once again. Two more hours elapsed before we saw the glint of the truck's cab appear behind a dune, reversing slowly back towards the river. We climbed back on to the camels to investigate. Mamat-Jan at last conceded that the lorry could go no further. We had no choice but to embark upon the disheartening process of retracing our steps to Charchan.

Night closed in fast and at eight o'clock we were entering the oasis once again. We were intrigued to find how different it was travelling by night. People were no longer focused on heading to work; instead, relaxed couples cruised past on their motorbikes, ensconced in their own world, and paying us little attention. We were less observed, more observers, and felt ourselves caught up in the bustle of their lives. Donkey carts stopped by the wayside, laden with extended families who idled away the hours in carefree chatter. Fathers returned to their families, husbands to wives, as fires were kindled, exotic fumes exuding from small doorways. We passed the abattoir and rode on to a small dusty hotel, set around a central open courtyard. We were ushered into two simple and not very clean rooms while the camels were tethered in the courtyard. By the time we lay down to sleep, exhausted and worried by the day's events, Mr Li and Mr He had still not returned with the truck.

The next day Wic wrote in her diary,

> It would either be a blatant lie or an act of insanity if I said that the sight of Mr He first thing in the morning filled my heart with happiness. Yet today was an exception. I was convinced, after he and Mr Li had failed to return last night, that they had abandoned the truck and gone off in search of noodles and a bus back to Beijing. After all, it was way past office hours. So, as I emerged from my room at the leisurely hour of seven o'clock, I was actually genuinely thrilled to see him and his black-toothed grin striding across the courtyard towards me, clutching his precious jam-jar of tea.

'Mr He!' exclaimed Wic. She receiving nothing but a grunt. 'Truck?' Still nothing. 'Broom, broom … ' she tried, accompanied by vigorous motions of turning a steering wheel. With that came a few more grunts and a finger pointing to the other side of the street. By the time she had turned her head back again, he had waddled off in his sandals to his room. '*Hen hao*' ('good'), she yelled enthusiastically after him, to be greeted only by a slammed door in her face.

Mamat-Jan now appeared from the next-door room, proudly telling us that he had rung Mr Ma but nothing could be done today because it was Sunday. We did not know whether to applaud him for this unprecedented act of initiative or berate him as a convenient scapegoat. Instead, we opted for a large breakfast of warm bread, freshly boiled eggs and an enormous bowl of yoghurt and honey, after which we felt a lot better.

We then escaped to the local bazaar with Egem and Rozi, who bought us corn on the cob for lunch and a 'perty' copper bracelet. I had previously said that I wanted to buy a sheepskin hat, so Egem spent a long time looking for one, earnestly scouring every stall. He appeared very disappointed when we could not find any. He and Rozi were generally so polite to us, helping us with our saddlebags and sharing their food, in contrast to Mr He and Mr Li, who were pointedly rude, never helping us to lift our heavy rucksacks into the truck and quite happy to watch as we struggled away.

Charchan was as hot and dusty as all the other oasis towns and the bazaar consisted of stalls selling anything from tin teapots to boiled sweets, protected from the blazing sun only by pieces of ragged canvas. After an hour we were ready to faint from the heat and noise, so we returned to our rooms to wait for news from Mr Ma, which never materialised.

The next day an electricity cut meant we could neither make nor receive telephone calls. Fate really seemed to be working against us and, depressed, we did not stir from our rooms. It was so hot outside that even to cross the courtyard to the lavatory, a hole behind the opposite wall, became an ordeal. The only water supply was from a hosepipe, but this too had been cut off.

In the afternoon some new arrivals appeared in our courtyard – about twenty Uighurs, squatting on top of two lorries loaded with sheepskins and one live sheep. Luckily they did not disturb our monopoly of the restaurant but set up a table of their own outside.

Rozi and Egem sat giggling together for most of the day. Rozi had persuaded Mamat-Jan to teach him the words 'I love you,' in English, which he used several times on Mouse, fleeing with embarrassment on one occasion. Meanwhile, when I came back after supper I found Lucy on her bed and Egem curled up on mine. Apparently he had stroked my pillow and said, 'Alex perty?', to which Lucy had loyally replied, 'Yes'.

The third day of our captivity was spent hunting for camel shoes. The poor camels' feet were beginning to crack and blister while a couple of them had even developed holes, which visibly gave them great pain. Up until now when we had broached the idea of 'camel shoes' it had been met with hoots of laughter, but today we were surprised to find that Mamat-Jan and Mr He were willing to accompany us to the bazaar on our search.

At length we found a tailor who seemed happy to undertake the unusual task of creating camel shoes out of his best black leather. In fact, he was so enthused by the idea that he set off on his motorbike, Mamat-Jan clinging on behind, to fetch more materials. We took the opportunity to lunch on yet more kebabs and noodles. The Uighurs seem to eat the most restricted range of food; in restaurants, the only choices are noodles and vegetables, always cooked in an identical way, or kebabs. Whenever we entered a restaurant Mamat-Jan would go through the formality of asking us what we wanted and we would ask hopefully whether there was anything except noodles and kebabs, to which he would reply, 'Fried noodles.'

Later that afternoon we collected the camel shoes, ingeniously created out of black leather exteriors, with felt inners, mounted on soles of tyre treads. Taking them back to the courtyard, we decided to try them out on the camels. Moon Boot was chosen as the first victim. While Rozi held a leg still, Egem pushed the shoe on, attempting to secure it round his ankle with string. But this operation provoked a dramatic reaction in Moon Boot, who began to roar and spit, finally giving an almighty kick that flung the boot across the courtyard. We decided to delay any further attempts at shoeing the camels until we resumed our journey. That evening Mamat-Jan finally spoke to Mr Ma, who assured us a four-wheel truck was being sent from Kashgar to accompany us for the rest of our journey.

The fourth day at last brought some news – although not exactly what we wanted. Around midday Egem entered our room, plonked himself down on my bed, as he had done everyday, and started fiddling with the contents of my wash bag, finding his reflection in my hand mirror particularly fascinating. Lucy and I looked up from our books briefly, smiled and continued with our reading. We did not wish to be impolite, but he and Rozi were constantly floating in and out of our room like two bored children. Our lack of interest, however, did not deter him. He launched into some story about cars and Mamat-Jan, throwing in the odd 'good' and 'no good' now and then. What he appeared to be telling us in his singsong tones was that we were not getting a new truck after all but that Mamat-Jan had gone to check whether the 'birch' outside Charchan had been mended. Our blood began to boil once more.

'Where have you been?' Mouse asked when Mamat-Jan finally reappeared.

'I go to birch.'

'Why?'

'Because I am thinking the road is good and the truck can go.'

'Where is our promised four-wheel drive truck?'

'No, I don't think new truck arrives.'

'Why not?'

'Mr Ma says road is good for old truck.'

It emerged that Mr Ma had instructed Mamat-Jan to find out more about the road, so he had duly set off to inspect the bridge. He told us it was mended and we could begin riding again the next morning. We were far from convinced that the road beyond the bridge would be passable, having been informed by road workers the day before that it was covered in sand. But Mamat-Jan chose to cite the hotel owner, who had driven along the road to Dunhuang a whole two years ago and told him it was clear. Yet again we were powerless to do anything.

Having woken early the next morning, Mouse was scuttling across the courtyard when, on passing Rozi and Egem's room, she was taken aback by a vision of whiteness through the window. She came dashing into our room to impart the news: the vision of whiteness was a girl and, moreover, she was lying in Rozi's bed. We rushed into the courtyard to watch as first Mamat-Jan entered their room and began conversing with her and then as she sat down on their doorstep in her flimsy nightdress. Most surprising was that, despite having been seen in Rozi's bed, it was Egem who held her hand longingly and tickled her chin as he said goodbye.

The dawn hours found us retracing our steps out of Charchan for the second time, following the new road until we turned off along the old one. Having travelled twelve miles in a straight line over the bridge and along a gravel track crossed occasionally by desert streams, we realised that our four wasted days could easily have been avoided by a simple reconnaissance trip on the part of the back-up team.

In Central Asia we had spent over three months crossing desert, complicated mountain passes, marsh and forest, but never did we encounter a delay. Our Russian back-up team had shown great initiative in planning and researching our route, anticipating our wishes and overcoming problems when they did occur. The world of our Chinese back-up team, however, was like a microcosm of Communism. Except for Mamat-Jan, who was just starting out on a career in the civil service, there was no incentive for any of the others to show resourcefulness or accept responsibility. Even Mamat-Jan's motivation amounted to little more than concern with following his chief's instructions, rather than satisfying his clients, while Mr Li and Mr He were guaranteed jobs for life with the government agency we had employed. There was no relationship between salary and performance. In contrast, the team in Central Asia had been privately employed and therefore had every incentive to provide a recommendable service. Throughout our time in China we missed their presence.

Around midday we reached our first camp outside Charchan: a liberating feeling after five nights inside. We settled contentedly into the routine of an itinerant life once more, only to be interrupted by Rozi and Egem, whose turn it now was to cause trouble. Henceforth, they had decided to alternate their workload, so that each day one would work, leading the camels, while the other slept. This rebellious move was instigated by their dislike of rising at four o'clock.

'If in contract it says they get up at four then they do – they are not lazy people,' Mamat-Jan told us solemnly. Rozi and Egem had obviously been taking tips from Mr Li, telling us that they were not obliged to start work before eight, Xinjiang time, because it had not been specified in their contract. However, they could not read, so we doubted the existence of such a contract, and in addition we knew they came from a remote village in Xinjiang, where it was inconceivable that office hours were practised.

First, we told them they could not be paid a full wage to work only half the time and second we tried to show them that, whatever time they got up, they would always do the same amount of work. Since they were constantly complaining of the heat themselves, we attempted to persuade them that it was only by travelling in the early morning that we could avoid the midday sun. But no amount of explanation or cajoling had any effect until finally we simply told them it was their job and if they did not both get up the next morning we would tell Mr Ma, whom they fortunately seemed to hold in great fear.

Rozi and Egem were ready at five the next morning, as promised, and we set off under clear skies, signalling an especially hot day ahead. The evening before Mr Li had spoken to a passing truck driver who had told him it was possible to take a short cut over the desert. There was apparently a large kink in the road which we could avoid by continuing in a straight line, towards the Kun Lun mountains and Charklik. Mamat-Jan told us only to begin this diversion from the road when we could see the telegraph poles on the opposite side of the kink, and not before. But after a mile or so of walking we noticed that the camel drivers had already veered off into the desert, heading for the mountains. This seemed like a sensible idea because, as long as the latter were in sight, we knew that the road must lie between them and us. The early morning sun was directly in front of us, confirming that we were heading east. We plodded on, in as straight a line as possible, towards the mountains, hazy in the morning light.

At one point Mouse panicked us, saying that no mountains came within two hundred miles of our road and therefore they must be vast sand dunes, obstructing our path to the road. But Rozi and Egem reassured us, saying, '*tagh* – yes.' ('*Tagh*' is the Turkic word for mountains.) Our doubts obviously had an effect on them, however, because they suddenly seemed to lose confidence and began to head south-east, despite our entreaties to continue in our original bearing. But they were far less receptive than usual, blankly ignoring us. So, fearful of antagonising them further, we sat back on the camels and watched the mountains hove further into sight. Finally, at one o'clock we spotted the reassuring telegraph poles and came back on to the road, a mile or so before our agreed camping spot. We continued along the road, dismayed not to see the truck, then clambered down into an old riverbed to cut across a bend in the road. As we crossed the bottom of it we saw the truck appear over the horizon. Having given our caravan a cursory glance and established that the truck could not negotiate the ten-foot drop, Mr Li turned around and drove off again. By this point it was three o'clock. We were hot and bleary-eyed from the unrelenting glare of the sun. Where had they been? Why had they not waited at our agreed meeting point?

Eventually we turned the last corner and found the back-up team sheepishly waiting for us by the side of the road. I flew at Mamat-Jan. This seemed the last straw in a list of blunders. He looked very upset, so I quickly retreated to the mess tent in order to avoid more confrontation. It gradually emerged that actually Mamat-Jan had done his duty efficiently and it was the camel drivers who were at fault. They had ignored his instructions to wait until the telegraph poles were visible before crossing the desert and therefore we had emerged much further along the road than he had predicted. When we had not arrived, he had become very worried and scoured the road backwards and forwards, looking for us. He had walked six miles into the desert trying to find us when, driving back along the road, he had finally seen the camels in the riverbed. In my diary I wrote, 'I felt incredibly remorseful on hearing this explanation and apologised several times, but he still looked very unhappy. Later he pathetically showed me how he had fallen over in the desert and hurt his leg.'

Next day it was war. As usual, we woke at four o'clock to a beautiful starlit night, packed away our sleeping bags, brushed our teeth and applied our sun cream. At half past four we woke the camel drivers with a gentle 'good morning, Rozi and Egem – lunch time!' ('Lunch time' was used as a summons for any food or meal.) We then sat down to eat our way through the daily ration of hard bread and boiled eggs, mysteriously flavoured with fish. Every couple of minutes one of us would walk over to the camel drivers and give them a nudge. This became a torch in the face, then a yell of 'Rozi and Egem – WAKE UP!' At a quarter to five Egem graced us with his presence at the table. He had had his hair cut very short in Charchan and now presented a rather terrifying figure. 'Is Rozi coming?' He shrugged his shoulders. They had obviously made a pact to follow their earlier plan of working in shifts.

Mouse marched up to Rozi and yelled at him again. One eye flickered as she shouted, 'It's five o'clock, we must go – get up!' He grinned wickedly and pulled the quilt over his face. 'That's it, get up now!' And she whipped away the quilt completely. 'Rozi, up – camels!' – pointing in their direction.

Rozi rose to his feet, only to skulk off to the other side of the camp and sit on his haunches. Meanwhile, Wic was organising the camels as Egem methodically undid every rope she had secured. In the end we set off on foot, unsure as to whether they and the camels would follow. Having covered ten miles, we sat waiting at our first watering hole, made up of two dilapidated sheds, until we thankfully spied the camel drivers approaching on the horizon. Unfortunately, the river had dried up completely. When Egem gestured for us climb on board we protested, 'No, the camels haven't drunk for three days – we must water them.' Still fuming and avoiding any eye contact, the camel drivers mumbled 'No water'.

'There must be a well,' we protested. 'They must drink.'

After a great deal of sighing, the camels were given a bucket of water each. We set off again on the long straight road with only tufts of tamarisk to relieve the monotony. At one point we noticed a small deer standing on top of a dune in the distance. It was strange to see life in this desolate landscape; we were baffled as to what it could survive on. Fourteen miles later, with not one word uttered by Rozi or Egem, we arrived in camp.

The last of the melons finished, we ate dry bread and quizzed Mamat-Jan about the camel handlers' dramatic change in behaviour. The following reasons emerged: Rozi and Egem said, i) we shouted at them in the desert; ii) we treated them like slaves, waking them at 4.30 am in such a rude way; iii) we always told them what to do with the camels, i.e. water them, and interfered, i.e. helped with the shoes; iv) they were bored.

We laughed and called them girls because they could not do what we had been doing for 150 days on the road without complaining. This made them furious and they began hurling insults at us in Kyrgyz. We then asked why they were so friendly before. Their 'revolting answer' was translated by Mamat-Jan: 'Maxi and Alkeez, ask yourselves why.' Mouse and I, who were known by these variations on our names to Rozi and Egem, paled, lost for words. It was insulting to realise that they were implying we had been anything more than good-natured.

'Mamat-Jan, you know the camel drivers don't always tell the truth, don't you?'

'What do you mean?'

'What we mean is that they seem to like you, yes?'

'Of course.'

'Well, they tell us everyday – "Mamat-Jan – no good".'

Mamat-Jan looked hurt, as it slowly dawned on him that Rozi and Egem had been attempting to play us off against each other. His misguided sympathy for them evaporated and he reassured us that from now on they would work properly.

That evening Moon Boot accidentally stepped on our washbowls and cracked them. Now we had no vessels. I asked Mr He whether we might borrow his small red plastic bucket but received only a torrent of abusive Chinese in return. I grabbed the bucket and marched back across the sand towards the others. But Mr He and Mr Li chased after me and began to wrestle the bucket out of my hands. I clung on to it, so we had a tug of war until they won, the others laughing in the background.

'Mamat-Jan, why can't we borrow the bucket?' I asked.

'Um, the Mr He says you are too dirty and might have disease.'

'What?'

'He says you have different skin.'

Even after I had offered to disinfect it, Mr He would still not relent. He spat, cursed and waved his arms frantically. I gave up and instead we took it in turns to wash out of the camels' food bowl. I went to sleep under the stars, thinking it was impossible to imagine Shamil ever refusing to get up because it was too early, or not wanting to share his bucket.

Next day's battle was fought with very different tactics. We delegated the job of waking the camel drivers to Mamat-Jan. He, desperate to appease both parties, agreed, and made a much better job of it than we had.

In a way, it was a relief that Rozi and Egem had begun to dislike us, as their admiration had become annoying. They were now behaving like sulking children, so it was funny to smile at them and watch them trying to conceal their smiles as they scowled back. Before our fall from grace, Mouse and I had always been allocated the camels behind our respective champions, but now we were relegated to the back.

A day later Mamat-Jan called a meeting about 'being nice to the forners'. He managed to extract a promise from the team that they would try to get on with us and change their petty ways. As an incentive, the camel drivers were promised a trip to an Urumchi nightclub on their return, and, if possible, they would also be provided with women.

As we were walking, tiny lizards crossed our path, darting across the desert floor. Occasionally they flung themselves underneath our boots, killing or maiming themselves. We passed no vegetation and camped by the side of the road on the flat, exposed gravel plain. Before long we were crying out for cover as the wind swept up patches of sand. Twenty minutes was enough to bury one of our rucksacks.

The storm continued throughout the day while at night we sought cover under the lorry, beneath a starless sky. The desert no longer felt peaceful, but frighteningly oppressive. We slept in goggles and scarves wrapped tightly around our heads and woke covered in sand. It was a relief when dawn rose, even though it brought with it an acute heat, which, when combined with the dusty air, was suffocating. The winds died down for a few hours, only to blow up again by mid-morning. The air became dark once more and we could not see more than a few feet ahead.

After a couple of hours we came to a strip of road covered in sand blown in from the dunes. This continued for nearly three miles. We became nervous that the lorry would not be able to cross it, but decided to keep going, if only to prove that a new truck was imperative. We continued further and further, but still no truck, until we reached a huge riverbed, dry except for a trickle, with deep, vertiginous sides. Our camels could only just clamber down, so we had great doubts about the truck. As we were deliberating over what to do, a truck appeared, inside which were three Uighurs, whom we stopped and asked to pass a message to Mamat-Jan. They also very kindly gave us all their bread, grapes and melon.

By this time we had already covered nearly twenty-four miles, so we decided to wait on the other side of the dried-up riverbed. At that very moment, the truck drew into sight, accompanied by a tractor. A man jumped out and attached a tow wire to our truck, then dragged it down the first bank of the riverbed and across to the opposite bank. This was more difficult to negotiate, being steep and uphill, but after several attempts it arrived at the top. We camped only a few yards away, under the shade of the first tree we had seen for weeks. Luckily, the winds had diminished and we were able to wash off some of the grime and dust we had accumulated.

After a week of barren desert, we were overjoyed to find ourselves entering the Wasa oasis the following day. Tamarisk, poplars and willows lined the road, while rows of sunflowers divided solicitously tended fields of maize, potatoes and cabbages. Small adobe houses covered in rambling vines were hidden down leafy avenues, away from the dust of the main road. Bullocks were particularly numerous here, pulling carts, ploughing fields and standing in the shade of the tall poplars. It still amazed us how such a wealth of plant life can suddenly appear in so lifeless an environment.

Strangely, the small oasis of Wasa seemed to possess a large Chinese population, all dressed in conical straw hats as they set off for the fields in droves, hoes slung over their backs. Generally, the Chinese population of Xinjiang tend to live in the big cities, Urumchi and Kashgar, while the villages and oases are principally populated by Uighurs. Rozi's head began to swivel as he strained to examine every girl we passed, starved as he was of this luxury since Charchan.

We camped three miles out of the shade of the oasis. Although the sun had reached its zenith and the wind was trying to destroy our camp, we were happy: Mamat-Jan had bought us freshly baked bread and melons. We pitched camp next to the camels to try and gain some protection from their huge bulks. Unfortunately, this plan backfired. First, they released overpoweringly pungent smells all night and, secondly, they kept moving around. I woke at one point with a fright to find Frankincense's head inches from mine, staring solemnly at me.

We were now only days from the end of August and were steadily becoming more excited about the approach of autumn. Convinced that the mornings were already colder, we started to wear jumpers at dawn, but as the sun rose we regretted our hastiness, as even an extra layer around the waist became unbearable. Still these were our favourite hours: the air was motionless, the light a warm orange and the temperatures cool enough to walk in without working up a sweat. The peaks of the Kun Lun mountains, which now lay only ten to fifteen miles south-east of us, were clearly defined until they became blurred in a hazy screen of heat. By ten the wind would pick up, sending spirals of sand hurling across the plains.

After nine consecutive days on the road we reached the oasis of Charklik, where we would have our last rest day before Dunhuang, another full three weeks ahead. Again, as in Wasa, we found many Chinese faces, watching us from the fields of sunflowers. However, in contrast to the previous oases, the willows and poplars here were grown not in strictly uniform rows but more randomly. Birds flew chirping between the branches and we realised that it was a long time since we had heard birdsong. The fields and trees soon gave way to adobe buildings. We passed a high-walled building with turrets at each corner, no windows and a guard parading around the top. Mamat-Jan informed us it was a prison. Our hotel was close by, so we lay inside for most of the afternoon, trapped by the unbearable heat outside.

Charklik had an uninspiring Chinese heart, which only livened up at sunset. The mosque to the west of the town crowned the skyline against a sky streaked in pink. One of the main squares became a night market and, as the heat of the day subsided, people began to emerge from their houses to spend the evening sauntering through the stalls and restaurants. What had been an empty, dusty square transformed into a mass of flaming braziers, thronged by Uighur people of all ages. These oasis towns only come to life at night, like Mediterranean towns. Children join their parents for a supper of noodles, while even the smallest babies are not left at home.

Lucy and I amazed ourselves that night by finding yet more fascinating topics of conversation after five months together. We stayed up until late talking, only to be woken early the next morning by Mamat-Jan, proudly knocking on our doors to present us with a local washerwoman.

9

The long march to Dunhuang

THE NEXT STAGE presented one of the greatest challenges of our journey: a 24-day march to Dunhuang. We had decided to sacrifice all rest days during this leg because we would pass through no oases and preferred to reach Dunhuang as soon as possible. This legendary Silk Road oasis, which links the northern and southern routes around the Taklamakan desert, had become the guiding beacon of our journey. All our dreams were focused on this small town, where Mouse had told us many times we would find fruit, chocolate and other long missed luxuries. It also marked the official end of the Taklamakan, although a stretch of the Black Gobi still lay ahead of us.

Our second night in Charklik was restless, as we nervously anticipated the long, unbroken march. Leaving in the early dawn, we strode through the empty streets, past adobe houses and stables, surprised at one point to see pigs, which were rare in this Muslim region.

The day passed uneventfully in ever-increasing heat. Our hopes of cooler temperatures were dashed, though. Mouse recorded a peak temperature of 45°C. The mountain range that divided us from Dunhuang beckoned tantalisingly from the east, but sadly we would not reach them until the following day. We went to sleep doubting that this inhuman heat would ever retreat.

The next day, we ascended our first slope in two months. Looking back across the open plain with its ribbon-like road snaking through the sand, we bid farewell to the Taklamakan with relief. Then we turned back to the mountains, excited at the thought of the valleys and peaks ahead of us.

It took two days to climb up through the foothills of the Argyn Shan. This mountain range is a part of the larger Kun Lun range that separates

China from Tibet. It was only in 1876 that the Argyn Shan became known to the outside world, when the Russian explorer Colonel Nikolai Mikhailovich Przhevalsky returned from his historic expedition to the Desert of Lop, in the east of the Taklamakan. His discoveries, concerning the location of Lop Nur, a previously uncharted saline lake, created a sensation at the time in geographical circles. When the first telegram containing his story was flashed around the world, the geographer Dr E. Behm wrote, 'So at last the darkness which surrounded Lop Nur is put to flight, and we shall soon see the lake on the maps as it really is. But who could have guessed that there was a mountain range [the Argyn Shan] to the south of it? Our ideas of the Gobi are about to be revolutionised.' The route we were to follow passed along the high and utterly barren slopes of this range. In the days of the Silk Road it took traffic when the desert route from Charklik to Dunhuang was closed between late spring and winter, on account of the saltiness of the wells by the shores of the ancient dried-up bed of Lop Nur.

Steep valleys soon replaced the gentle slopes of the bases of the mountains and we turned back and forth along hairpin bends, following a gravelly track. Arid and severe, the mountains provided a welcome contrast to the flat uniformity of the desert. Wic shouted Rozi's name at one point and the echo ricocheted around the valley. As we all took up the call, Rozi turned around, terrified and bewildered, even looking up to heaven to discover the origin of this unearthly noise.

Our first night in the mountains was spent in a small valley with patchy vegetation. For the first time in two months we saw wild flowers – little yellow petals on bright green stalks, which the camels found delicious. Our path that day had followed a riverbed and where the road had climbed out of the river we had felt sure the truck would not be able to get up the steep, rocky slope. Sure enough, eight hours after we had set out, there was no sign of the truck, so we decided to stop anyway. We had waited for two hours before Mamat-Jan surprised us by appearing on foot around the corner of the valley. Having left the truck stuck in the riverbed, he had walked seven and a half miles to bring us some food. Half an hour later, a dishevelled Mr He came into view, having walked for an hour in flip-flops after the tractor on which he had hitched a lift had broken down. We were pleased to note that he immediately grabbed a bottle of water from Mamat-Jan, draining it in seconds. Perhaps in future he would be more sympathetic to our pleas for increased rations.

It was ironic that on the first cold night for months we were stranded without our sleeping bags and tents. Mamat-Jan told us the truck was wedged firmly in the riverbed and, although we had passed a small road workers' depot on the road, their tractor would not be available to help until the next day. We looked for firewood to keep us warm as the sun dipped behind the mountains, leaving our valley cold and gloomy. Wrapped up in our camel quilts we lay as close to the embers of the fire as possible, watching the moon as it rose, illuminating the whole valley.

Reluctant to lose time, we decided to continue the following morning, leaving Mamat-Jan to solve the problem. After all, the back-up team had assured us so many times that the truck was capable of following us wherever we went. We set off at five in the cold dawn light, climbing further into the Argyn Shan, up to the 10,000-foot Tashi pass. Admiring the spectacular view of the snow-capped Kun Lun mountains beyond, we sat down to enjoy the sun and a watermelon. Rozi and Egem followed half an hour behind us, complaining that Moon Boot had lain down to sleep. At this very moment, we spied a chain of camels giving vent to a leonine roaring, winding their way up the sinuous road towards us, accompanied by a dozen ponies and two men. This unexpected encounter raised our spirits, although Rozi scuttled up a rock face, frightened that the men were 'bandits', while Egem explained this cowardly behaviour by pointing to his heart and repeating, 'Small, small.'

There proved to be five camels, one an unusual white colour. All of them, however, towered over our diminutive caravan. Ridden by two swarthy Uighur men, their pegs were inserted underneath their nose cartilage, as opposed to above, like ours. The ponies were small but they suddenly kicked up their hooves, in unprovoked annoyance, and trotted away. Egem and Rozi having approached the Uighurs, we inferred the following meagre information: the ponies were being brought down from their summer pastures while the camels were being taken from Dunhuang to Charklik for use by foreigners. Egem told the men to speak to Mamat-Jan about possibly buying the camels when they passed him on the road and we left, praying this providential meeting would not prove fruitless.

The walk down the other side of the pass was less strenuous and warmer than the ascent. Argyn means 'gold' in Chinese, and the mountains were indeed a yellow colour, from the layer of sand which coats them on their lower slopes. They made a beautiful scene, the golden sand contrasting vividly with the blue of the sky.

After a few more hours Amec lay down and refused to move, resisting even Rozi's thick stick. Moon Boot was still also very reluctant to move, so we decided to leave Egem with these two camels while we continued, covering another eight miles before coming to a halt. Mamat-Jan had not passed us in the road workers' truck by this point, so we anticipated a repetition of the previous night's experience. We collected piles of the abundant thyme bushes in preparation for a fire and lay down to rest after a wearying day. The sun was beginning to sink when suddenly we saw Egem approaching round the corner, leading only Moon Boot. Apparently Amec had been dragged to a few miles away but had collapsed again. We were very upset to think of him stranded alone, but there was nothing we could do. We could only hope that the vegetation would provide him with enough sustenance to recover and live wild.

As dusk fell we lit our fire and lay beside it on our camel rugs. While we were trying to warm ourselves we saw a road workers' truck passing us from the opposite direction. Rozi ran over to stop it. We thought we heard the surly tones of Mr Li but dismissed this as an impossibility, as the truck was approaching from the wrong way. Indeed it was him though, coming from Simianqiang, an asbestos mine high up in the mountains ahead of us. Now he was returning to pick up Mamat-Jan. We were furious to learn that Mr Li would have to return all the way to our truck, still stuck in the riverbed, then back again to us before we could have our sleeping bags or food. By now it was freezing and we lay close together under the quilts, trying to forget about our useless back-up team, as well as, of course, the fate of poor Amec.

At nearly one o'clock in the morning, a pair of headlights eventually loomed round the edge of the mountain, sending a beam of light across the valley: the road workers' truck again. We were so relieved that we forfeited any supper to jump straight into our sleeping bags. Mamat-Jan then told us how Mr He had flouted his careful arrangements of the previous day, to use the road workers' truck to transport our belongings, and instead had sent Mr Li off in it in the middle of the night to buy a new axle for our truck. Mr Li, never a careful driver, had sped through the dark only to crash the truck, falling over the edge of a broken bridge. He had apparently been rescued by a second road workers' truck, in which we had met him. Poor Mamat-Jan had been left alone all day at our camping spot of the night before. Mr He's obstinacy seemed to have reached giddying new heights. We never understood why Mr Li had not left us our provisions as he passed us on the road to Simianqiang, or why he had not waited until the next morning to buy the axle.

We were woken the next morning by Mr He yelling at Rozi. The sun was breaking over our little valley and Mr He was frying chips, perhaps feeling guilty about the previous night's escapade. Having had nothing to eat for forty-eight hours, we ate voraciously while arguing heatedly with the back-up team. We needed new camels urgently: Amec had collapsed, Neurotic, the smallest camel, was too weak to be ridden, and Moon Boot was fading fast, incapable of crossing another pass. The obvious solution was to follow the camel train we had passed the day before, back towards Charklik, and buy two of their animals. Unsurprisingly, this suggestion met with great opposition. Mr He wanted to wait until Simianqiang to telephone Mr Ma before making a decision. To us, and even to Mamat-Jan, this seemed a crazy plan: we had just seen our first camel train in China and could not forgo such a providential gift. After much shouting, Mamat-Jan was given permission by Mr He to return along the road to Charklik in search of the camels. Mr Li was to mend the truck while the road workers had kindly agreed to deliver Mr He and our belongings to our campsite for the next two nights. We would meet up in Simianqiang three days later with Mr Li, the truck, Mamat-Jan and the new camels.

So it was that we set off once more through the truncated spurs of the Argyn Shan, still enjoying the novelty of mountain breezes and lower temperatures. Mamat-Jan travelled with us for the first hour until we came to a small bus stop. He jumped down to wait there for a bus to Charklik, which the road workers had assured us ran a couple of times a day. One of the Argyn Shan's many rivers had destroyed part of the road and we edged carefully along the crumbling cliffs at the water's edge. A couple of miles further on the river had swept away half a bridge. This was where Mr Li had driven over the edge into the water. The truck was still there with its back wheels suspended on the broken bridge and its front wheels hanging over the riverbed. We were horrified, as well as surprised, that Mr Li had escaped with no more than a few cuts and bruises.

We continued down a much wider valley that opened out into some spectacular grasslands. Dressed only in thin shirts, we wrapped ourselves in the camel quilts to stave off the cold, intermittent rain. Meanwhile, Moon Boot had been slowing all morning, his nose thrust forward in an effort to loosen the permanently taut rope. Blood was beginning to run out of his nostrils and his eyes watered with exhaustion. Eventually, we decided it was pointless to drag him further; he would never recover his strength at the pace we were going. However, if he was to rest with food and water he would clearly survive. We looked around: a mile back was a clear, wide river in a valley of grass and thyme bushes. Egem unroped the fading Moon Boot and led him off towards the river. He had come so far with us, it was difficult not to feel a pang at deserting him, but thankfully he made no attempt to follow us. We continued on our way, watching him until he had become a mere speck in the distance. We were now down to five camels, one of which was poor Neurotic, so only four rideable ones. We took it in turns to ride and walk.

The grasslands turned to marsh, thick with rushes, and then to gravel and more thyme. At half-past four we espied our mess tent looking very vulnerable beneath the barren mountains, looming on every side. After Mr He had cooked us a supper of rice and vegetables, still almost fresh from Charklik, we laid out our sleeping bags in the mess tent, frightened by the prospect of rain. Rozi chose to sleep outside.

'Rozi, why are you sleeping outside?'

'Bandits,' was the ominous reply.

'What will you do if they come?'

'Me, Maxi, camel, Xian,' he replied simply, pointing to the east.

No longer having to contend with the heat of the desert, we were now able to rise at a more civilised hour: around six o'clock each morning. After five days of riding over the peaks and valleys of the Argyn Shan, we arrived in Simianqiang, the asbestos deposit, high up in the mountains.

As we approached, a bleak landscape of pylons appeared from nowhere, indicating that we were reaching the outskirts of the town. We came over a hilltop to find ourselves confronted by towering chimneys and mounds of asbestos dust. Then we suddenly felt the ground reverberate. An explosion threw tons of rock into the air, with clouds of dust drifting over us. Great flakes of asbestos settled on our clothes and hair as we hurriedly wrapped jumpers round our faces to try and protect ourselves from the toxins.

Everything was grey, from the sky to the road to the people, who slowly appeared from behind the mounds of dust wearing white facemasks with their hair matted by asbestos flakes. They looked prematurely aged, with their white hair and dusty faces. This eerie scene, where it seemed impossible that the sun could ever penetrate, appeared like a science fiction scene. We urged Egem and Rozi to hurry past as quickly as possible.

We emerged in Simianqiang's sole street, where the visibility was equally poor and the people bore the same resigned expressions. After twenty minutes of questioning we were directed to the one hotel in town, and entered its courtyard to find Mr He standing there waiting for us in his flip-flops. He directed us to a small room with rickety beds that had no mattresses, dirt floors and one small window that we kept firmly closed. Mr He also intimated, through the medium of his customary grunts, that we were not allowed to leave the room. (Later Mamat-Jan told us we had been placed under house arrest because this place was forbidden to foreigners.)

I was reading Marco Polo's account of his journey along the Silk Road at the time and was surprised to discover that he too had encountered the asbestos deposit. He wrote:

> ... and you must know that in the same mountain there is a vein of the substance from which Salamander is made. For the real truth is that the Salamander is no beast, as they allege in our part of the world, but is a substance found in the earth ... The substance of this vein was then taken and crushed, and when so treated it divides as it were into fibres of wool, which they set forth to dry. When dry, these fibres were pounded in a great copper mortar, and then washed, so as to remove all the earth and to leave only the fibres like fibres of wool. These were then spun and made into napkins. When first made these napkins are not very white, but by putting them into fire for a while they come out as white as fire.

The fable of asbestos being a substance derived from the Salamander was prevalent in the Middle Ages, both in Asia and Europe. Although nowadays asbestos is mined for more appropriate uses than white napkins, we later discovered that this haunted town is in fact a hideous gulag settlement, and people from all over China are deported to come and work here.

We were eager to leave as quickly as possible, so were excited to be woken the next morning by familiar roars. Outside our door we found two new camels, dwarfing our remaining five. Mamat-Jan was standing beside them, glowing with pride at his work. He had arrived the night before with the camels in the back of a lorry. Meanwhile, Mr Li and our truck had been transported from the riverbed in another lorry. He finally appeared, screeching in his usual dramatic fashion into the courtyard, obviously keen to impress on us that the truck was back in full working order.

Unfortunately, our time in the mountains proved to be short-lived.

From Simianqiang we headed back down into the endless, flat plateaux of crusty sand around the edge of the Tsaidam basin, through which Peter Fleming had crossed on his way from Xining to Kashgar in 1935. Special travel correspondent for *The Times*, he travelled from Peking to Kashmir along a branch of the Silk Road. His account of this journey has become a classic of travel writing and is filled with adventure as well as humour.

We were at a constant height of ten thousand feet, so the temperatures remained cooler and our days, if monotonous, were at least not as uncomfortable as previously. The only highlight was the appearance of hundreds of rotivators with small trailers, piled high with grime-covered men, pots, pans, spades, wooden poles and bulging hessian sacks. These machines moved with the velocity of crippled snails, their drivers invariably wearing a large pair of black goggles and a furry hat.

When we asked Mamat-Jan who these people were, he answered, 'Ah, they are business men.'

'Are they Hui?'

We knew that the Huis, or Tungans, were of mixed Chinese and Muslim parentage. Marco Polo refers to their ancestors as 'Argons', saying that they 'sprung from two different races: to wit, of the race of the Idolators of Tenduc [Buddhists] and that of the worshippers of Mahommet. They are handsomer men than the other natives of the country, and having more ability, they come to have authority, and they are also capital merchants.' The Tungans are said by one account to trace their origins to a large body of Uighurs transported to the vicinity of the Great Wall during the T'ang Dynasty (618–907). However, another theory traces them back to Samarkand. Claimed by Fleming to be the best fighters in China, bar the communists, they instigated several bloody uprisings in the twentieth century, the most famous being the 1931 rebellion against President Jin Shuren led by General Ma. The men on the rotivators indeed looked different from both the Chinese and the Uighurs, so we assumed they were Huis. Mamat-Jan, always reluctant to clarify a situation, answered simply, 'They are Muslim.'

I laughed. 'If they're business men, where are their briefcases?'

He looked thoughtful. 'Oh, they are in Charchan or Charklik.'

It proved that the Huis had been given a special licence by the Chinese government to dig for gold, in the eponymous Argyn Shan, where they comb the mountains in droves.

One night, we camped among a host of oil wells, ugly and incongruous in this barren landscape. Tar-filled streams flowed from the small town that had sprung up around them and the next day we passed a semi-permanent camp of military green tents where the oil workers obviously lived. It was lunchtime and hundreds of men were squatting on the sand, banging their metal tins and spoons in anticipation of food. It seemed an only marginally preferable existence to that of the asbestos workers in Simianqiang, yet this was not forced labour.

The weather had changed dramatically by now. It was cold, with bitter winds blowing in from the east, unrestrained by the flat landscape. Boredom became a greater problem than ever and we tried everything to create a feeling of novelty. One morning I broke with our rigid routine of travelling the first ten miles on foot by beginning on the camels, hoping to pass the day more quickly but to no avail. It was at this time that Lucy happened to be reading an account by two female missionaries, Mildred Cable and Eva French, of their time travelling through the Taklamakan at the beginning of the twentieth century:

> What faced me here might be the burden of boundless monotony. Should I ever distinguish one stage from the other? Might I not even die, not, as some had done, of thirst and fatigue, but of boredom? In the end, shall I make good my quest or would the desert prove too much for me? Where would it all end? How would it end? Anything might happen and it might end anywhere.

We felt similarly desperate.

After a week the flatness of the plains was broken by wind eroded sand dunes. Sometimes we would find ourselves walking through gorges made by the ferocity of the wind; at others the wind had gouged out furrows in the sand so that it seemed like ploughed fields stretched to the horizon. Although it was a relief to encounter a change it became exhausting, as we scaled up and down these neverending slopes, slipping and sliding in the crusty sand. Just when we thought we had reached a flat expanse, a small valley would open up below and another steep bank would rise up ahead of us. However, from these peaks the view was magnificent. Miles of dappled golden sand spread out to the horizon, contrasting with the deep azure sky.

Our two new camels, although larger and stronger than the others, were beginning to exhibit some very irritating habits. One of them continually spat, covering us in stinking streaks of regurgitated maize balls, while the other would not stop roaring. I sometimes found it impossible to ride in the caravan because the noise grated in my ears so, precluding any chatting or reading. The others were more patient, so I often found myself journeying alone.

One day we found ourselves in a bare stretch of landscape where shards of quartz-like stone littered the ground. Occasionally, the sun picked out the stones and they glistened like millions of stars in a sandy sky. Workers were collecting these rocks which, with their heat-retaining properties, are apparently used to manufacture solar panels. We spent a night camping in the workers' temporary base, consisting of two sheds. To the north-west we could see the shadowy form of the Argyn Shan re-emerging on the horizon; as the sun set, it left a pink haze floating above their opaque blue and grey peaks.

The first point of inhabitation after Simianqiang came ten days and two hundred miles later, in Lenghu, a small oil-manufacturing town. The hills surrounding the town must have been beautiful at one point, with their wind eroded pinnacles of sand, but now they are criss-crossed by dynamite wires and punctuated by oil-refining stations. On the edge of the town we found Mamat-Jan and a roadblock. The Chinese had apparently been waiting for us to come through before blowing up the road. Mamat-Jan had only discovered their intentions on his arrival in Lenghu and, not having time to turn back and halt our caravan, he had shown uncharacteristic initiative by radioing through to the dynamiters, requesting them to wait until we had passed.

Within minutes of our turning off the main street, which boasted the only tree in town, into a shabby hostel, Lenghu's police had arrived *en force* at our door. Through Mamat-Jan, they told us that they were not happy with our sleeping arrangements since our hostel, like the rest of the town, was out of bounds to foreigners. When they suggested we book in at the expensive hotel designated for aliens at the other end of the main street, our hearts leapt. However, after negotiations, we were disappointed to find the police gave way a little too easily: having confiscated our passports until we left the following morning, they banned us from leaving the hostel instead. It was apparent that where money was involved Mr He was able to negotiate effectively on our behalf, whereas when it came to our truck or the camels, he was unable to do anything.

Incarcerated in our dusty hostel, we whiled away the hours with everything the tired traveller could ask for. First, great quantities of food from the restaurant, not only delicious but varied – mangetout and French beans with garlic and ginger, cabbage and courgette with baby spring onions and cumin, eggs, noodles with baby Chinese spinach, fresh tomatoes, bean sprouts and large wedges of fried potatoes, and, best of all, pork – our first meat for nearly three weeks. Second, a shelter from the freezing winds that whipped up at night. Third, a small grey fluffy kitten, and fourth a trashy English film they played in the restaurant. Meanwhile, Rozi and Egem, practising Muslims of sorts, were having a less enjoyable time: we saw them tiptoeing past a pair of piglets playing in the courtyard with a look of horror on their faces.

The next morning brought another luxury: a wash. We plunged our heads into two inches of heated water in the enamel bowls provided and tried to wash as many other limbs as possible. Having eaten several eggs each for breakfast, and freed now from our house arrest, we continued our journey along the rim of the Tsaidam basin with renewed purpose.

At the end of August we had received an e-mail from a John C. Z. Thomas of Knoxville, Tennessee, USA, who had chanced on our website and was planning to travel part of the Silk Road himself in September. We had replied immediately, extolling him to meet up with us, with pleas for Hershey's chocolate bars. He readily agreed.

He was scheduled to cross our path that day, and I had calculated that he would arrive during the morning. Panic set in very quickly when 'John See Zee' did not materialise and we climbed despondently back on to our camels. However, twenty minutes later two land cruisers appeared in clouds of dust, drawing to a halt on the road. Several elderly gentlemen climbed out. One approached at a gentle trot and asked, 'Are you guys English?'

'Yes,' we cried.

'Are you the girls …?'

'Are you John C. Z. of 2071 Rodeo Drive?'

'Yes!'

We jumped off our camels as Rozi and Egem looked on, astonished at this apparently chance meeting. Smallish, with thick glasses, a grey moustache and wearing a checked shirt and khaki shorts, John was exactly as we had envisaged during hours of desert talk. Introductions over, John C. Z. produced the promised Hershey bars. We thanked him profusely, then questioned his companions about their journey. We also discovered that

John C. Z. was an avid Peter Fleming fan. 'Oh yes, it's because of Peeder that I'm doing this route.' Sadly, time was pressing on, so we reluctantly said goodbye, wishing our American friends the best of luck with their journey and waving until they were out of sight. The only disappointment to the day was when we came to try the Hershey's bars: we greatly regretted not having asked for English chocolate.

As we headed towards the Nan Shan mountains the next day, we found out that the plateau we were crossing was at the mercy of sudden and unpredictable changes of weather. The autumn sun was still warming our faces when we were overtaken by an unheralded storm that blew up from the north east. The wind increased in strength, becoming too strong for us to walk against, so we sat on our camels, ineffectively wrapped in our quilts. It blew so ferociously that we could not even hear the roars of the camels, let alone each other talking.

Now we approached some hills, a range of snow-covered peaks to our left. At one point a small squall of snow blew across our path. We were becoming more and more unhappy at the thought of a night on the flat wind-blown plain when Mamat-Jan suddenly emerged from a desolate grey building ahead of us. Turning into the courtyard and tethering our camels to the wall, we found that Mr He, Mr Li and Mamat-Jan had swept the rubbish and dust from inside the building and arranged a basic table. We were greatly relieved to have escaped the cold and spent the evening trying to teach Mamat-Jan the rules of whist. Apparently the Chinese always play card games anti-clockwise, but having overcome this small handicap he managed to learn quickly. To add an incentive, we designated forfeits to the loser – the most popular being to kiss Mr Li. I was unfortunate enough to suffer a protracted run of poor cards.

The winds howled throughout the night but clear blue skies and a gentle breeze greeted us the next morning. The mountains looked deceptively close. As we approached a 12,600-foot pass, we were amazed to find we had still not reached it after two hours of walking. As Cable and French had observed, when embarking on their similar mission across the Gobi: 'The air is so clear that there is no perspective. Trees, walls and landmarks which appear to be but a mile distant are, in fact, half a day's journey away.'

Eventually we reached the mountains and began our ascent by a steep path. As we climbed higher scrubby bushes appeared, along with animals, the first evidence of wildlife we had seen for weeks. We spied enormous hares, as well as some mice and rabbits. Over the brink of the first hill three wild black ponies appeared, foraging for grass. But we were soon halted by two figures, swathed in black material from head to neck, with tiny holes cut for their eyes. They were riding very small ponies, which is perhaps why we were not frightened. Rozi shrank back in terror, but Egem, being braver, spoke to them in Kyrgyz. They were Kazakhs, apparently returning to collect their horses from the mountain pastures. They removed their masks to reveal rosy-cheeked faces and huge, childish smiles – apparently the masks were designed for protection against the sun. Rozi looked rather abashed when we started laughing.

The pass is known as the Dangjin Shankou pass, or Golden Mountain Mouth, because of its shimmering yellow slopes. The camels heaved and puffed their way to the top, skidding down the other side on their pads, as we gripped on nervously. We wound our way down through dry riverbeds, the end of the Argyn Shan range disgorging us into steep barren valleys inhabited by Kazakh *yurts* and flocks of sheep.

As the sun threw its last pink rays over the peaks, we drew into our camp for the night, which Mouse described, accurately, as a 'rubbish dump'. The back-up team had chosen the only crowded refuse tip in a hundred-mile radius. Too tired to protest, we untied the camels to forage for grass among the discarded shoes and bottles. A large group of people gathered to watch us eat, so we were relieved when Mamat-Jan informed us there was an empty garage we could sleep in. He also advised us to lock the door.

'Why?'

'There is a mad crazy man who lives opposite in the courtyard – you should be careful.'

But there was nothing to block the door with. It took a long time to fall asleep that night.

'Oh, thank goodness you're still here!' exclaimed Wic the next morning, as she found Mamat-Jan dozing on a rickety bed he had dragged into the yard. 'The mad man didn't get you?'

'Ah! But I saw him!'

Mouse, who was crossing the yard during this conversation, announced that she had seen the 'mad man' strolling near the truck and that he appeared perfectly harmless.

'Where's Mr Li?' continued Wic. He too had been sleeping outside, but both he and his bed had vanished. Wic had visions of Mr Li being carried off by a lunatic with wild hair and foaming mouth.

'He moved into room.'

'Was he also scared of the mad man?'

'No. I don't think so. He was cold.'

Wic chortled in disbelief.

At lunchtime we reached New Aksay, a rectangular town of bland, white blocks lining wide, empty streets. Mamat-Jan appeared from a shop and joined us for the rest of the afternoon. Wic was riding in front of him on Frankincense.

'Mamat-Jan,' she shouted over her shoulder, 'would you like to live here?' She pointed towards the lifeless, dusty streets of Aksay.

'No, I don't think so.'

'Why?'

'I think I have bored.'

'Yes, me too, and it's rather ugly.'

'You think so?'

'Well, yes, look at those white buildings. They may be quite clean but don't you think they're a bit dull?'

'No, I don't think so,' Mamat-Jan's favourite words.

'You see, Mamat-Jan, I find that type of building much more interesting to look at.'

He followed her finger to an old brick factory.

'You like that?'

'Yes, it's got character. You'll never find another building exactly the same.'

'I think you very strange,' Mamat-Jan replied while frowning at the factory.

When we arrived in camp we somehow began comparing our leg muscles.

'Oh dear, Mamat-Jan,' Wic said, prodding his thigh, 'we are much stronger than you.'

'OK, I will walk twenty miles tomorrow.'

'But I can't, Mamat-Jan,' cried Wic. 'My feet are covered in blisters.'

'Ah yes, me too. My foot-fingers are hurting very much.'

'Oh Mamat-Jan, I will miss our conversations very much.'

Finally, after almost three months in the Gobi, we gained a glimpse of the rolling sand dunes one associates with a desert. On one of our last mornings before Dunhuang they rose up to a golden height of sixty feet, undulating down to a riverbed. But their beauty was short-lived and we once more found ourselves transversing a pebbly plain.

In Dunhuang our back-up team were to be replaced by a new team. To mark our last evening together, Mamat-Jan produced a bottle of Chinese red wine while we offered them some of our Cock o' the North whisky liqueur. Before sleeping we implored Mamat-Jan to join us. 'Tell us about your home, we love hearing stories about your family and Kashgar.'

'Kashgar is the prefecture with 300,000 populations. There are eleven counties in the prefecture and Kashgar county is the largest ...'

'Uh, Mamat-Jan, could you add a little more spice?'

'Spices? In the market?'

'No, we meant maybe you could tell a more personal story.'

Mamat-Jan began to discourse further on the government departments. We relented and plied him with questions about 'China today'. But sadly Mamat-Jan's knowledge was limited to propaganda.

'Were your parents affected by the Cultural Revolution?'

'No, I don't think so. But some of their friends were killed by Tibetan bandits.'

We tried to explain that, from our perspective, the Tibetans had been cruelly abused by the Chinese, but the idea was incomprehensible to him. He told us he rued the dawn of socialism in China. 'Under communism it was much better – people didn't have to pay for hospitals,' he observed profoundly, perhaps in regretful reference to our battle with Mr He. After that, we let Mamat-Jan go to sleep and lay looking at the clear desert stars.

We woke up the next morning to find Mr Li in a very jovial mood, talking loudly and even laughing with Mamat-Jan. This was the first occasion on which we had seen him smile and he showed no embarrassment in revealing how happy he was that this was to be the last leg of our journey together. He even became quite tactile, grabbing Lucy's shoulders animatedly for a photograph. Whatever their faults, the back-up team had indeed endured extremely tough conditions for the last three months. We suspected Mr Ma had given them no intimation of what lay ahead of them and they could not be held fully accountable for all the problems we had encountered. None the less, we were equally excited about their imminent departure.

Approaching Dunhuang, we could hardly contain our impatience. Suddenly we saw our truck – it had previously overtaken us – with a smaller vehicle on its trail. This caused great disappointment because Mr Ma had promised us that an 'Italian joint venture' truck would accompany us for the rest of our journey. This one's chassis was hung perhaps even lower than that of our first truck and there were gaping holes visible in its tarpaulin roof. Our new driver and guide sprung out and we were introduced. The driver, who was huge, immediately attracted Lucy's attention for being the first person in China to be taller than her. Wearing a baseball cap over shoulder-length hair, he obviously considered himself very attractive as he swaggered towards us and graciously shook our hands.

'This is Mr Hor,' said Mamat-Jan, as we tried not to smile at this unfortunate name. 'It means "fire".'

'This is Jason,' he continued, as the guide, looking very serious and conscientious, stepped forward. (The Chinese have a strange custom of picking European names, to use when talking to 'forners'.)

Then they climbed back into their 'driving chamber', as Jason referred to the cab of the truck, and headed towards Dunhuang. Mr He and Mr Li grimaced at us grotesquely from their own driving chamber and accelerated violently, clearly overjoyed to be travelling their final few miles.

At last our impatience was satisfied and we found ourselves in the outskirts of Dunhuang. We wound our way through small streets before emerging in front of a large modern hotel. Outside, Jason stood looking very formal in his green army trousers, then ushered us in. The hotel struck us as paradise after the desert. We had baths, mini-bars, fluffy white towels, telephones and televisions, each an unsurpassable luxury, although the televisions apparently did not work on Tuesdays.

Dunhuang is famed for its Mogao caves – 'the Caves of a Thousand Buddhas' – dug high up in a cliff that rises dramatically out of the desert some fifteen miles outside the oasis. The caves were traditionally a stopping point for all Silk Road travellers. Those entering the desert would come here to pray for a safe journey, while those leaving would come to thank the gods for a safe delivery. In 1907 the caves yielded up innumerable treasured manuscripts to Sir Aurel Stein when he managed to induce the wary Daoist Abbot Wang, self-appointed guardian of the library, to part with some of its thousands of manuscripts. Thus the British Library is now home to, among other texts found here, the Diamond Sutra – the oldest known printed book in the world.

Jason accompanied us on our visit to the caves the following day. As we entered them by a network of ladders and scaffolding that line the front of the cliff, I wondered if the Silk Road pilgrims would have used the same approach. The small wooden doors of the caves gave no intimation of what lay behind them. As we stooped under their low beams we were astonished to discover vivid frescoes emerging in the light of our torches. Thousands of exquisite representations of Buddha lined the walls, painted in mineral colours of green, red, turquoise, black, rust and blue. Portrayed in the past, present and future, the earlier depictions of Buddha show him with Indian features, while later ones give him more rounded Chinese characteristics, as the influence of India waned along the Silk Road.

Some of the caves possess an anteroom, divided from the shrine of the inner cave by a corridor. In one such corridor we found several terrifying guardians – giant wooden monsters, with fanged mouths and crossed arms, crushing devils beneath their webbed feet – and in between the legs of one of these we spied a diminutive figure of Mr Tao, the tenth century patron of that particular cave. Inside the shrine we found that the golden faces of the Buddhas had turned black but the turquoises and navy blue in a frieze of *asparas*, or flying angels, remained as vibrant as ever. Interestingly, these angels possessed ribbons instead of the Christian wings.

As we were passing through one cave Mouse spotted a primitively drawn human face and four-legged beast. Our guide's reply to her enquiry was curt: 'Tourist vandals.' 'Tourist vandals, when?' Not turning his head, he replied decisively, 'In the Qing dynasty.' Whenever a statue was missing or a face damaged he informed us it was the fault of 'the American people', or even that it had been 'stolen by the American people'. By 'American' we inferred he was referring to anybody non-Chinese. At one point we attempted to intimate that the Chinese had had their own iconoclasts, above all in recent times, but we received icily blank stares and decided not to pursue this antagonistic course further.

Staggered to think that Silk Road pilgrims and merchants had offered thanks and prayers at these caves for over two millennia, we too made our own tributes for a successful skirting of the Taklamakan desert.

Back in Dunhuang we headed for Shirley's, a western café where we hoped to find 'forners'. After three months in the desert we were desperate to meet people we could talk to normally, but we were disappointed to find ourselves alone, save for two Chinese middle-aged men, who showed no interest in anything except their food.

A day later we were due to leave for our final leg of the journey – a two-month stretch through China proper to Xian, the traditional terminus of the Silk Road. While Wic and I were enjoying a last breakfast in Shirley's, Mouse and Lucy had advanced into yet another battle with Mr He. Their request for a photocopy of the hospital receipt had met with outrage from Mr He, who still refused to accept that our satellite telephone bill had redressed the balance of debts. Eventually he squelched off in his flip-flops, the vital document still firmly wedged in his bulging wallet. There was absolutely nothing we could do, and Lucy and Mouse were obliged to concede defeat.

After lunch we said goodbye to the back-up team, who were heading back to Kashgar. We all agreed with Wic when she wrote, 'In all honesty, I felt no sadness at all when saying goodbye to Mr He and Mr Li, and I know the feeling was mutual,' although we had been touched over the last week to see that Rozi and Egem's animosity towards us had been only temporary and they had become very helpful once more. However, when we asked Mamat-Jan whether Mr He and Mr Li would miss us, he hesitated. Mouse filled the embarrassing pause with, 'No, I don't think so,' as Mamat-Jan, seemingly oblivious to our teasing, remained deep in thought before finally agreeing with us. 'No, I don't think so, too,' he answered, breaking into nervous giggles.

Our discrimination showed, perhaps a little too much, in our farewell presents, which thankfully they did not open in front of us. Mr He and Mr Li received DHL T-shirts. Egem had shown intense interest in our Everyman Koran, despite being illiterate, so we presented him with this as well as a pair of walking boots, (the latter was not a great act of generosity because he had borrowed them for the previous two months and they now smelled particularly unpleasant). Rozi also received a pair of boots and a waterproof jacket for which he had shown a penchant. Mamat-Jan, our favourite, was given a grey cashmere jumper and abridged versions of *The Prisoner of Zenda* and *The Thirty-Nine Steps* in English. Wic observed that she 'wanted to give the latter three one enormous hug, they had all done a fantastic job. However, for Mouse and Alex's own personal safety we resorted to formal handshakes as we stepped back into the hotel.' Only now did we realise how fond of them we had grown, despite the many low points we had suffered together in the desert. Now they were going on their separate ways and we would never see them again.

10

The black Gobi

WE WERE EXCITED to be leaving the Taklamakan firmly behind us, although it was only to be replaced by a finger of desert that joins it with the Gobi. This is known as the Kara Gobi, where small rough-shaped, yet burnished, black stones cover the surface of the earth, hence the name. Marco Polo wrote of this section of our journey: 'On leaving … [Dunhuang] … you ride ten days between north-east and east, and in all that way you find no human dwelling, or next to none, so that there is nothing for our book to speak of.' This remains pretty well the case today, the landscape never being more than a flat stretch of monotonous gravel, which presents no obstacle to the winds that come howling in from the Gobi Desert.

On the morning of our departure we met Mr Shu and Mr Wu, our new camel drivers. They were cherubic looking, with round faces that rarely stopped smiling, but we soon discovered that they had never ridden a camel before, only driven them in front of a plough. Unable to steer the camels, they were forced to walk on foot all day, so we did the same, in order to spare them unnecessary embarrassment. Occasionally, we would glance surreptitiously behind us to see how they were faring and found them smiling away in their matching red caps. At the end of their first day they hobbled around the camp, nursing their bruised feet, having worn only canvas slippers. We expressed our concern to Jason but he proudly dismissed our fears, saying they would quickly adapt.

The winds were blowing so strongly the next day, increasing in ferocity by the minute, that Mr Shu and Mr Wu did indeed make a valiant attempt to ride. We were grateful for the layer of black stones on the ground because they prevented the winds from blowing up the sand. It was nevertheless impossible to walk, as each step became a fight against an invisible force. Riding on the camels was not much more comfortable: books could not be opened and we could not hear each other speak as the wind howled in our ears. It continued all day without remission, so we were overjoyed when, despite Marco Polo's ominous observations, Fire and Jason found as our resting place for the night a cluster of adobe houses, built with a double layer of walls to keep out the incessant winds, and used by road workers. The latter slept on *kangs*, raised brick beds, heated from underneath by coal and wood, while we laid our mats out in their garage.

We reached Anxi, a small unprepossessing town, after four days' journey from Dunhuang. Famed as the windiest place in China, it appeared to be another 'one-storey' town with no distinguishing features or landmarks. It would have been forgettable were it not for one incident that happened there. As we made our way down the main street the camel train suddenly and inexplicably lost control. The Roarer, as our noisy camel had been christened, leapt out into the middle of the road, tugging the other camels behind him. Frankincense, second in line, was startled and began to buck. Mouse lost her balance and started slipping round the side of her saddle. Catching sight of her out of the corner of his eye, Frankincense bucked even more vigorously, sending Mouse flying on to the hard tarmac.

A huge crowd of spectators immediately gathered round and we only just prevented them from carrying Mouse off to the local hospital. Luckily, she was able to stand after a few apprehensive minutes, her only injury a large bruise on her leg. Now three of the camels, who had snapped their ropes, were proving very reluctant to be caught again, so we were faced with the awkward task of reaching their nose-pegs in order to re-attach the ropes. Standing at seven feet, Goliath, our other latest addition along with the Roarer, was particularly awkward, for he knew that by sticking his nose in the air he would put the peg well out of reach. Mr Shu and Mr Wu, lacking the aggressive manner of Rozi and Egem, spent ages gently stroking the camel's neck until they got within inches of his nose-peg, only to receive a vicious spitting. The next step was to draw up a tricycle taxi alongside the difficult animal. Mr Shu and Mr Wu clambered up on to the cart and attempted to reach the nose-peg from there. Goliath, unfortunately, just stuck his nose further into the air.

At least half an hour later the situation was no less embarrassing: the camel drivers were still hopping up and down from their precarious position in the tricycle cart making wild swipes at the unattainable nose-peg.

Then the crowd suddenly fell silent and parted down the middle. In Wic's words, 'The sky (almost) darkened and I (almost) heard an almighty clap of thunder ... striding (in slow motion) through the mass of on-lookers came FIRE! Woosh!' Acknowledging us with a nod, Mr Hor coolly wrestled the spitting camel to the ground, retied his rope and disappeared back into his 'driving chamber'. The crowd cheered as the truck slowly made its way down the street. (We were always surprised that Fire, despite his 'suave' exterior, drove with incredible caution.)

The day was longer than usual – twenty-seven miles and still windy – but we found the extra distance was well worth the effort because it meant we could stay the night in what Jason termed a 'cott'.

Not wanting to question his English on only his fourth day, we accepted his 'cott' for the time being, only realising on arrival at our destination what he meant.

'Oh, a court!' Lucy exclaimed, as we walked into a very clean and empty courtyard, similar to the road workers' stations.

'Yes, a cott!' Jason told us proudly.

This was an ideal place for us to set up camp as it offered at least some protection against the constant wind. An hour later we were feasting on Fire's cooking, which was exceptionally good. Each evening he prepared several dishes of fried meat and vegetables, often with delicious spices and pieces of fresh ginger, which we ate with steamed rice. We were introduced to the owner of the 'cott' who was also the 'director' of a spirit factory that produces rice wine. Later he announced that he would like to present us with a bottle of his product.

'Oh, thank you,' we pronounced nervously, for our previous experiences had made us more than a little wary of this potent alcohol (in Wic's opinion 'about as appealing as a shot of four-star'). However, there was little we could do. The diminutive owner soon rejoined us with all his family and friends, including one Chinese lady who had dressed up in a silky black-tie outfit. As they gathered around our small table and bombarded us with questions, suddenly, through the gate of the 'cott', appeared a film crew. A powerful strobe light was shone into our faces, illuminating the entire courtyard, as a camera started to roll. Jason explained that they had decided to take advantage of this unforeseen opportunity to make an advertisement. The director presented us each with a bottle of the rice wine, then staged four lengthy handshakes, as statesmen do before the world's media. Next he poured out the liquid into large bowls and raised his for a toast.

'Cheers!' we all shouted, before draining the liquid and turning to the camera for a final 'satisfied look' shot. Then, thankfully, the light went out. As we sat down our attention was drawn to the box in which our wine had been presented. On the front was a picture of a very vertical and robust-looking cactus, while on the back, written in English, was a brief introduction to the wine, whose merits included that of 'reviving flagging body parts'. It appeared that we may inadvertently soon be promoting the benefits of Gobi Viagra across the billboards of China.

The camels had been persuaded to wear their shoes over the past month, despite their initial reluctance. We were glad to find that their blisters were beginning to disappear, so no longer felt anxious about covering up to twenty-five miles each day. Four days after leaving Dunhuang, we decided to change the worn-out shoes for new ones that we had been storing in the truck since Charchan. We looked everywhere before coming to the frustrating conclusion that Mr He must have taken them back to Xinjiang with him. We were furious to discover this legacy of his pettiness but there was nothing we could do until we reached the next town.

The next day we passed an ancient adobe fort. We tried to peep inside its little museum, but our view was obstructed by a sea of Chinese faces. They obviously did not receive enough visitors to justify their large staff, so we felt guilty as we sloped off without even looking round. (We did not have any money and Mr Shu and Mr Wu were equally penniless.) However, later that evening, Jason told us the story of the fort. Apparently a Chinese emperor, having dreamed about a silver mountain and a solitary tree with a golden crown hanging on its branches, had commanded one of his generals and his son to find the spot and build a magnificent palace on it. The general settled on this particular place because the snow-capped peaks of the South mountains, which were visible from here, looked silver in the desert haze, while he found a single tree growing nearby with a straw hat hanging on its branches, which he rather liberally interpreted as the 'golden crown'. But the general, knowing that the Emperor was unlikely to ever visit this remote spot, decided to exploit the situation. He took most of the emperor's money for himself and built a very modest fort. One day another general who was passing by thought he would stop at the fort. When he told the Emperor how small it was, the Emperor was so enraged that he killed both the general and his son and made their skin into drums. These engaging relics are said to be in the small museum that we had seen.

That night we began our usual routine of washing in a bucket of water behind one side of the truck when we realised that our camp was surrounded by strangers whose truck headlights were embarrassingly close. We then saw them begin to examine Neurotic, our youngest camel, whom we had never ridden because of her sore feet. We had agreed earlier with Jason that it would be a good idea to exchange Neurotic for a new camel and these people were apparently interested in buying her for breeding. After some quick negotiating she was sold for the sum of five hundred yuan, equivalent to forty pounds, and led off. It was sad to see her disappearing into the dark after three months with our caravan, but Jason reassured us that the rutting season was not until January, so she would have a few months' rest before her duties began. We were now down to six camels, with none to spare. In addition, only the two new camels we had acquired in Simianqang were entirely healthy, the others showing increasing signs of fatigue.

The journey between Anxi and Jiayugan, our next resting place, was a six-day leg across the last section of the Black Gobi with only two brief respites from the monotonous and windy desert landscape. The first of these was Yumen, a small oasis halfway between these two towns. As we approached it, greenery enveloped us. Women in brightly coloured headscarves picked apples and pears in the orchards, oxen-led ploughs tilled the dry earth and small boys laid out maize cobs to dry, in anticipation of winter. The winds of the previous few days was superseded by the ripening heat of the sun. We did not explore Yumen properly, however. By now we all shared an excited anticipation of our journey's end, and our conversations were focused on England and what we would do on our return.

After a few miles of civilisation, we returned once again to the 'nothingness' of the Gobi, where we followed a railway line, busy with freight and passenger trains. The only other object to catch our eye was a squat, well-rounded camel that bounced along the edge of the railway track, attached by a rope to the back of a small tractor. Having overtaken us, it would carry on for a few miles before being allowed to stop and graze. Then it would set off again, trotting in a steady rhythm with its head held high and its round body swinging from side to side as it overtook us once more. Every time we passed it Frankincense became wildly overexcited, skipping around with his admiring eyes fixed firmly on this voluptuous beast. Mouse, on the other hand, had both eyes fixed firmly on the frayed rope straining from his lop-sided nose-peg. We presumed that this passing camel was a female on heat, but later discovered that it was in fact a castrated male that had rolled in a pile of fresh dung and whose enticing fragrance attracted Frankincense.

For a few weeks Wic had suspected that DHL was pregnant – her stomach had blown out, despite no increase in her feed. In addition, her feet were very sore and the shoes did not seem to be offering her enough protection against blisters. Consequently, we had decided to try and exchange her. This providential meeting with the voluptuous camel provided us with the opportunity we had been looking for, so Jason entered into negotiations with its owner. He assented, accepting DHL and a sum of yuan in exchange for his camel, which we christened Ben after a friend of ours in London.

Ben was secured to the back of one of our camel trains and we set off once more. Seeing her friends leave, DHL desperately tried to follow, but the bush she was attached to would not relent and she ran round in circles instead. Her new owner looked kind and knowledgeable (he had adroitly removed a cluster of ticks from Meredith-Jones' stomach) and her new life would certainly be less strenuous. As we looked back, we saw her being tied to the tractor and then jog down a dusty track.

The second oasis we encountered between Anxi and Jiayuguan was Chikhin Pu, pronounced, more respectably, 'Churjin Pu'. Trees once more lined the road; ponies, camels and mules grazed in fields of stubble and the maize harvest was in full progress, although unfortunately this late in the season the corn was suitable only for animal feed. Chikhin Pu was followed closely by a tiny village called 'Clear Water', named after its stream, out of which we drank. We found our camp, nine miles further on, in front of a clump of beautiful autumnal trees of sand jujube, or 'desert dates', which have a very bitter fruit. I remembered we had eaten some of these before, at Merv, over six months ago, and my mind was cast back to that far-off time.

From here it was one short stage to the town of Jiayugan and 'China proper'. Jiayugan, which stands on the border between China and her Turkic neighbours, boasts a great adobe fort as well as the most westerly section of the Great Wall. The last few miles to the town took us over the black sands of the previous ten days, with the fort looming large from afar. It was easy to imagine how welcoming this sight must have been to Chinese soldiers, merchants and travellers returning to their homeland from the land of the 'hideous barbarians'. This fort, which dates from the Ming dynasty and stands strategically in a narrow bottleneck between two mountain ranges, was used in defence against the marauding Huns north of the Tarim basin. It was occupied, as a small town, until the 1930s, when General Ma's followers swept through it, decimating the population.

We entered the fort by the West Gate, or 'Travellers' Gate'. In front of the 12-inch thick studded wooden door stands a large mound of earth, blocking the entrance from desert demons and devils, who apparently were considered too stupid to negotiate such an obstacle. The fort encloses an enormous area and its walls stretched up high and windowless to the cerulean sky above. It is made up of two enclosures: outer and inner. The former would have been reserved for travellers and traders but we found it populated only by ponies and a dishevelled camel, used for tourists' photo shoots. Before entering the inner enclosure we passed a small temple, decorated with a red papier-mâché Buddha, horses and warriors. In the centre was a small open courtyard where we found a wizened old man consuming a bowl of noodles and an incense stand emitting pungent vapours in a slow-rising plume of greenish smoke. We headed into the heart of the fort, passing through an arch in the fortified inner walls. These were at least ten feet thick, and thirty feet high, surmounted by fifty-foot high towers with flying eaves – the whole effect was very belittling. Having climbed a steep ramp up on to the walls, we walked around the ramparts, with the Gobi stretching out in front of us and the 'Black' Mountains rising imperiously to our left. It was a scene that could not have changed for hundreds of years.

The week of 1 October saw massive celebrations throughout China for the fiftieth anniversary of the People's Republic of China. The festivities around here, however, were confined to the domination of the thirty or so national television channels by the glitzy ceremonies taking place in Beijing, as well as several different soap operas based around the life and endless good deeds of the benevolent and compassionate Chairman Mao. Lucy spent our night in Jiayugan's hotel watching them, gripped by a strange fascination.

Jiayugan also marked our departure, at last, from the monotonous landscape of the desert and the beginning of the fertile Hexi Corridor, with its endless villages. This strip of land, sandwiched between two mountain ranges, was famous in days of old as a breeding ground for the 'heavenly horses' brought back from the Ferghana valley to China in 138 BC. The villages differed from those of Xinjiang in certain characteristics: pointed eaves adorned every building and we no longer saw Uighur people or mosques but only Chinese faces. However, essentially the villages were of a similar agricultural nature: adobe houses, with piles of straw heaped on their roofs, were fronted by tiny courtyards full of people and animals.

The predominant feature of the first village was maize. It was everywhere, on the ground and on the roofs, laid out in giant circles, to dry in the autumn sun. Its beautiful golden colour accentuated the autumnal poplar leaves that lined every street. Everybody we encountered was working with it – Jason told us that this was the principal maize-producing area for the whole of China. Overburdened tractor trailers filled the roads, carrying maize plants to threshing floors where the cobs were cut off the stalks and laid out in neat patterns. Next they were de-corned, then, once this had been done, columns of maize were to be seen flying into the air as the women patiently separated the maize from the dust, leaving mounds of corn ready for packaging. Finally, the maize stalks were collected into vast bundles, tied up into sheaves and lined against the walls, roofs and courtyards of the houses, to be used as winter fuel. In the fields oxen steadily ploughed the stubble back into the earth with one-furrowed ploughs while donkeys, hitched up to carts ready to gather in the autumn fruits, looked on. From the maize villages we passed to those where only onions were harvested, their pungent odour permeating everything. (In China, rural areas are allocated certain crops and given a quota for each year.) I remember at this time walking with Wic on our own one day and her saying, 'It's such a pity we can't stop and spend more time in these places.' I agreed – it was sometimes frustrating to have to keep moving and I would have liked to have had more rest days in China. Wic and I also had less desire to return home than Mouse or Lucy and I think we both felt a bit lost about what we would do on our return.

We tried to keep off the main road that sweeps down the Hexi Corridor, but occasionally the intensive cultivation forced us on to the tarmac. A week after leaving Jiaguyan we were walking ahead of the camels when a tiny open van drew past us with two gigantic camels in the back. Frankincense and Meredith-Jones, two of our three original camels, had both begun stumbling over the last few days, so yet again we had decided to acquire new animals. Jason and Fire told us that good camels were only to be found in villages nearer the mountains, and had left us that morning to investigate. We were pleased to discover that these two healthy animals were intended for us.

They were beautiful specimens, indeed. One had especially pert humps and soft coat; Fire was clearly infatuated. 'It's a model,' he said, stroking it gently. Consequently, this camel became known as 'The Model' while her less fortunate companion became 'The Model's Friend'. Despite her looks, The Model was prey to the unfortunate habit of tripping as she walked, but The Model's Friend was an invaluable addition to the caravan, since she headed the line without needing anything but vocal encouragement.

Marco Polo passed through the Hexi Corridor on his way from Italy to Karakoram, seat of the Mongol khans. It is claimed that Kublai Khan, founder of the Mongol Yuan dynasty in China and grandson of Genghis, was born in Zhangye, our next stopping place. En route to Karokoram Marco Polo visited the town (which he called Campichu), noting 'the great idols … which … lie at length'. We arrived there to find that the whole city was suffering from a power cut. But we were still able to visit the Temple of the Sleeping Buddha, one of the town's few mediaeval remains, housing China's largest reclining Buddha, at 112 feet long. Although lying down, his eyes were open and he did not look very peaceful. It was depressing to walk around later and find the ubiquitous white-tiled buildings in the place of wooden pagodas. Even the town's bell tower had been spoiled, with gaudy nylon flags draped over it.

As we left Zhangye, the temperatures suddenly dropped, bringing with them an extraordinary clarity in the air. The mountains enclosing the Hexi Corridor on both sides now became distinct forms, their snowline changing daily. One night, Jason and Fire unwisely chose to camp at the top of a small pass. The sun had dipped behind the mountains and it was freezing. We huddled against the truck and woke up with a layer of frost on our sleeping-bags and the wind whipping up our belongings.

On the other side of this pass we found a crowd of mules and donkeys. There were also sheep tended by shepherds dressed in long sheepskin capes, tied with string around the neck, who looked like huge white stag beetles standing on their hind legs. The snow clouds of the morning cleared to let the sun light up the adobe houses and piles of hay and maize. The two big camels, Roarer and Goliath, had struggled up the mountain pass, breaking their nose-pegs several times, so we had become worried that they were on the brink of collapse. However, they recovered on the journey down, even able to trot a little as we entered the school where we had been invited to camp for the night. Here we were ushered into the headmaster's office, plastered with posters of Mao, but ate our supper outside in the playground, watched by an audience of children and their parents. They gaped at us, apparently unable to believe that we ate Chinese food.

It was becoming colder all the time. We were waking up in the mornings to find our water cylinders frozen with several inches of ice. Too lazy to put up our tents, however, we continued to sleep outside, often waking up with a thin layer of snow on everything. But the days, which were beautiful and sunny, passed quickly as we walked and rode through the villages. One night we met two German boys who were cycling from Germany to Beijing and invited them to camp with us. It was fun to talk to some Westerners after such a long time; however, Jason and Fire became extremely agitated. They said they could be 'punished' by the police if they were found with two extra foreigners in their camp. We explained that the Germans had all the proper documents to be travelling through China, but to no avail. Jason told us that because they were not detailed on our documents we could incur a heavy fine.

Jason also explained to us that the Chinese government constantly instils a distrust of foreigners in its people. This did not however temper their curiosity. Wherever we camped, we attracted a crowd of people, young and old, even in the middle of nowhere. Brightly clad, grubby children pressed each other forward until we were hemmed in on all sides by the throng (the one child per family policy seemed not to apply here). Old women with broken and bound miniature feet tottered uncomfortably on the fringes, commanding respect by brandishing battered walking sticks. They must have all been well over fifty, since it was on Mao's assumption of power in 1949 that foot-binding was banned. Laughing and pointing, these crowds seemed unperturbed by our inability to respond and would even lean over us to interfere in our card games. Once they had watched us unload the camels, write, eat and read, the entertainment moved to the next scene: preparing for bed. They politely stepped back a few paces, as if heading for home, before curiosity won them over and once more they peered at us rolling out our mats and sleeping bags before finally undressing.

We now began to feed the camels double rations of maize balls, Jason being far more receptive to our pleas than either Mr He or Mamat-Jan. But Roarer suddenly refused to eat anything and wailed more plaintively than ever, flailing spit over everything. Its pungent odour would linger for days on our clothes, so we all fought not to ride on the camel in front of him. Fire's attachment to The Model meant that he had forbidden us from riding her. We had initially humoured his infatuation, but now we insisted that The Model should no longer be shown such preferential treatment, and Roarer was allowed to rest at the back of the train.

The next town we passed through was Wuwei, another Silk Road posting point that had been destroyed by the Chinese during the Cultural Revolution. We rode quickly on, pleased to leave the traffic and fumes for more adobe villages. The countryside was becoming more and more densely populated. Every piece of land was meticulously cultivated regardless of size, shape, gradient or soil. Fields clung to the mountainsides, snaking their way in long thin stripes up narrow sheer-sided ravines. When travelling off the road we had to edge our way, in line, between carefully defined fields on tiny ridges. Our clumsy feet were not suited to this delicate task and we constantly stumbled into the mud. Until recently, we had been surrounded by ploughed fields, etching their immaculate stripes of varying browns, oranges and yellows into the landscape. With the drop in altitude, however, tiny shoots of emerald green winter wheat had begun to appear, making a stunning contrast to the stark mountains that surrounded them. This first real expanse of green we had seen since the verdant pastures of Kyrgyzstan made a welcome change.

On our first night outside Wuwei we camped next to a field of radishes. As we ate our supper, we asked Jason about communism. He told us that he considered the Cultural Revolution the most shameful part of Chinese history. His father, a teacher, had been forced to become a peasant for five years, after leaving the army, and Jason had not been able to go to school until he was eight. Lucy then changed the conversation by asking about discos in Lanzhou, perhaps, we teased her, in the hope of luring Fire on to the dance floor. Jason told us he did not like dancing, but went on to say that his teacher had told him he must learn to dance if he wanted to work in tourism. Consequently he had gone to great pains to learn both the tango and the foxtrot. He began to dance a very solemn tango across the camp, which made us laugh for hours. There was something touching about Jason; he was so earnest and showed such reverence towards Fire, who really did not deserve this attention. Several times Jason dejectedly told us that he did not have a girlfriend, while Fire had many beautiful girls chasing him.

That evening a vet came to look at Roarer and prescribed a sticky brown medicine. He said there was something wrong with his stomach, probably from eating bad grass. The next few days were spent climbing up towards the Wu Shao Ling pass, 9,860 feet high, with Roarer suffering more and more as the altitude increased. We began our ascent from a village that had evidently been allocated a huge cabbage quota by the government. Everybody, young and old, was helping to collect in the cabbage harvest that surrounded their homes for miles around. The heart of the cabbage was sliced from its dark outer leaves, then flung along a long chain of hands until it landed on a small tractor. These piles of cabbage hearts towered eight feet high, while the outer leaves were collected into bundles for animal fodder. As our path continued on up the hills we noticed an enormous sloping wall to our left. It was not until we had reached a point where it dipped in height that we realised it was a dam. On the other side lay a big reservoir, its bright water a still reflection of the hills that rose up from it on all sides. After months of parched desert and highly cultivated land, we appreciated such a large body of water. Having stood for a while admiring the reservoir's calm expanse, we moved on.

As we rounded a twist in the road we were confronted by another scene of activity. There sat several huge stacks of straw. A number of labourers were busy working on the harvest and in front of us an old man was standing in the middle of a large circle of flattened straw. Around him two mules were striding round in wide circles, dragging rollers behind them. Further up the road men and women were hurling the straw high into the air with pitchforks, sending a shower of dust over everything. One man was balanced on top of a ten-foot heap of straw piled into a small tractor cart. Below him, another man was tossing up the straw with mighty swings from a pitchfork. The man at the top received a showering each time, before padding it down.

The road turned and our truck came into sight again, thankfully. It was parked a good distance from a cluster of bee hives guarded by a young man. Although we had left the camels only a couple of miles behind us, it took them a good hour to reach camp. Roarer was in a bad way, and had refused to go any further at one point. Mr Wu and Mr Shu removed his saddle and put it on Frankincense, whom we had been resting, and with a lot of effort had dragged the camels up the hill to the camp.

As the other camels grazed, Roarer just stood immobile, not moving an inch from the spot where he had halted. In the morning he had shown some signs of recovery from his diagnosed stomach problem, but just before sunset Wic had noticed that his eyes had shut and tears were falling from them. Now he was lying down, a pitiful sight. Mr Wu and Mr Shu gave him a small heap of grass, which he attempted to eat, but even that seemed too much exertion. Eventually we covered him in a couple of blankets and hoped that a night's rest might help him.

Mouse and Lucy, in the meantime, had pulled out a tent from the back of the truck, shaking off the dust and sand. Even the zips were stiff, after months of disuse, but Fire came to the rescue with his vegetable oil. Wic and I were too lazy to put up ours but as we were rolling out our mats Jason asked us whether we would like to use his and Fire's tent.

'Why don't you want to use it?'

'We must stay up all night to guard the camp from backward people.'

We guessed he was referring to the beekeeper, who had begged us for some rice wine.

The next morning we saw that Roarer had managed to eat all his grass during the night and his eyes had opened a little. Having set off to climb the pass, we found Fire and Jason waiting for us at the peak, an hour later.

'Don't take any photos and stay on the road. This is mitary control zoh!' ordered Jason.

As the tail of the truck crept around the corner we took to the hills: the other three across the rolling plains while I scaled a ridge high above the road. I managed to get deep inside the hills, far away from any habitation, where suddenly it felt like a different world. Alone for five hours, climbing up and down the steep slopes, with panoramic views of a wild and uncultivated landscape, I felt a sense of freedom that I had not experienced since we left the desert. Finally dropping back down to the road, I found the others waiting on the side of the road for the camels. Our camp that night was in a birch grove. It made a picturesque scene, as the camels moved around slowly, munching through the autumnal branches. We woke up to find it as beautiful by sunrise as by sunset, with the morning sun glancing off a stream and lighting up the golden leaves.

A couple of days later we reached Lanzhou, our first resting point for twenty-one consecutive days. To our disappointment we found a large, grim, industrial city, which we approached by the busy principal road that enters it from the west. Peter Fleming, in contrast, had seen 'the pagodas and machicolations of a great walled city' when he was there in 1935. Jason had found a 'folk village' on the outskirts, where the camels would stay while we spent a couple of nights in one of Lanzhou's hotels. On arrival, Jason told us with great importance that two national television companies wanted to interview us and had invited us to join them for dinner. They had chosen the folk village's restaurant as their location, eager to film us with our camels. We agreed before enjoying baths and an all too brief rest on the soft hotel beds.

11

The end of the road

WE LEFT LANZHOU for the terraced hills, wiggling our way over the ploughed landscape. Despite his day's rest, Roarer showed even greater signs of exhaustion. It became painful to watch him. His neck was outstretched, his rope taut and his nose-peg tugged at his nostril with every sluggish step. Finally, the rope snapped and a feeble 'roar' told us that he could carry on no more. It was decided that Mouse and Wic should wait with Roarer while Lucy and I continued with the other camels. (Mouse told us later that Jason had reluctantly agreed to her demand to sell or exchange Roarer and had then driven on to send Mr Shu back to collect the poor animal. It had taken him two hours to cover the few miles to camp, as Roarer had repeatedly stopped and tried to lie down.)

We camped in front of a solitary hut that belonged to a quiet, elderly man with two fat pigs, several plump chickens and a small, yapping dog. It was the first evening for a couple of months that we had to entertain no audience. The next morning we ate a hurried breakfast of tea and boiled eggs before persuading Jason to leave Roarer with the old man. He was reluctant because the old man would only agree to pay a minimal sum of money for him – so small that Jason was too ashamed to tell us exactly how much. And so we left the ailing Roarer behind, having handed over his stomach medicine to the old man. We hoped he would recover to experience a less strenuous life than in our caravan.

By now it was the end of October, and we regularly awoke to a crisp layer of frost, or snow, on our bivvy bags. The days were spent climbing up and down the terraced hills. It was sometimes difficult to differentiate the villages from the hills from which they seemed to grow, for they were exactly the same brown colour. Occasionally we would pass an old man sitting outside a mud building, surrounded by vast piles of maize while smoking a loosely rolled cigarette through a clay pipe. Husbands and wives worked alongside each other, guiding their two-donkey ploughs, only stopping briefly to stare at us. Stacks of maize stalks lined the fields, often hiding a family of hungry donkeys behind their huge bulks.

Now it was becoming colder and colder riding on the camels, even when the sun came out, so we walked as much as possible. One evening we passed through a tiny cluster of adobe houses, taking a path that cut through the hillside and led us into a courtyard. A woman stared at us in amazement, putting down her broom to get a better look. The courtyard, its floor swept of every straw, was full of beautifully neat haycocks. Each animal had its individual pen and her house looked very cosy, nestling in the hillside. The people obviously took great pride in keeping their houses clean, giving them the appearance of well-ordered dolls' houses. The woman pointed us in the right direction for our camp, which was in the courtyard of another house. Behind it was a pigpen, housing a piglet the size of a rat that darted in and out of a tiny bricked up hole. Our mess-tent had broken long ago but only now did we begin to suffer from its absence. We ate our supper outside as quickly as possible before huddling into our sleeping bags.

On 2 November Wic wrote in her diary:

> It's hard to believe we are now so close to the end. Only two weeks to go. In a way, I find this concept a hundred times more difficult to cope with than when we set out at the beginning, knowing we had eight or nine months ahead of us. The idea tortures our minds with virtually every step. Lucy hit the nail on the head when she said it wasn't so much the thought of returning home to our family and friends that provokes so much excitement, instead, it is the thought of finally ending our routine. She is right.

It was hard to imagine the day when we would not have to get up and walk or ride our twenty miles.

Meredith-Jones, like Roarer before him, suddenly refused at this point to eat his maize balls and we feared that he too was suffering from a stomach problem. Jason promised to find a vet, and one morning we found him and Fire waiting for us with a 'vurry famous anima docta'. Half the village collected to watch the vet's examination and diagnosis.

From a small leather briefcase he extracted a stethoscope and listened earnestly to the sound of Meredith-Jones' bowels. 'His fourth stomach is not good,' translated Jason. We had no idea camels had so many stomachs. The vet sent us away with bags full of medicine, which we administered that night. Meredith-Jones retched for an hour, then uncharacteristically spat at us. However, we continued to feed him at least one hundred pills, as advised by the vet, every twenty-four hours, and within days he had recovered his appetite.

The next few days saw the road wind up into the mountains along precipitous ledges. The cliffs above us were littered with tiny arches, each marking the entrance to a troglodyte's home. Patchwork curtains shielded the caves from our inquisitive eyes as old men squatted outside next to piles of pumpkins. We saw a man coming down from the hills, carrying a stick with two dead rabbits, a pigeon and a pheasant suspended from it. We wanted to buy them but unfortunately Jason told us that Fire was unable to cook them, so we settled for a couple of pumpkins that, when steamed, made a delicious respite from the fried vegetables and rice.

Ten days from our expected arrival in Xian, we approached a tunnel that stretched for two miles. We had planned to ride through this tunnel, so avoiding the steep mountain pass above, but Jason informed us that it was unlit and would be too dangerous for us, let alone the camels, to enter. Instead, we must take the road over the mountains.

It was only four miles to the top, but the road's precipitous gradient made it hard work. All the way up we followed a man, probably in his late fifties, who showed absolutely no signs of discomfort even as we shed our layers, frequently stopping to catch our breath. By the time we reached the top, sweating and panting, he had lit a fire in his hut and was preparing a meal. Next a video camera was thrust in our faces. Jason's 'collegurs', who had been following us all the way from Lanzhou, had returned, cameraman in tow, to 'help us get to the top of the pass'.

Marking the summit was a small shrine named 'The Memorial Hall'. It was here, in 1935, that Mao and his troops had met during the Long March. Now we had this memorable spot all to ourselves, apart from the old man in his hut. As soon as he saw us coming he dashed out of his tiny home, clutching a handful of tickets. We had no money with us, so we were unable to view the Memorial Hall in detail. We felt bad, not at being unable to see inside the shrine, but because we feared the old man might have raced up the hill simply to sell us his tickets.

Contrary to our fears, the camels also made it successfully up the mountain and we joined them on the journey down the other side. We found our camp situated in a wide river valley with a gravelly bottom. As it was early, we decided to take advantage of the extra hours of light and sort out our equipment, in preparation for our journey's end. Jason and Fire looked on intently as we tipped our belongings into a heap. Lucy was particularly meticulous, removing every last item from the truck, 'in her eagerness to impress Fire with what a worthy Chinese wife she would be', according to Wic. As she sifted through her rucksack, Lucy suddenly turned to Jason and asked him, 'Jason, do you find us annoying?'

'Yes, sometimes.'

'Oh dear, why's that?'

'All girls are annoying.'

'But who's the most annoying?'

'Yes, you both,' he said, pointing an accusatory finger at Lucy and me. 'Mouse is the best, you two are the most naughty.'

'Why?'

'I don't know, but you are.'

Unenlightened, we left Jason and Fire to go to bed.

The next day we reached Pingliang, our last resting place before Xian and home to the first holy Taoist mountain in China. We found the grey, modern town shrouded in mist, so were unable to see the magnificent view it is said to afford. As we set off on the final leg of our journey, the frost and snow of the previous few weeks turned to rain, which proved an even greater discomfort. The roads became a slippery quagmire, which made it difficult for the camels even to stay vertical at times. We slid off our camels one by one and trudged despondently through the mud, walking a mile apart from each other, until we finally arrived in our camp. After we had eaten a miserable supper by candlelight, Jason and Fire slung a flimsy piece of tarpaulin along one side of the truck and we slept underneath this improvised shelter, our sleeping mats swimming in pools of mud and water. The rain gathered on the tarpaulin as we slept, slowly dripping through on to our bodies below. The entire camp had become awash, while the camels looked very dejected as the rain continued to trickle over their large, dark eyes and flattened coats.

Setting off in the drizzle, we found the going slippery and tiring. With our arms outstretched to aid our balance, we slowly worked our way along the road, the camels plodding behind. These exhausting conditions continued for a few days, the visibility deteriorating all the time. One morning we woke up to find we could not see more than ten yards in front of us. We spent the morning keeping close to the road, wary of losing our way. At one point we found ourselves on a plateau topping the mountains, with only the occasional ravine. Then the mist melted away to reveal a circular patch of blue sky above our heads. Looking to the horizon we felt as if we might fall off were we to venture away from the road, which was wide and straight, cutting through small fields of wheat and apricot orchards. Then it dipped back down into the misty valleys, and once again our vision was obstructed.

On the third day of travelling through this mist, Lucy and I were walking on foot when we spied a faint crowd ahead. As we approached, we discerned Wic and Mouse clasping huge bouquets of flowers, surrounded by men in red jackets with microphones poised at their mouths. When we joined them, we too had flowers thrust at us, as well as tangerines. Mouse explained that this was a television company from Xian who wanted to interview us.

'So, why did you come to China?'

'Because we're interested in the Silk Road.'

'Um, so what was your reason for coming?'

'Well, we'd all read about the history and are interested by it.'

'Right, so I'll say culture.'

They were eager for us to ride the camels but we were reluctant to do so right now because the poor animals were exhausted. We persuaded the film crew to meet us again in a couple of hours, when we would start riding. Having set off, we found Fire and Jason waiting for us in the truck on the edge of the road. We told them what had happened and asked them to meet us so that they could prevent the television company from detaining us.

'Pay no attenshun – they are extra company – not Mr Ma's,' was Jason's advice, accompanied by a ferocious hand gesture, as though to behead them.

At the agreed meeting point, Lucy and I found Mouse and Wic hiding behind a wall. Having been coaxed out, we were all subjected to more questioning on our physical training as well as about thirty rolls of film.

The rest of the day was spent relatively peacefully as we rode through a beautiful valley, cleft deep into the hills. We camped outside some Buddhist caves carved in the rock face, which were fronted by a delicate pagoda.

From here it was only two days' riding to the western gate of Xian. We hardly knew how to react, whether to feel excited or sad that the end was so close. Mouse's parents had arranged with mine to fly out from England and meet us as we entered Xian, and the thought of seeing them after eight months away contributed not a little to our state of nervous anticipation. We could hardly sleep.

On the final night of our journey we stayed in a small hostel on the side of the busy road that leads into the west of Xian, while our camels were lodged in the muddy courtyard. We did our best to clean ourselves, sluicing buckets of cold water over our hair and dusting our boots down. Our clothes were filthy from eight months on the road, but there was little we could do to improve them, so we satisfied ourselves with scrubbing our faces.

The next morning we woke far too early, packed up our belongings and waited impatiently for the time to pass until we could set off on the final short leg of our 5,000-mile journey. Our parents were due to meet us at around eleven o'clock only six miles away from our hostel, so there was no point in departing before nine. We tried to distract ourselves with endless games of cards.

Finally, the moment came and we stepped out of the courtyard with more energy than we had shown for months. Too excited to ride the camels, we strode ahead of them, scanning the horizon.

Lorries and buses sped passed us on the busy thoroughfare, pushing the camels off the edge of the road. Suddenly we spied a small white mini-bus approaching us slowly, with hands waving from the window.

'It's them!'

The bus drew to a halt. I could hardly contain myself as my parents jumped out. Throwing my arms around their necks, I felt the tears spring to my eyes as I was overwhelmed by the happiness I felt to see them. It was only when I became aware of a gentle tugging at my coat that I realised Mr Shu and Mr Wu were keen to continue on with the journey to Xian. I reluctantly resumed my place with the camels, but it was only another half an hour before we reached a statue of mediaeval merchants on their camels, built in the last decade, to commemorate the spot where the Silk Road officially ended.

Approaching on our camels, we felt an incredible sense of elation as a large group of students began to cheer and take photographs. Cars and buses drew to a halt around us, allowing a clear passage for our procession. We had done it! Five thousand miles and eight months of continual travelling towards this point and now we had finally arrived. All the difficulties we had experienced were forgotten as an incredible feeling of achievement surged through us and we lifted up our arms to wave at the crowd gathered in front of us.

The television crews asked us to line up on our camels as the students made a small presentation, gingerly handing us four china camels. We thanked them and smiled, holding the statuettes in one hand and raising the other triumphantly for the cameras. Unfortunately, Lucy's camel chose this moment to lower itself gently to the ground, crumpling first its front and then back legs. The photographs show her looking like a dwarf several feet below us, but still waving enthusiastically.

Our next and final concern was the fate of our camels. For the past couple of days we had been asking Fire and Jason what would happen to them, and how we could secure them a good home. They had been evasive but as we dismounted for the last time Jason approached us with a beaming smile.

'The camels will live with Fire's brother,' he announced.

We discovered that Fire's brother lived outside Xian and he promised that our animals would lead a healthy existence. It was very sad to see the camels being led away. Their long-lashed eyes looked more doleful than ever as they lumbered slowly off, obedient to the last. It also made us realise that our journey had truly come to an end and a whole era of our lives was over.

Xian sadly suffered the fate of most Chinese cities during the Cultural Revolution, and very little remains of the old Silk Road terminus. However, we were happy to enjoy the company of our parents and revel in no longer being on the move. It was indeed a strange sensation after eight months of itinerant life, and one that we relished. A week later we flew back to London and I felt that our adventure slowly became like a distant dream. The remote passes of Kyrgyzstan and windswept expanses of the Taklamakan seemed so far from the rolling English countryside, it was hard to believe we had ever really been away. But to this moment I can picture clearly each and every day of our journey, so distinctive and lasting an impression did they create on my mind. Never will I forget the feeling of romance and excitement those magnificent landscapes and peoples generated in me. The sense of timelessness we experienced will stay with me for the rest of my life as a cherished memory in our all too quickly changing world.

Select reading

Bailey, Colonel F. M., *Mission to Tashkent* (London, 1946)

Cable, M. and French, F., *The Gobi Desert* (London, 1942)

Fleming, Peter, *News from Tartary* (London, 1936)

Hopkirk, Peter, *The Great Game: On Secret Service in High Asia* (London, 1990)

Hopkirk, Peter, *Setting the East Ablaze: On Secret Service in Bolshevik Asia* (London, 1984)

Hopkirk, Peter, *Foreign Devils on the Silk Road: The Search for the Lost Treasures of Central Asia* (London, 1980)

Hopkirk, Peter, *On Secret Service East of Constantinople* (London, 1994)

Kipling, Rudyard, *Kim* (London, 1901)

Knauer, Elfriede Regina *The Camel's Load in Life and Death* (Switzerland, 1998)

Larner, John, *Marco Polo and the Discovery of the World* (Hong Kong, 1999)

Maclean, Fitzroy, *A Person from England and other travellers to Turkestan* (London, 1958)

Maclean, Fitzroy, *Eastern Approaches* (London, 1949)

Spence, Jonathan, *The Chan's Great Continent: China in Western Minds* (London, 1998)

Stein, Sir Aurel, *On Ancient Central Asian Tracks* (London, 1933)

The Travels of Marco Polo: The Complete Yule-Cordier Edition (London, 1993)

Thubron, Colin, *The Lost Heart of Asia* (London, 1997)

Whitfield, Susan, *Life along the Silk Road* (London, 1999)